Planning, Risk and Property Development

Urban regeneration schemes involving a wide range of actors and dependent on private investment are increasingly deployed in Europe's cities with the aim of delivering private, merit and public goods. This book explores the relationships, objectives and strategies of the actors engaging in these schemes in cities of three advanced European economies. It researches the outcomes of actor interactions as these transform under the influence of changing market circumstances and associated risks. The book focuses on the way this change is reflected in the provision of mixed-use developments within a context of increasingly polarised housing markets and urban growth patterns. It argues that although these schemes can and do deliver much-needed dwellings, their exposure to market risks may in many cases cause them to fall short of the desired socio-economically sustainable outcomes.

Nikos Karadimitriou is Lecturer in Planning and Property Development at the Bartlett School of Planning, UCL.

Claudio de Magalhães is Reader in Urban Regeneration and Management at the Bartlett School of Planning, UCL.

Roelof Verhage is Lecturer in Urban Planning and Development at the Institut d'Urbanisme de Lyon, Université Lumière Lyon.

Housing, Planning and Design Series

Editors: Nick Gallent and Mark Tewdwr-Jones,
The Bartlett School of Planning, University College London

A series of books examining the interface between housing policy and practice, and spatial planning. Various facets of this interface are explored, including the role of planning in supporting housing policies in the countryside, the pivotal role that planning plays in raising housing supply, affordability and quality, and the link between planning/housing policies and broader areas of concern including homelessness, the use of private dwellings, regeneration, market renewal, and environmental impact. The series positions housing and planning debates within the broader built environment agenda, engaging in a critical analysis of different issues at a time when many planning systems are being modernised and prepared for the challenges facing 21st century society.

Housing Development
Ron Blake, Andrew Golland

Decent Homes for All
Nick Gallent, Mark Tewdwr-Jones

Housing in the European Countryside
Nick Gallent, Mark Shucksmith,
Mark Tewdwr-Jones

Private Dwelling
Peter King

International Perspectives on Rural Homelessness
Paul Cloke, Paul Millbourne

Planning and Housing in the Rapidly Urbanising World
Paul Jenkins, Harry Smith,
Ya Ping Wang

Housing Market Renewal and Social Class
Chris Allen

Politics, Planning and Homes in a World City
Duncan Bowie

Planning, Risk and Property Development
Urban regeneration in England, France and the Netherlands
Nikos Karadimitriou,
Claudio de Magalhães, Roelof Verhage

Planning, Risk and Property Development

Urban regeneration in England, France and the Netherlands

Nikos Karadimitriou,
Claudio de Magalhães
and Roelof Verhage

 Routledge
Taylor & Francis Group

LONDON AND NEW YORK

First published 2013
by Routledge
2 Park Square, Milton Park, Abingdon, Oxon, OX14 4RN

Simultaneously published in the USA and Canada
by Routledge
711 Third Avenue, New York, NY 10017

Routledge is an imprint of the Taylor & Francis Group, an informa business

British Library Cataloguing in Publication Data
A catalogue record for this book is available from the British Library

Library of Congress Cataloging-in-Publication Data
Karadimitrio, Nikos.
Planning, risk, and property development : urban regeneration in the
England, France, and the Netherlands / by Nikos Karadimitriou,
Claudio de Magalhaes, Roelof Verhage.
p. cm.
Includes bibliographical references and index.
1. Urban renewal–Great Britain. 2. Urban renewal–France. 3. Urban
renewal–Netherlands. I. Magalh?es, Claudio de. II. Verhage, Roelof, 1971–
III. Title.
HT178.G7K37 2013
307.3'416094–dc23
2012034355

ISBN13: 978–0–415–48110–6 (hbk)
ISBN13: 978–0–415–48111–3 (pbk)
ISBN13: 978–0–203–88626–7 (ebk)

Typeset in Galliard by
Keystroke, Station Road, Codsall, Wolverhampton

Printed and bound in Great Britain by the MPG Books Group

Contents

Illustrations

Figures

Boxes

About the authors

Nikos Karadimitriou is Lecturer in Planning and Property Development at the Bartlett School of Planning, UCL. He has conducted research and published on a wide array of topics, including how space and place are socially constructed in urban regeneration, the interrelations between UK planning policy and housebuilders' business practices, the evaluation of regeneration projects in London and the new forms of social segregation in Athens. His research has attracted funding from UK research councils, research foundations such as the Foundation for Urban and Regional Studies and the Royal Institution of Chartered Surveyors Foundation, the UK housebuilding industry and from British and overseas government departments.

Claudio de Magalhães is Reader in Urban Regeneration and Management at the Bartlett School of Planning, UCL, with a background in architecture and urban planning and with research interests in planning and the governance of the built environment, the provision and governance of public space, property development processes and urban regeneration policy. He has conducted research for British research councils, professional bodies such as the Royal Institute of Chartered Surveyors, the Council for Architecture and the Built Environment, UK government departments and local authorities and has published widely on these topics, including the books *Urban Governance, Institutional Capacity and Social Milieux* (2002) and *Public Space: The Management Dimension* (2008).

Roelof Verhage is Lecturer in Urban Planning and Development at the Institut d'Urbanisme de Lyon – Université Lumière Lyon 2 and a member of the research laboratory CNRS UMR 5206 Triangle. His research interests are in urban development and urban regeneration, with particular attention to issues related to land development. Much of his work has a cross-national comparative character, concentrating on countries of Western Europe. He has conducted research projects in France and the Netherlands on behalf of ministries, local authorities and research councils, and has published on these topics in English, Dutch and French professional and scientific journals and books.

Preface

The three decades since 1980 have witnessed enormous social, economic and spatial transformations, with dramatic effects on the ways in which Europe's cities are developing. Urban regeneration as a field of policy and practice emerged in an effort to manage this process and to tackle the undesirable effects of those transformations. However, in spite of the rhetorical similarities, the countries of Western Europe (certainly the three countries examined in this book) display a noteworthy degree of variety in the ways in which urban regeneration is approached and practised.

Our intellectual curiosity was aroused by the new forms of cooperation that have become widespread throughout Western Europe, boosted by the booming property market of the early and mid-2000s. Could it really be the case that such a crucial field of public policy had been co-opted by 'the property market', as some would argue? Or was it the other way around: was 'the state' piggybacking on the profits of property developers? This book reflects an attempt to uncover the complex relationships between private, public and third sector actors in regeneration partnerships. It looks into how these arrangements may affect the physical outputs of regeneration schemes and how public, private and merit goods are provided through such schemes. Finally, it looks at how the different institutional frameworks and configurations of actors engaging in each of six case study regeneration schemes have responded to the prolonged period of economic turbulence that continued apace throughout the time it took to complete the research and write this book.

It is hoped that this book will answer questions of interest to academics and built environment professionals and provide useful insights in so far as the context, content and organisation of urban regeneration in all three countries is concerned. There are many other important areas that the book did not delve into, and it is hoped that future research will do so. Clearly, the six cases looked into have their own specificities, but what their examination reveals could be more widely applicable in many instances. In each of the schemes studied, an intricate pattern of interrelations between public, private and third sector actors emerged. The main purpose of these constellations of actors was to create value through a process of urban regeneration, to monetise it or otherwise capture it to some extent and to come to an arrangement with regard to its distribution, bearing in mind the risks and uncertainties that each actor was taking on. Apart from a very complex managerial and technical endeavour, this negotiation is an intensely political process, the outcomes of which substantively affect citizen well-being and the citizen–state relationship.

Nikos Karadimitriou, Claudio de Magalhães and Roelof Verhage

Autumn 2011

Acknowledgements

This book would not have been possible without the support provided by many people in different capacities. Our profound thanks are due to all those in academia, regeneration partnerships, development companies, local government and housing associations who agreed, on condition of anonymity, to be interviewed by us for our six case studies and helped us to obtain the information we needed to write the book.

We would also like to thank the British Council in France ('Alliance' Franco-British Research Partnership Programme) and the Bartlett School of Planning, UCL, for their financial support of the research project titled "Major Urban Renewal Projects in European cities: examining the adjustment of economic, social and environmental objectives", which provided the core material used in writing this book.

Last but not least, particular thanks go to Michael Manlangit undertaking a substantial chunk of the desktop research for the English and Dutch case studies and the team at Routledge for their patience and guidance.

Abbreviations

ANRU	Agence National pour la Renovation Urbaine
AWF	Amsterdam Waterfront Finance
BID	Business Improvement District
BNG	Bank Nederlandse Gemeenten
CABE	Commission for Architecture and the Built Environment
CDC	Caisse des Dépôts et Consignations
CIL	Community Infrastructure Levy
CT	Community Trust
DETR	Department for the Environment, Transport and the Regions
DoE	Department of the Environment
EP	English Partnerships
EPF	Etablissements Publics Foncier
GOL	Government Office for London
GSB	Grote Steden Beleid
HCA	Homes and Communities Agency
HC	Housing Corporation
HMR	Housing Market Renewal
ISV	Investeringsbudget Stedelijke Vernieuwing
LEP	Local Enterprise Partnership
LOV	Loi d'Orientation pour la Ville
MCC	Manchester City Council
MMHG	Manchester Methodist Housing Group
MUURS	Mixed Use Urban Regeneration Scheme
MXD	mixed-use development
NAO	National Audit Office
NDC	New Deal for Communities
NEM	New East Manchester
NRF	Neighbourhood Renewal Fund
NWDA	North West Development Agency
OBR	Ontwikkelings Bedrijf Rotterdam
ODPM	Office of the Deputy Prime Minister
PAE	Programme d'Aménagement d'Ensemble

PFI	private finance initiative
PLAI	Prêt Locatif Aidé d'Intégration
PLH	Programme Local d'Habitat
PLS	Prêt Locatif Social
PLUS	Prêt Locatif à Usage Social
PPP	public–private partnership
PRP	Paddington Regeneration Partnership
PSPA	Paddington Special Policy Area
PWP	Paddington Waterside Partnership
RDA	Regional Development Agencies
RSL	Registered Social Landlord
SCOT	Schema de Cohérence Territoriale
SEM	Société d'Economie Mixte
SERL	Société d'Equipement du Rhône et de Lyon
SEU	Social Exclusion Unit
SRB	Single Regeneration Budget
SRU	Solidarité et Renouvellement Urbains
TfL	Transport for London
TfP	Time for Paddington
UDC	Urban Development Corporation
URC	Urban Regeneration Company
UTF	Urban Task Force
Vinex	*Vierde Nota over de Ruimtelijke Ordening Extra*
WCC	Westminster City Council
WELPUT	West End of London Property Unit Trust
WEQ	West End Quay
ZAC	Zone d'Aménagement Concerté

Chapter 1

Urban transformations and policy responses in Western European cities

Introduction

This book discusses on-going changes in the way in which demand for what could broadly be defined as merit and public goods, particularly but not exclusively for non-market housing,[1] has been met in three Western European countries in the context of urban regeneration schemes. These schemes point to structures and mechanisms of provision that differ markedly from those that were established in the early post-war years. Where once this provision was closely associated with the duties of the (welfare) state, it is now increasingly contingent upon the outcomes of a much wider array of processes and actors. Moreover, whereas non-market housing, in particular, used to be part of strategies for coping with the growth pressures of manufacturing-based cities and national economies, it now often is a key element of efforts to regenerate declining urban areas in the internationally more porous economies of Western Europe.

Kemeny (2001) points out the four main pillars of welfare provision, namely housing, education, health and social security. He notes that housing is the most capital intensive of the four, which makes it rather unique and, in our view, hints at why it was linked to private property development via urban regeneration. He also argues that the state plays a complex role in the provision of housing that is difficult to untangle from the role of market actors. What also makes housing rather unique, as compared to the other three pillars, is the higher level of commodification and market involvement in its production (Harloe, 1995). Although this difference is less striking today than it was in 1995 it does indeed pose some difficulties in defining and researching housing within the context of welfare provision.

The effort of governments to achieve public policy goals whilst increasingly relying on market mechanisms and private actors for the provision of merit and public goods, typical of regeneration policies of the last 30 years or so, was based on specific assumptions about the role of private actors and the role of the state, as well as about the way they can pool resources in order to achieve public policy goals. Depending on the extent and scope of the partnerships that emerged, novel risk-/return-sharing arrangements between private, public and third sector actors have appeared that make the concept of public–private partnership a rather diffuse one (Miraftab, 2004).

The logic of the public–private partnership arrangements that gained momentum in the last few decades in all types of welfare provision suggested that the involvement of the private sector would offer increased effectiveness and efficiency gains, whereas state involvement could lower risk premia and thus would allow projects to be financed at rates closer to sovereign debt rates without necessarily expanding state expenditure. Arguably, however, offloading those liabilities from the state's balance sheet is not the same as not expanding state expenditure.

One has to note here that the dichotomy between planning and markets can be rather misleading when taken as anything other than an analytical device. In several Western European countries, for example, the third sector played a crucial role in the delivery of public services throughout the post-war years and the concept of the social market economy draws on ideas which first appeared in Germany in the intra-war period. It is thus more illuminating to focus any inquiry on which governance mix could or should be chosen (Alexander, 2001). Insofar as welfare systems are concerned, this point has been iterated by Hamnett (1998) or Marcuse and van Kempen (2002), who argue that as the state continues to be ever present in the processes of urban transformation, the changes in its role with regard to welfare provision are as much an outcome of local political processes as they are a consequence of global restructuring and market forces.

Concerns about the potential consequences of the public–private partnership approaches to welfare provision pursued in the last three decades or so, especially so far as housing is concerned, have been raised throughout the period in question (for example, see Iglesias, 2009). These concerns obviously extend to the provision of public goods, like amenities and the public realm, which are crucial ingredients in place making and for human well-being. The crisis in the financial markets that started in 2007 and the subsequent downturn in many property markets provided a stark reminder of what these consequences may be and how likely the associated risks are. At the very least, the public–private risk/return arrangements underpinning regeneration schemes throughout Western Europe have had to be rethought and adjusted. In many cases, this adjustment has resulted in the partial or complete withdrawal of private sector actors from schemes and/or increased state intervention and expenditure in the name of social cohesion.

This chapter situates the transformations discussed above in the context of the recent socio-economic evolution of many Western European cities. For that, we introduce themes and concepts that underpin the book's approach to the relationship between urban regeneration schemes and merit and public goods provision in Western Europe. We present a brief historical overview of the range of factors that has led to current forms of provision through urban regeneration schemes and summarise our understanding of the emergence of urban regeneration as an important field of policy. We also focus on changes in the practice of urban regeneration that reflect new forms of public–private cooperation away from the New Public Management approach (see for example Brandsen and Pestoff, 2006).

The argument pursued throughout the rest of this book highlights how these processes of production of the built environment mesh public policy objectives and the delivery of merit and public goods with the logic and the priorities of property developers and investors, especially linking them with the risks and uncertainties embedded in the property development process. The resulting forms and types of urban quarters in turn create path dependencies that further affect the achievement of public and private objectives and priorities. It is interesting to note that in each of the countries that the book looks into, the roles and ambitions of the actors engaging in the process, especially the roles of public sector actors, differ markedly between them. These differences highlight the deeply embedded cultural and ideological factors that affect the behaviour and worldview of the agents engaging in the regeneration process, as well as the institutional framework within which they operate.

The rise and decline of the European industrial city

In most of the world, and certainly in the three countries examined in this book, the process of industrialisation has led to massive growth of cities. In some cases, this has meant the rapid emergence of large urban centres where previously there were small towns, whereas in others it had led to the transformation of former merchant or administrative cities into industrial metropolises and sites for the transport infrastructure that accompanied industrial production. For many cities, it has meant the replacement of the pre-existing physical fabric with one more suited to the dynamics of manufacturing and its labour force. For others, particularly in European countries which industrialised late, it had meant the accretion of industrial suburbs to the pre-existing urban tissue. Thus, during the nineteenth and early twentieth centuries the needs of an industrial society were inscribed in the physical structure of many contemporary cities. Concentrations of manufacturing plants, workers' housing, warehousing and transport infrastructure came to define a considerable proportion of a city's fabric.

The problems that accompanied that spatial logic were acknowledged very early on. The insalubrious mix of industry and housing; the very low quality of much of the housing stock; the appalling environmental conditions in which the fast-growing numbers of industrial workers lived; all this came to form the background for a raft of public health legislation that by and large was the precursor of modern planning systems in many Western European countries. Slum-clearance programmes through the later part of the nineteenth century and first half of the twentieth century were also part of that approach, as were zoning policies and the newly created industrial districts. However, the logic of the European industrial city was part and parcel of nineteenth- and early twentieth-century capitalist space-economy and, as such, became associated with economic development, progress and modernity. By the eve of the Second World War, the industrial city was an integral part of the European landscape. Moreover, faith in the industrial city and the economic geography that supported it was very much a part of the thinking about cities and urban policies. The modernist project had it at its core, as did the reconstruction plans elaborated during and after the war years, which were to shape the contemporary city. The efforts to reconstruct war-damaged cities, to do away with the social, economic and spatial injustices of industrialisation, to build a more equitable society, were framed by a belief in the stability and permanence of an urbanised industrial economy and its attending spatial structure at a time when, compared to the present day, nation-states exerted significantly more control over capital and labour (Fraser, 2003a; Hall, 1990).

Much has been written about the broader changes in the world economy in the final decades of the twentieth century that ultimately led to the decline of whole sectors of manufacturing in the industrialised economies of Western Europe and to the concomitant growth of the service sector, often with a distinct geography (Beauregard, 2003; Castells, 1989; Sassen, 1991; Schoon, 2001). In spite of the many contested interpretations of the meanings of those changes, there is some consensus on what their elements are. Most accounts point to the growing internationalisation of the economy, to the emergence of global elites, to the increasing mobility of capital looking for lower production costs, and subsequently of labour too; to technological changes that have made labour redundant in the production process or have allowed the 'down-skilling' of blue-collar jobs and their replacement with low-skilled jobs elsewhere; to the reduction of the impact of distance, allowing for a much wider spread of production than previously; to the emergence of information technologies and their progressive incorporation into all stages of production and consumption, leading to new patterns of concentration and dispersal of people and activities; to the increasing proportion of value added by information and knowledge; and so on.

Whatever views one might hold on the relative importance of these changes, their social and spatial consequences are widely acknowledged: the decline of the economic basis of many places leading to loss of jobs, population and tax incomes, physical dereliction and a raft of social problems. Significantly, the capacity of the state to control its tax base and thus its incomes has also been undermined by increased capital and personal mobility. Increased mobility combined with changing demographics also poses new challenges for welfare provision systems.

Given the new circumstances, some of the mechanisms that were created during the growth era in order to improve life conditions through welfare provision were weakened and in some cases contributed to the entrapment of the very people whom they set out to support. Paradoxical situations arose whereby welfare structures often increased the risks and costs associated with re-entering employment, migrating etc. and thus reinforced the isolation of those less able to adapt or fit into the new economic structures (Forrest, 1987; Hills, 2007).

In some places, the economic decline and loss of jobs happened side by side with the growth in service-related activities, impacting differently on locations within a city or an urban region. In other places, it meant the demise of whole regional economies, like coal-mining areas or textile-production clusters everywhere in Europe, as well as larger industrial cities at a distance from preferred service industry locations, such as the industrial conurbations of Liverpool, Glasgow, Manchester, Lille or parts of the Ruhr area.

However, economic change in itself does not explain the intensity and acuteness of the problems that industrial cities have faced over the last decades. The growth and decline of places are not historically new processes: each cycle of growth and decline in the economy has depended on its own particular sets of dynamic and profitable economic activities with their own location requirements.

A prominent feature of late twentieth-century de-industrialisation is the relatively short period of time in which major changes have happened within a context of liberalisation of both intra-European and global flows of trade, capital and people. Although some cities in Europe had been experiencing a decline in their economic basis since much earlier – e.g. heavy engineering and ship building in Tyneside, in decline since the interwar period (Hudson, 2005) – for many industrialised cities and regions in Europe the loss of manufacturing jobs and the decline of long-established economic structures happened relatively rapidly after trade barriers were removed. For example, it took around 10 years, from the mid-1970s to the mid-1980s, for entire branches of the secondary sector to close down, and this exerted enormous pressure on planning and spatial policy frameworks that were predicated on the stability and growth dynamics of an industrial, manufacturing-based urban development.

The speed of the economic decline in places like the Midlands, Nord Pas de Calais, the Ruhr or Wallonia in the 1970s and 1980s stretched governance systems and welfare regimes alike and hindered an orderly transition that could have attenuated the economic and social consequences of that decline through a long-term process of adaptation.

The welfare state and urban decline

Cities are certainly more than buildings and physical infrastructure, but they are those too. Urban layouts, buildings and infrastructure have a long life and tend to outlast the economic and social context in which they were produced. Some European cities have developed along a basic design laid out by Roman roads two millennia ago and many still show evidence of medieval plot structure in the position and size of present-day land parcels. Many contemporary urban developments are therefore shaped by site parameters that derive directly from long-disappeared forms of land use that have been crystallised in the plot structure and the footprints of buildings and infrastructure.

The extensive and substantial urban growth in the last two centuries associated with industrialisation, of which the reconstruction of cities after the Second World War is a short but substantive episode, was therefore likely to produce physical structures that could shape cities for a long time to come. It is not surprising to find cities in post-industrial, service-based economies that have to contend with buildings and infrastructure networks that might have suited well the previous economic cycle, but will not necessarily suit the economic, social and environmental requirements of post-industrial economies. This applies to a variety of spatial scales, from parts of a city that might have thrived in a previous period but that are currently obsolete, to the region, the nation and the world (Couch, 2003). It is important to keep in mind this association between the nature of many of the urban problems of the late twentieth century and the transformation of the economy and of society, the consolidation of the spatial structure of European industrial cities and the urban policies of the post-war years. The interconnection of these different aspects can provide the basis for understanding the genesis and formulation of many current urban problems.

Another important development that helped to consolidate the physical structure of the industrial city, and thus define the nature of the challenges facing contemporary cities, was the emergence of the welfare state and the consequent growth of state-driven provision of a range of goods and services, partly because it was essential for the improvement of social welfare and social justice (and thus for maintaining a more equitable society and social peace) but also because it supported consumer demand as part of strategies for managing economic growth (Barlow and Duncan, 1994). Importantly, this included housing, as the provision of adequate accommodation had been historically problematic for a substantial proportion of the population.

The history here differs from country to country, but in general the activities of pre-existing networks of charitable providers of services such as education, health and housing for the poor (private charities, church organisations, trade associations, workers' unions, etc.) were gradually complemented or absorbed and expanded to cover wider social strata by local and national governments in the late nineteenth century and the first half of the twentieth century (Leach and Percy-Smith, 2001). In England, for instance, state-driven housing provision became significant in the interwar years and reached its climax in the decades immediately after the Second World War when a fully developed state-based welfare provision emerged (Balchin, 1996). In France, it started in earnest in the 1950s, with a vast programme of state-subsidised social housing construction (Blanc and Bertrand, 1996).

The development of European welfare states took place in the context of economies and labour markets over which nation-states had more control than the case is today. The massive investment in social infrastructure in the post-war years happened within the framework of industrial economies with substantial blue-collar employment located in urban areas. Considerable amounts of national wealth were put into solving the urban problems of the pre-war years with mass production of social housing – often as large ensembles – relocation of polluting industries away from housing areas and into industrial estates at the fringe of cities, construction of a transport network connecting industries, workers' housing and markets etc.

This investment was predicated on, and reciprocally reinforced, the assumption that the structure and trajectory of these economies would remain relatively stable in the long run. Such an approach, typical in investment appraisal, could therefore provide short- and long-term justifications for the significant commitment of social and economic resources. With hindsight, it also contributed to fixing that structure in the territory of cities and regions, helping to form the base conditions for some of the urban problems of the following decades (Couch *et al.*, 2003; Hall and Tewdwr-Jones, 2011).

In parallel with the growth and later decline of the economic and tax bases of the industrial city, another factor has contributed to weakening the ability of cities to manage economic change: the long-lasting process of urban expansion, sub-urbanisation and peri-urbanisation of population and of businesses, compounded by insufficient re-arrangement of urban governance structures. This has been a prominent characteristic of North American and British patterns of urbanisation, but elements of it have been present in the evolution of cities elsewhere in Europe throughout the twentieth century. As a result, many areas in cities throughout

Europe have been abandoned by businesses and higher-income residents who favour edge- and out-of-town locations. This gradual loss of population, employment and economic activity often left behind those who could not afford to move – often residents of public housing built closer to the manufacturing jobs they once depended upon.

In the UK, and to an extent in the Netherlands too, the outmigration of businesses and wealthier residents, combined with the loss of jobs and falling incomes for large parts of the population, meant that many of the areas where large social housing estates had been built became enclaves dominated overwhelmingly by social renting (see, for instance, the social housing belts around Newcastle, Manchester-Salford and Liverpool). In countries such as France or Italy, with relatively late large-scale urbanisation and already under the influence of a modernist approach to planning, spatial polarisation has followed a different pattern: many social housing projects were built in the periphery as self-contained settlements, sometimes replacing irregular housing built there by increasing numbers of rural migrants who moved to the cities to benefit from the rapid expansion of industrial jobs in the post-war years. In these countries, in spite of the population leakage, parts of the urban core and of the nineteenth-century belt around it retained their function as middle- or upper-class residential areas.

Whatever the nature or the particular characteristics of this process, this rearranging of population and of the services catering for them along lines of income within an expanding city-region with a rapidly changing economic structure facilitated a self-reinforcing geographical concentration of economic and social problems. In countries where local government revenues are directly related to the wealth of the residing population and businesses, this reduction in income and population has adversely affected the tax base that could finance remedial policies. Those trends have created their own dynamics and have not necessarily been arrested by more recent economic growth. In places like Manchester or Rotterdam, the economic dynamism of the early 2000s has not always been matched by population gain, although there was clearly a trend towards a return to city living, especially among young, educated adults with no children (ODPM, 2006). Besides, any population increase associated with this return has often taken place in narrowly defined pockets.

Decline, urban regeneration and the market

This depiction of the process of urban decline has so far left aside the role of the policies and initiatives that have tried explicitly or implicitly to address its causes and consequences. As far back as the 1930s, the British government was promoting the development of industrial estates in the North and West of England as a way of shoring up a declining manufacturing base (Scott, 2001). In the same vein, British regional policies in the 1960s and 1970s tried to relocate manufacturing, offices, government agencies and government-owned utility companies away from more economically dynamic regions, especially London, and towards northern cities whose economies were faltering (Balchin *et al.*, 1999; Couch, 2003; Hall and Tewdwr-Jones, 2011).

Throughout Western Europe significant state interventions such as infrastructure investment, government subsidies and tax benefits were put in place to try to counteract the forces of economic decline. More recently, as will be discussed in detail in the next chapter, these interventions have come to fall under a new field of policy – 'urban regeneration' – concerned with dealing with the physical, social and economic consequences of urban change within the context of a retrenching welfare state. Although it is debatable whether any set of urban policies could or should have entirely prevented the economic and physical decline of industrial cities, it is arguable that 'prevention' rather narrowly describes their scope, remit and outcomes. On many occasions, such policies and their results have not only influenced the degree and nature of decline and the deprivation that came with it but are also to some extent responsible for affecting the future trajectory of places and people.

The vast majority of these responses to urban transformations have depended – and to a large extent still do – on the ability of the state, its agencies and the actors it can enrol, to reshape the spatial effects of economic and social processes and to channel these processes in ways that societies deem desirable. However, as will become apparent in the discussion of urban regeneration strategies in the next chapter, changes instigated by the latest wave of globalisation have affected the very basis of the post-war welfare state and thus the mechanisms relied upon to provide policy responses to those phenomena (see Couch *et al.*, 2003; Goss, 2001; Leach and Percy-Smith, 2001; Sullivan and Skelcher, 2002). This means not only that cities and urban regions have gone through fundamental economic, social and spatial changes in the last few decades of the century but also that the tools and mechanisms that try to address the consequences of those changes have themselves changed in the process.

Although the details might vary from country to country, urban policy initiatives up to some point in the 1970s relied upon state machinery with a high degree of specialisation and professionalism (Goldsmith, 1993; Leach and Percy-Smith, 2001). This machinery took the form of large, self-contained policy-delivery units, organised around specific areas (e.g. housing, education, health, regional development), that could deliver public services and goods en masse to the growing industrial economies of the 1950s and 1960s. This form of specialisation was at the heart of what was later decried as the 'silo-mentality' that came to dominate the thinking and the delivery of public policy. It is characterised by an exclusive focus on one particular field and a difficulty to deal with the connections and linkages across services and policy areas (Richards *et al.*, 1999). These silo-type structures were behind the conception and implementation of policies addressing employment, economic productivity, housing needs and the spatial imbalance of national economies. The coordination of their actions and their impacts was guaranteed by means of strong policy frameworks linked to a powerful and well-resourced policy-delivery machinery.

The decline of manufacturing and of the pattern of job stability that characterised it, the parallel growth of flexible work in the service industries, together with the globalisation of the economy (of capital, production processes, labour markets, taxation and consumption), which made it less predictable and less controllable by conventional national economic policy instruments, have undermined the financial basis and some of the legitimacy of the post-war European welfare state (Esping-Andersen, 2002; Pierson, 1996). Moreover, prosperity, patterns of migration, changes in demographics in general and family structures in particular (fewer children, single households, erosion of familial support structures), as well as flexible work patterns, have led to the emergence of multiple concurrent and often competing lifestyles, with their different needs, vying to different degrees for increasingly constrained resources. General willingness to accept top-down and centralised solutions to social problems – and the taxation rates implied by these – has also decreased (Pierson, 1996). These changes have challenged hierarchical, 'command and control' forms of government and have led to a rethinking of public sector cultures, structures and procedures (Goss, 2001; Leach and Percy-Smith, 2001; Pierre and Peters, 2000).

In parallel, an increasing urban policy focus on problems such as the environment, social exclusion, personal safety etc. that cut across specialised policy areas, seemed intractable, persistent and not amenable to simple solutions (i.e. the 'wicked issues' of the literature – Clarke and Stewart, 1997) has strengthened the case for collaborative forms of making, managing and delivering policy involving multiple policy actors and interested parties. These have caused policy actors to replace the previous focus on the formal structures of government and on the state as the central governing actor with a focus on the process of governing and on the multiple state–society interactions that constitute it (Kooiman, 2003).

In the UK, more than in the rest of Western Europe, it was the commitment of Conservative governments in the 1980s and early 1990s to solutions for economic, social and spatial issues that allocated a greater role to private sector actors. This logic, inspired by idealised notions of the efficiency and effectiveness of perfect markets, was not fundamentally altered by subsequent administrations.

The constant push from the European Union to promote a single European market for goods and services also meant that several widespread practices of state involvement in the provision of goods and services fell foul of competition and state aid regulations. Therefore, in the UK and to a lesser extent elsewhere in Europe, solutions to problems of urban decline have come to rely increasingly on the dynamics of markets and on the resources that market agents and civic society could also bring into the process. As Couch *et al.* (2011) also note, however, while the 1980s in the UK were a period of a radical break with past policies, other countries in Western Europe had "the political inclination to seek solutions within their existing structures of local governance and economic relations" (p. 9). Arguably, that approach was in line with their tradition of third sector engagement in the delivery of public goods and services.

Public sector and local government reforms in the 1980s and early 1990s were often translated into privatisation, agencification and the flowing of power to subsidiary bodies within and outside the formal boundaries of the state (Rhodes, 1997; Stoker, 2004). This has led to a multiplication of agencies with a stake in the delivery of urban policies, which typically involve a plethora of privatised public sector bodies, private utility providers, area-based urban regeneration organisations, local authority departments, semi-public delivery agencies and so forth. For some commentators this has meant the unacceptable intrusion of private interests into the making and delivery of public policy (see discussion in Bailey *et al.*, 1995 or Swyngedow *et al.*, 2002). For others it has signalled the unavoidable transformation of the forms of collaboration between different sectors and jurisdictions in policy making and delivery, essential in an increasingly diverse, fragmented and complex society, in which no single social actor has the solutions for the policy problems at hand or the power to implement them (Sullivan and Skelcher, 2002).

For urban policies, this shift meant a substantial redefinition of the principles guiding their funding and delivery and the way they should respond to social needs more generally. An increasing emphasis on cost-effectiveness, on competition among providers and on consumers' choice has underpinned the retreat of central and local government from direct service provision and, especially in the UK, the transfer of public management responsibilities to private and community stakeholders in an effort to strike an increasingly fragile balance between cost-efficiency, service quality, public control and accountability.

This shift is at the core of the notion of the 'enabling' state, whose main role as far as public services are concerned, is to "stimulate, facilitate, support, regulate, influence and thereby enable other agencies and organisations to act on its behalf" (Leach and Percy-Smith, 2001, p. 162). Therefore, at the same time as previously prosperous urban areas were facing economic decline, with its social and physical consequences, the governance mechanisms to deal with them were increasingly relying on private sector actors and civil society, with a concomitant change in the nature of the complexities and uncertainties of the urban regeneration process.

Arguably, the processes described above were most striking in UK urban policy, though many elements are present in policies dealing with urban change and decline elsewhere in Europe. Urban policy makers in much of Europe have recognised that previously existing mechanisms could be insufficient in altering the economic, social and physical dynamics of cities and sought to understand and engage more with market actors and civic society in order to effect change (Anderson and van Kempen, 2001; Couch *et al.*, 2003).

This shift in the balance between state operations and the function of markets in urban policy has caused novel institutional relationships between the two to emerge. In a way, urban policy and regeneration became an epitome of the new forms of welfare provision typifying the late twentieth century, often involving the retrenchment and sometimes the residualisation of the welfare state. Given the spatiality of many of the problems brought about by urban decline and the frequent lack of public funding, influencing the behaviour of property markets either as a goal in itself or as a means to other ends became an important component of urban policy. The next chapter explores in detail how this has taken place in the UK, France and the Netherlands.

An important consequence of the redefinition of the relationships between state and market actors is that the problems of urban and regional decline and its physical consequences have been often read from the perspective of the property market (Adams *et al.*, 2005; Colenutt, 1999; MacLaran, 2003; Turok, 1992). This has affected the way these problems are perceived and defined and, consequently, the solutions proposed to tackle those problems. From this perspective, the consequences of the decline of a locality suffering from the loss of economic activity – including the existence of run-down houses, derelict buildings and vacant spaces – can be interpreted as a problem with land and property values in that area, associated with falling demand for that location. The assumption that a healthy property market is a precondition for economic and social regeneration has affected urban policy and regeneration initiatives since the 1980s (see Turok, 1992).

Since then, there has been a long debate as to what the relationship is between a dynamic property market and a growing economy and prosperous society (Adams *et al.*, 2005; Turok, 1992), and the current consensus is that the relationship is more complex than one of constant unidirectional causality between property investment and economic development. However, few deny the importance of investment in the built environment in reversing declining urban areas. In a context in which a large part of this investment had to come from actors other than the state, the problem and its solutions were formulated, at least in part, in terms of property markets and their functioning.

Therefore, in this light the problems of declining urban areas were often recast as related to a lack of demand in the property market. This lack of demand would mean that no private investment would come forward to provide the new or refurbished spaces that could attract and accommodate more dynamic economic activities or the housing and amenities for the labour force coming to serve them. Making available the 'right' kind of public, merit and private goods like commercial buildings, facilities, homes, amenities and infrastructure would therefore be an important element in attracting those businesses and an adequate pool of labour, provided that other economic, social and institutional parameters were favourable.

In order to achieve its objectives, this type of policy needed to restore the function of the property market in those areas in order to secure their regeneration in the long run. Thus, various constraints to development were identified in the form of e.g. fragmented landownership, costs of land decontamination, poor transport access, lack of adequate infrastructure, costs of and access to development finance, lack of confidence and excessive risks, uncertainties and low profitability (Adair *et al.*, 2003; Jeffrey and Pounder, 2000; Nappi-Choulet, 2006; Syms, 2002). State involvement aiming at securing the provision of buildings and infrastructure in cities across Western Europe was largely predicated on the premise that these constraints have to be lifted.

Moreover, in societies where homeownership has a significant household investment function, increasing dwelling prices often create a substantial 'wealth effect' whereas lack of demand and falling prices inevitably lead to a decrease in the value of many households' most important asset, their homes, affecting their mobility and consumption (Barker, 2004; Gregory, 2011). Saddled with mortgages for homes whose market value drops significantly, homeowners can be trapped in increasingly more derelict locations where falling consumption creates self-reinforcing spirals of decline (Nevin and Leather, 2006). Thus, securing a buoyant housing market was, and to an extent still is, seen as important for public policy as argued in government-funded regeneration programmes tackling housing market weakness through supply-side measures such as selective demolition, stock transfers, refurbishment and reconstruction in order to establish and inflate a housing market (Nevin and Leather, 2006). Selective demolition and reconstruction has been used not only in large public housing estates across Europe such as Bijmelmeer in Amsterdam or Marzahn in Berlin but also as part of plans to revive entire cities (e.g. Leipzig) or regions (e.g. the north of England). Similarly, interventions aiming at reshaping housing markets in deprived areas have been used to remove the stigma that might have been created around them.

The examples above illustrate urban policies explicitly aiming at influencing the function of property markets in order to counteract urban decline. All assume that the desired social and economic outcomes that those policy interventions are trying to achieve cannot be brought about by public sector or private/third sector action alone and depend, to an extent, on the mobilisation of property market interests. This type of approach is predicated on the delivery of societal goals and policy objectives by articulations of public, private and community players (Sullivan and Skelcher, 2002). It has become particularly important in the provision of housing, especially when one takes into account the increasingly pervasive asset-based forms of welfare provision in which part of the responsibility for that provision (pension, minimum income) is transferred to asset-holding households (Watson, 2009).

Urban regeneration and housing provision

State involvement in housing provision in Europe dates from the nineteenth century. Subsidies by the French state to facilitate access to homeownership were part of that early involvement in housing provision, as were the incentives to the construction of salubrious workers' houses by charitable organisations and local governments across most of Europe (Balchin, 1996). However, this rarely meant direct state involvement in the construction of housing. Large-scale, systematic and direct state involvement in housing provision became more common in the interwar years, and developed into a fully fledged policy field and integral part of the welfare state only in the post-war period.

In most European countries, including the UK, France and the Netherlands, the main housing policy objective in the middle part of the twentieth century was to meet shortages of adequate housing, which in some cases had been building up since the previous century. Intervention included the direct provision of social housing (where the private sector participated as subcontractors, if at all), the demolition and replacement of slum dwellings and incentives to boost private sector provision of market housing. This was the dominant approach until the mid-1970s, when in many of these countries the historical gap between number of housing units and families needing housing was met. This statistical 'closing the gap' does not mean that actual demand for adequate housing was satisfied, only that the issue temporarily ceased to be one of quantity. In the UK this happened earlier, in France slightly later and in the Netherlands arguably this condition was never really achieved (see Balchin, 1996). From the mid-1970s, direct intervention in the provision of units (supply-side, 'bricks and mortar' programmes) was gradually replaced by subsidies to demand in the form of tax concessions, housing benefits etc. (Balchin, 1996).

This primacy of provision issues, which remained at the core of housing policies well into the 1970s, also meant that housing policy had its own agenda and dynamics dictated by the need to deliver annual housing construction targets. These evolved separately from the policies and initiatives that would come to constitute 'urban regeneration'. Although housing provision, especially in the form of large public housing estates inserted into existing urban areas, was in effect reshaping those areas, regenerating decaying neighbourhoods was not itself amongst the key drivers of housing policy.

It was only in the 1970s that the multidimensional and systemic nature of urban problems was recognised and urban renewal policies started to converge and link up with housing. On the one hand, this is related to mounting pressure to revive and renew historic city areas that had been detrimentally affected by the war and the lack of public and private investment and by often insensitive planning interventions in the post-war era. The fact that housing for low-income families constituted a significant part of the fabric of declining European city quarters meant that reviving these locations necessarily involved provision of housing in adequate quantity and quality. By the late 1970s community breakdown and wider negative side-effects associated with the conventional way of addressing low-quality housing (i.e. relocation of dwellers to newly built estates elsewhere) had already been acknowledged, and thus, policy initiatives started to focus on improving neighbourhoods in situ (Priemus, 2006; Roberts, 2000).

Concomitant with the increasing pressure for the renewal of declining urban quarters and the acknowledgement of the role of housing in that process, the need for integration of housing and regeneration was also being felt in the public housing estates built in the preceding decades. By the mid-1970s many of them were in need of substantial repairs (Balchin, 1996). This was sometimes the result of speedy construction with untested building techniques, poor and underfunded management and maintenance regimes or, on other occasions, the result of the over-concentration of economically and socially disadvantaged households into particular locations without adequate resources to support them. From the mid-1970s the physical and social renewal of public housing estates became increasingly an important part of the discourse of urban regeneration (McCarthy, 2007). If in France and the Netherlands this became associated with interventions throughout the city and even at the scale of the city-region, in the UK it added to pressures for the regeneration of the 'inner' cities (Balchin, 1996).

Furthermore, by the 1980s the argument that single-use, mono-functional environments were a contributing factor to a wide array of problems was gaining ground. The negative consequences of the over-concentration of office activities in city centres had already been noted as early as the late 1960s (Jacobs, 2000) and in the following decades many urban policy initiatives tried to introduce a wider array of uses into intervention areas, somewhat over-emphasising the importance of physical aspects. Housing especially was seen as a use that could support transport investment and small-scale retail uses and inject life beyond weekdays and office hours. The provision of housing in areas previously dominated by commercial uses became a tool of urban policies for introducing diversity into those areas (Urban Task Force, 1999; ODPM, 2003).

In the 1990s a similar rationale came to be accepted in the case of the regeneration of large, single-use, post-war public housing estates overwhelmingly dominated by one type of tenure, i.e. social renting. In this case, however, diversity referred to the introduction through regeneration projects of a variety of tenure types, with the encouragement of owner occupation and private renting (see van Beckhoven and van Kempen, 2003; Blanc and Bertrand, 1996; ODPM, 2003; Priemus, 1998). There is a long-standing debate on the potential social and economic benefits that can be achieved by mixing different tenures – and consequently income groups – in close proximity to one another (see Cheshire, 2007; Goodchild and Cole, 2001; SEU, 1998), but the principle of 'mixity' has largely been accepted by urban policy makers in Europe (see ECTP, 2003). Consequently, policies and initiatives for the provision of housing for different types of tenure has therefore become commonplace in the regeneration of social housing estates and other areas in which there is a large housing component.

With time, the ideas of 'mixed communities' and 'mixed uses' as key ingredients in urban regeneration initiatives have been extended beyond the regeneration of monofunctional, single-tenure social housing estates to all types of urban regeneration. This has been linked to the growing importance of the sustainability agenda and its assimilation of ideas about the compact city and the benefits accruing from the intensive reuse of previously developed land (CEC, 1990; ODPM, 2006). Such changes have contributed to the consolidation of the linkages between urban regeneration and housing policy by linking the provision of private, speculative housing to broader objectives of planning and urban policy. The more recent and increasing reliance on property markets and private development to achieve urban policy objectives of various kinds has only strengthened those linkages.

Therefore, if in the 1970s and 1980s the link between housing provision and urban regeneration was mostly through the need to renovate public housing estates and deteriorating city quarters, from the 1990s onwards regeneration has encompassed initiatives addressing a much broader range of types of property and tenure. Rather than simply physical renovation of a decaying stock, the key focus has shifted towards the creation of mixed communities in income and forms of tenure, the return of middle-class households to the city and the introduction of mixed-use developments in formerly single-use areas. These are to be produced mostly by private and third sector developers and financed to a large extent with private capital (Cadell *et al.*, 2008; Hoppenbrouwer and Louw, 2005; UTF, 1999).

Cooperation and the co-production of merit and public goods

The last issue in this brief introduction to the main topic of the book is that of cooperation in the production of merit and public goods in the context of urban regeneration interventions. Contemporary policy responses to declining neighbourhoods and deprived communities have tried to create sustainable social and economic life, i.e. a social and economic dynamic that ensures that a neighbourhood becomes a fully functional part of the city, through the introduction of a mix of different types of uses and housing tenures as well as public realm improvements, social infrastructure etc. As summarised earlier, this is not to be achieved by direct state provision, as in the past, but through cooperative development initiatives, often market-led, with the state trying to secure delivery of the expected goods and services.

This type of engagement with markets and the private and third sectors means that the final combination between private, merit and public goods, on which the delivery of policy objectives depends, is guided by a mix of policy directives and market signals. In this, current strategies for urban regeneration and housing provision mirror those adopted in other fields of state action discussed earlier. The term 'co-production' is used in this book to define this type of production of merit and public goods. It has been applied more frequently to describe the relationship between the state and voluntary sector organisations (see Brandsen and Pestoff, 2006) but it could be expanded to aptly describe the nature of the relationship between the public sector and private and third sector actors in contemporary urban regeneration. In this policy field, societal goals are to be met by a process of negotiation with, and transfer of a wider range of decision-making powers to developers, third sector providers, financial agents and the beneficiaries and users.

However, it should be pointed out that the issue in this case is that of relative changes in the roles of different social agents rather than a radical break with the past. Alexander (2001) and Linblom (2001), amongst others, have argued that the boundaries between state and markets are not and never have been as clear cut as part of the literature is suggesting. Therefore, it could be plausibly argued that elements of co-production have been a part of the delivery of social goals in regeneration and housing policy for a very long time. As an example, in all three countries examined in this book incentives and subsidies to private developers to produce housing units, or to households to meet their housing needs in the marketplace, have been a part of housing policies from their very origins (see Chapter 2 and discussion earlier in this chapter). What distinguishes the approaches of the last few decades is that co-production, in the sense suggested earlier in this chapter, greatly increased in importance as part of a wider move towards policy delivery through partnership arrangements between state, private and third sector actors.

In housing and urban regeneration, as with health, education and other areas of public policy, the boundaries between the state and private interests, state and civil society, between producers and users of policy are increasingly shaped by contractual relations and partnership mechanisms, which attribute rights and responsibilities in a way that makes tenuous the distinction between client and contractor, provider and user, or policy maker and policy beneficiary (Sullivan and Skelcher, 2002). The reasons for this were briefly summarised earlier in this chapter. The collaborative arrangements for co-production between the state and private agents in each country are described in more detail in the chapter that follows.

From the point of view of the social actors commissioning and delivering policy objectives, this shift from a 'provider' state to an 'enabling' one (Sullivan and Skelcher, 2002) and the move towards co-production have not been smooth processes. Organisational forms, skill sets and routines that might have been useful under one governance mode have proved to be inadequate under the other. For the public sector, the restructuring that has accompanied that shift is well documented (see Anderson and van Kempen, 2001; Leach and Percy-Smith, 2001; Stewart and Walsh, 1992; Stoker, 2004). There is also a growing literature on the implications of co-production of services for the voluntary sector, focusing especially on how organisations can maintain independence and responsiveness to their constituencies in the context of increasing contractual obligations and partnership ties with the state (Deakin, 2001).

Similarly, private sector players in regeneration have had to adapt their strategies to take into account the introduction of a multiplicity of new policy objectives into their business environment (Karadimitriou, 2005). Clearly, policy objectives have always been to some extent factored into property development, yet in more recent times an increasingly complex set of societal objectives is being required from private developments, well beyond those implicit or explicit in land-use planning and related policies. For example, the delivery of 'affordable' housing, forms of mixed-use and mixed-tenure, an attractive public realm, local employment initiatives, amenities and social facilities are now almost standard requirements in urban regeneration projects.

The long-term evolution and convergence of policies with a strong physical dimension (like housing), urban policy and social policy gave rise to present-day urban regeneration policy and practice. This transformation took place in the context of changes in urban governance regimes favouring new modes of collaboration. So far as the physical expression of that process is concerned, it has taken the form of a Mixed Use Urban Regeneration Scheme (MUURS). MUURSs now play a key role in the delivery of a wide range of policy objectives, housing policy included.

Given the nature of policy delivery systems described above – in which the distinctions between provider and user, contractor and client, public and private are increasingly blurred – processes of change in governance imply changes in the organisational profile, strategies and ways of doing things on the part of the actors involved, whether in the public, third or private sector. They also imply changes in the physical form of cities and set the scene for their future development, in the same way that previous rounds of investment affect our present reality (see above, section on European industrial city). How this happens and what the implications are will be some of the main concerns of this book.

The structure of the book

This book explores the ways in which merit and public goods, like non-market housing, social infrastructure, green space etc. have been provided through urban regeneration projects in three countries in Europe. It looks at how in the UK (or England, more specifically), the Netherlands and France urban regeneration schemes bringing together public, private and third sector partners combine their aspirations and strategies to produce both private gains and social and economic policy objectives. This is not necessarily a harmonious and conflict-free process, as the different parties involved in it are engaged in a continuous process of risk and return allocation. In all three countries, legal and institutional frameworks are in place to try to regulate how the distribution of risks and appropriation of rewards might happen and how disagreements might be negotiated. These frameworks shape the outcomes of regeneration schemes as well as the limits and the potential of the policies relying on those schemes.

In order to investigate those frameworks in the three countries and the kinds of urban environments they might lead to, the next chapter takes a closer look at urban regeneration, what it means and how it is conducted on all three occasions. It looks in more detail at the relationship between regeneration policies and practices and non-market housing, a most important component of urban regeneration policies as of late.

Chapter 3 introduces the analytical framework deployed to investigate how private and public sector objectives are brought together in large-scale, mixed-used urban regeneration schemes in the Netherlands, France and England, and how risks and rewards are apportioned between partners.

Chapters 4, 5 and 6 present two cases each of mixed-use urban regeneration schemes in the Netherlands, France and England respectively. For each country, one of the cases refers to an area of previous commercial and/or industrial use that is being reintroduced into the city's property market through a combination of public and private actions. The other case deals with attempts to introduce market dynamics to failing social housing estates, again as a way of delivering public policy objectives.

Chapter 7 concludes the book with a discussion of what the six cases can tell us about the different approaches to urban regeneration in each country, the differences and similarities in the roles of actors and, more broadly, the limits and potentials of this form of policy delivery.

Note

1 With the term 'non-market housing' we tried to capture the meaning of what elsewhere has been called 'non-profit' and/or 'subsidised' housing. We mean housing normally available at prices and rents below those that would be achieved in open market transactions and the production of which does not necessarily and exclusively come from purely profit-driven market actors. This includes social housing, municipal and cooperative housing, the 'affordable housing' of UK housing policy etc.

Chapter 2

Urban regeneration and property market dynamics in the Netherlands, France and the UK

Changes in urban policies: urban regeneration and market mechanisms

The 'recycling' of previously developed land became an important objective of current public policies throughout Europe (see also Couch *et al.*, 2003; Karadimitriou, 2005) in an attempt to bring about a more sustainable urban development, control urban sprawl, reduce travel distances and responsibly use land as a scarce resource. Chapter 1 explored how, due to macro trends such as technological development and globalisation, certain parts of the existing urban fabric have gradually become unfit for current demand and not attractive for investors, employers and inhabitants alike. In all three countries, frameworks and methodologies were developed that would measure and spatially locate deprivation, in an effort to assist area-based interventions. That approach has been criticised as a factor reinforcing stigmatisation, but although the terminology may have changed, the logic of area-based measurement still remains a core element of urban policies. The shift in focus of public policies towards these areas and away from urban extensions resulted in the increase in the proportion of urban development taking place as part of urban regeneration projects.

These urban regeneration projects would typically have two important characteristics. First, they would be a purposeful attempt to intervene in a particular area in order to transform it socially, economically and physically. Second, this transformation process required some form of cooperation between the state, the private and the third sectors in order to instigate change towards a desired direction. Broadly speaking, in the 1960s and 1970s the public sector readily intervened in the part of the urban fabric that was deemed to be ripe for 'renewal', whereas, depending on the country, the private sector became more involved during the course of the 1980s and 1990s, mainly due to the need to reduce public spending, but also because of expectations of greater effectiveness and efficiency. There is now an increasing body of evidence suggesting that these expectations have not necessarily materialised (NAO, 2011; Siddiquee, 2011).

During that time, starting from the US and the UK, an argument gained credence according to which in the areas concerned there was no buoyant market for property and, as a consequence, these areas would not attract the investment that is necessary to renew them (Guy *et al.*, 2002; Healey, 1991; Piron, 2002). Therefore, the argument continued, interventions from the state should in the first instance try to make the area attractive for private investors and developers. If they managed to do so, market mechanisms would take over and regenerate the area by re-establishing the supply–demand interactions at a level that would make it meaningful for private businesses to become active.

By its very nature, private sector investment in projects of urban regeneration is only feasible if value is created that can then be monetised through the market. However, in many regeneration projects it is public involvement that puts in place and sustains the preconditions for value creation. The main reasons why the public sector is prepared to get involved fall into three broad categories: social welfare objectives, economic development objectives and a concern for the urban form related to ideas about the relationship between space and social and economic well-being (nowadays largely encapsulated in the concept of sustainability).

As discussed in the previous chapter, urban regeneration objectives and public investment have been strongly associated with the provision of housing, and especially non-market dwellings. The delivery of housing – and the realisation of housing policy objectives – is therefore a goal of many regeneration projects, whether or not housing units is their main output. Non-market ('public', 'social', 'affordable') housing is a key merit good delivered through most regeneration interventions, and around which other services and facilities with strong merit and public good characteristics (health, education, public spaces etc.) are organised. The delivery of housing is therefore a key element in the negotiation between public, private and third sector actors around the apportionment of risks and rewards, and the way this is done shapes to a large extent the nature of urban regeneration as public policy.

In comparison with earlier debates on access to housing, the discourse since the early 1990s was characterised by the attention to housing issues for middle-income households and 'key workers' (Raco, 2008). The important price increases over the early and mid-2000s in particular have compromised the possibility of middle-income households, particularly the non-homeowners among them, to enter or move upward in the housing market. This phenomenon was exacerbated by the fact that by that time most countries had gone through a process of retreat from public provision of housing.

State-centred structures of housing provision have effectively been dismantled (in the UK) or have been made more autonomous and less directly linked to the public sector (in the Netherlands) and direct public subsidies for housing production have been drastically reduced (in the Netherlands, France and the UK).

As a result, the public sector has become less involved in the production of housing. Partnerships with private developers, and the attraction of private sector investment, have become crucial elements of housing provision.

At the same time, documents like the European Commission's Green Paper (CEC, 1990) underpinned the Europe-wide redirection of urban policy towards sustainability, later reflected in a series of documents like the Lille Action Programme (in 2000), the Bristol Accord (in 2005), the Leipzig Charter (in 2007), the Marseille Statement (in 2008) and the Toledo Declaration (in 2010). As Couch *et al.* (2003) and Verhage (2005a, 2005b) point out, from the mid-1990s many countries have turned their attention to the regeneration of the existing urban fabric, eventually framed by initiatives like the 'Loi Solidarité et Renouvellement Urbains' (SRU law) in France in 2000, the Urban Task Force (UTF) Report in the UK in 1999, and the Investeringsbudget Stedelijke Vernieuwing (ISV – Investment Budget for Urban Regeneration) in 1997 in the Netherlands.

Throughout Western Europe, the idea that an important proportion of newly built spaces, and consequently of housing, ought to be provided on brownfield land obtained a central position in urban policy. In this chapter we trace the emergence of these trends in the Netherlands, France and the UK since the beginning of the 1980s. This description highlights how in each national context the interrelation between policies, institutional settings, physical realities and economic situation has led to a particular approach to urban regeneration. It also shows how this approach is characterised by an increased reliance on market mechanisms for the delivery of merit and public goods. Public sector intervention in such schemes has often been necessary not only in order to instigate investment, but more importantly from a policy point of view to affect the balance between types of housing and to steer it closer to affordability goals. In that, it has been effective to varying degrees in the three countries in question.

In all three countries the provision of merit and public goods depends not only on urban regeneration projects but on a wide range of policy measures and initiatives. Especially so far as housing is concerned, in the UK, following the aggressive rollback of the welfare state the provision of 'affordable housing' through urban regeneration came to assume a dominant position, whereas in France and the Netherlands it has played an important role but as part of a wider mix of complementary measures. These trends are discussed in more detail in the sections that follow. The aim is not to provide an exhaustive account of regeneration, housing and urban policies in all three countries for the last three decades, as this has been done much more thoroughly and comprehensively by several other authors, on some of whom we also draw. Rather, the goal is to highlight some key characteristics and trends of those policy streams and thus provide a general background for the case studies.

The Netherlands: a coalition of municipalities, housing associations and private housebuilders

The focus and the logic of urban regeneration policy in the Netherlands has changed significantly over time, especially since the 1990s, but still draws on that country's approach to housing provision, which is steeped in a corporatist/ social democratic tradition (for an extensive typological discussion see Hoekstra, 2003), and on a planning culture that favours a strategic and multiscalar approach (for further elaboration see, for example, Needham, 2007). A distinctive characteristic of the Dutch housing system is the high proportion of social rental housing in the total housing stock: in the early 2000s social housing comprised 36 per cent of the total housing stock and 75 per cent of the rental housing stock (Ministerie van VROM, 2001). Those percentages have remained relatively stable (Høj, 2011). Moreover, typical of what Kemeny called an "integrated housing system" (Kemeny, 2001; Kemeny *et al.*, 2005), social housing in the Netherlands functions as an alternative to the market rental sector for a wide range of social strata, whereas rents are regulated to a large extent. This situation is in part the result of long-standing public involvement with the provision of non-market housing but it also has to do with the particular character of the providers of non-market housing in the Netherlands, the *Woningbouwcorporaties* (Housing Associations).

The Housing Associations, which have their legal basis in the 1901 Housing Act, are independent actors that act as private parties. They remain non-profit organisations, whose capital has been built up with public money and who obtained significant autonomy when they were made financially independent in 1995 through the grossing (*brutering*) operation. They no longer receive direct public subsidies but instead they use their own resources for the construction of new dwellings or the refurbishment of older dwellings in their stock. They also have to cover loss-making investments with revenues from elsewhere, for example by selling dwellings or through rental incomes, but their social objectives and non-profit character remain, as does their main legal responsibility to provide accommodation for households incapable of acquiring satisfactory housing on the open market (Ouwehand and van Daalen, 2002). Housing provision in the Netherlands is largely structured around them, especially since the mid-1990s, when municipal provision was phased out.

The direct or indirect involvement of the public sector in housing is justified on the grounds that many low-income households cannot afford to pay for decent housing on the free market. The public sector sees it as one of its tasks to support these households. Apart from rent regulation, this support can take various forms, ranging from financial support to the supply side (i.e. to the housing associations), referred to as *objectsubsidie*, to financial support to the demand side (i.e. the households), referred to as *subjectsubsidie*. A third form of state support for the provision of housing is by reducing the development costs. This third option has been very important in the Netherlands, where municipalities often play a very active role in land assembly and development (see, for example, van der Krabben and Jacobs, 2011). This allows them to provide land under favourable conditions to housing associations. Land lease was used quite extensively in this respect, but is less and less practised. Since the middle of the 1990s, the position of the Dutch municipalities in the land market is changing and private developers play an increasing role (de Kam, 1996). As a consequence, providing land at reduced prices to housing associations is becoming more complicated, but new and inventive ways are being tested in order to continue this practice.

In order to support homeownership the government makes mortgage interest tax deductible, subsidises home purchases and backs a mortgage guarantee fund. Following the grossing operation of 1995, the housing associations no longer receive any *objectsubsidies*. Indirectly, public subsidies still play a role because the *subjectsubsidies* allow the housing associations to charge higher rent levels, thus increasing their revenues. The public sector approaches the whole sector as a 'revolving fund' whose income comes from rents and sales of the associations' housing production and existing stock. This does imply a more market-oriented strategy for housing associations, in which the creation of economic value in order to finance new social projects becomes a central element. There are two main institutions providing financial support to housing associations, the 'Central Housing Fund' and the 'Guarantee Fund for Social Housing', a fund constituted with money from the housing associations that secures the loans of the associations in the capital market.

Dutch municipalities play a very active role in the development process. They not only elaborate the legally binding land-use plans that designate areas for housing development, but they also play a very active role in the realisation of these plans (Needham and Verhage, 1998), e.g. by supporting housing associations through the assembly and provision of land at reduced prices. To that effect Dutch municipalities often operate organisations specialising in land trading and development. The Bank Nederlandse Gemeenten (BNG – Bank of Dutch Municipalities) plays an important role in funding local authorities and housing associations, and thus urban development projects, in a fashion similar to the Caisse des Depots et Consignations (CDC) in France. Funding for regeneration is also available through revolving funds that operate at the municipal level.

The period between the 1950s and the 1980s was characterised by a strong coalition of housing associations and municipalities in urban development (Priemus, 2006). Apart from the importance of public sector subsidies, there was a strong convergence of interests between municipalities, who wanted to expand and to renew run-down parts of their territory, and housing associations, who wanted to build new housing. In order to be in charge of their territorial development, municipalities used to acquire all the land prior to urbanisation and take charge of the land development. They then sold building plots to private housing developers or to housing associations. As said above, the land for housing associations was often transferred at a lower price than the land for market housing. In exchange, using their *objectsubsidies*, housing associations offered certainty that development would take place in the area concerned (de Kam, 1996). This reduced the financial risk for the municipalities engaging in land development and assisted them in achieving their planning and welfare goals.

This practice changed in the course of the 1990s, due to pressure from the European Union's market competition imperatives and because of a 'price shock' in the land markets, related to economic factors (mainly low interest rates), changes in the planning system (introduction of *Vinex* locations) and the reduction of the proportion of social housing to be realised in new urban development, which strengthened the role of private housebuilders. They were able to compete with and often outbid municipalities in the land market, thus assuring their involvement in development project proposals. At the same time, the municipalities still considered it part of their responsibilities to take charge of new urban development and developers were not always averse to this aspiration.

This new balance sometimes allowed developers to engage in land development without municipal intervention, but often gave rise to partnerships between the municipality and the private housebuilders in which the land is often transferred to the municipality in exchange for a 'building claim' of a specified number of dwellings, reflecting the amount of land that the private housebuilder owned on the site. This practice still allows the municipalities to transfer the required land to the housing associations and to influence the conditions of the transfer. However, the combination of more market-oriented housing associations and a bigger role for private housebuilders in the development process has resulted in a much stronger emphasis on economic arguments in the provision of housing.

Recent changes in the Spatial Planning Act of 2008 have introduced tools that allow Dutch local authorities to recover the costs of infrastructure and to ensure 'affordable' housing provision even in cases where the municipalities don't own the land. It is still rather early to see the effects of those changes on housing provision and the production of the built environment more generally. Any evaluation of the practices evolving as a result of the new Act should always bear in mind what the role of the state is or can be regarding the uncertainties inherent in the development process, the volatility of the land and property market as well as welfare provision.

Housing and urban regeneration

The production of housing in projects of urban regeneration has gained importance in the Netherlands since the beginning of the 1990s, when the provision of new housing on previously developed land gradually became an objective of public policy. Until then, urban renewal was an objective of public policy but it mainly aimed at improving housing conditions in existing residential areas that often had a substantial component of housing association dwellings. Development of new dwellings in extension areas was running in parallel but separated from those programmes. At the same time, the increasing influence of market mechanisms in housing development made property-led urban regeneration projects a focal point in the discourse surrounding the provision of housing.

The new discourse has its origins in the *Vinex* (*Vierde Nota over de Ruimtelijke Ordening Extra* – Fourth Report on Spatial Planning) of 1991, which introduced the notion of the compact city. New housing was to be produced in the existing city, and in the immediate proximity of the city if that was not possible. The *Vinex* indicated locations, mainly adjacent to existing conurbations, where housing was to be provided. Outside those locations a restrictive policy made new housing development more difficult. The attention to housing production focused on the *Vinex* locations but the production of housing in these areas took off more slowly than planned, mainly because of problems with land acquisition and with reaching agreements with private developers who had speculatively acquired land in the area. The important housing price increases of the second half of the 1990s and the first half of the 2000s resulted in pressures to accelerate housing production on *Vinex* locations, in order to increase the supply of housing. This pushed to the background the initial objective of providing housing in the already built-up areas of cities.

The objective of providing new housing through transformation of previously developed land was reiterated in the follow-up *Vinex* of 2004. This new national spatial planning document fixed a percentage of 40 per cent of all new housing to be built in projects on previously developed land. This overall number of 40 per cent was thought to be too generic to suit all situations, therefore national government changed it into 24–40 per cent in 2007 (Ministerie van Algemene Zaken, 2007).

As mentioned already, state involvement in urban regeneration in the Netherlands traditionally aimed mainly at the renewal of degraded housing areas with social housing. This was realised by local government in cooperation with the housing associations and was financially supported by central government subsidies. 'Building for the neighbourhood' was the central slogan. At the end of the 1980s and the beginning of the 1990s the primacy of the housing sector was questioned and the function of cities as 'motors of the economy' gained in importance (Ekkers, 2002). In the same period, the national policy report on housing policy *Volkshuisvesting in de Jaren '90* (Social Housing in the 1990s) initiated a more market-led housing policy. This resulted in a growing independence of the housing associations that was confirmed by the grossing operation after which the whole system of non-market housing reached maturity and housing associations became financially independent and did not receive any further central state subsidies.

The national policy for urban regeneration reflects this changing character. The subsidies in the 1970s and 1980s had specific criteria and procedures. In 1985, the Law on the Renewal of Cities and Villages (*Wet op de Stads- en Dorpsvernieuwing*) bundled existing subsidies in the Fund for Urban Renewal (*Stadsvernieuwingsfonds*). Municipalities and housing associations had to deal with only one procedure to obtain these subsidies. During the 1990s, however, starting with the "Urban Renewal Policy in the Future" paper (also known as 'Belstato'), policy began to shift towards less state involvement in urban renewal, especially with regard to funding responsibilities (Stouten, 2010). In 1995 this logic was taken a step further in the "Policy for the Major Cities" (Grote Steden Beleid – GSB) (Korthals Altes, 2002). The GSB acknowledged that the social and economic problems of the major cities (initially the 4 biggest ones but then expanded to 30) were spatially concentrated and their eradication would require a combined effort by central and local government and cooperation between public and private actors.

The GSB distinguished three fields of action, its three 'pillars': the social, the economic and the physical. To obtain subsidies, the cities were invited to draw up an investment programme in which they present their strategy for the next four years. Ever since, urban regeneration has to tie the three pillars of the GSB together and therefore to integrate sectoral policies of housing, urban planning, environment and the economy.

The policy of urban regeneration (*stadsvernieuwing*) was elaborated in the national report on urban regeneration, published in 1997 by the Ministry of Housing, the Environment and Spatial Planning (Ministerie van VROM). The objective was to create conditions that would facilitate qualitative improvements in the residential, economic and 'living' urban environment. Its focus was on post-war (i.e. mainly housing association-built) neighbourhoods in decline, with the aim of changing the balance between social rental and owner-occupied housing in what has been dubbed strategy of 'urban restructuring' (Kleinhans, 2009) specifically aiming at establishing 'social control' in the more deprived neighbourhoods (Uitermark *et al.*, 2007).

To this end, central government created the ISV. This budget regrouped subsidies from three ministries: VROM, the Ministry of Economic Affairs and the Ministry of Agriculture, Fishery and Nature. The ISV promoted a project-led approach to urban regeneration at the local level, and the increased autonomy that it offers was well received by local authorities (Priemus *et al.*, 2002). Local authorities elaborated strategies of urban regeneration and translated them into concrete projects in their investment programmes. In the 30 biggest cities, local authorities enter into long-term 'covenants' with the central government in order to implement these strategies whereas smaller local authorities can enter into agreements with the provincial governments. This approach, however, is not without its critics, and van der Schaar (2005) argues that many problems with the implementation of locally determined projects were due to the national level of government losing its direct means of influence and thus its capacity to enforce the strategic direction of national policy.

Since the introduction of the ISV, the mobilisation of private partners, or at least of private sector investment, is an important objective of the policy for urban regeneration in the Netherlands. In practice, the most common form of partner-ship still is between local authorities and housing associations. The way in which the Dutch municipalities can encourage housing associations to engage in urban regeneration is rather similar to the way in which private actors can be induced, i.e. by influencing the risk/reward profile of an operation (Guy *et al.*, 2002). They can do this, for example, by selling land for moderate prices, or by investing in public space in the areas for renewal, to increase the development potential of a site.

As Nijkamp *et al.* (2002) argue, the reconciliation of economic, social and environmental considerations in a joint decision-making process leads to a complex process architecture. In order to receive the required funding, public, semi-public and private actors have to agree upon the contents of a project and establish a partnership. They therefore have to address issues concerning the division of risks, responsibilities and rewards and fix the outcomes of the nego-tiations in contracts that from then on determine the margin of manoeuvre of the actors in the process. Detailed arrangements in the initial phases of the project can lead to a lack of flexibility in the later phases (Verhage and Sluis, 2003).

France: between public sector-led and market-driven urban regeneration

Underpinning French urban policy and public policy in general is a strong tradition "of the 'republican state' and its social obligations towards its citizens" (Dikec, 2006, p. 59). Dikec also notes that, despite market-liberalising reforms (ibid., p. 66), the obligation of the French state to provide a wide array of services and infrastructure to its citizens is combined with powerful cross-party political discourses emphasising the importance of social justice and social cohesion, as well as social order in what he calls the 'right hand' of the state.

The steady course towards devolution of power to the regional and local level from the early 1980s onwards has resulted in the transfer of significant planning, economic development and regeneration competencies to the local and regional governments. Central, regional and local government frequently collaborate with each other, often through a system of contracts that set out strategies and objectives for specific programmatic periods and link them to national government and (potentially) European Union funding. Collaboration between local authorities is also frequent and is encouraged by the legislative and funding framework. These collaborations are not always possible to achieve and the system has been criticised for being too cumbersome, fragmented and focused on welfare provision to the detriment of economic development objectives. As Nappi-Choulet (2006, p. 1518) points out, so far as regeneration is concerned for the period 2000–7, there were "247 *contrats de ville* involving more than 1500 neighbourhoods and over 1 million housing units".

In terms of urban planning, each agglomeration has to produce a Schema de Cohérence Territoriale (SCOT) a strategic document with which all other sectoral policies and plans should be compatible (see Programme Local d'Habitat – PLH – below). *Regeneration urbaine* (see Chaline, 1999) was traditionally related to more physical, urban renewal interventions, whereas interventions with a greater social focus would fall under the term *politique de la ville* (see Chaline, 2003; Cour des Comptes, 2002). The distinction between the two is becoming rather historical, as policy in the last couple of decades at least is increasingly focusing on integrated approaches to urban regeneration. However, as Dormois *et al.* (2005) point out, there are also elements of path dependency that act as obstacles to policy integration and to the redefinition of the roles of public, private and third sectors.

Two strands of urban regeneration interventions can be distinguished, as pointed out by Bonneville (2005). On the one hand, there is the regeneration of derelict industrial or mixed areas that have become underused, mainly because of changes in the productive structure of cities. The regeneration of these areas is usually initiated by local planning authorities and aims at making the area attractive for private investors. These types of projects rely on attracting private sector investment, which also means that they take place in areas that have potential for redevelopment (good accessibility, a waterfront etc.). On the other hand, there is the regeneration of mainly large-scale, suburban high-rise social housing areas of the 1960s and 1970s, known as the *grands ensembles*, even though some more centrally located and older housing areas are also included. Because of the difficulty in attracting private sector investment into these areas, and given the French republican tradition, such operations rely much more heavily on public sector investment. The central state plays a key role in this type of regeneration through the subsidies it provides and the criteria it uses for delivering these subsidies.

Since the early 2000s, the differences between the two types of projects are diminishing. Following the SRU law of 2000 and the Borloo law (*loi d'orientation pour la ville et la renovation urbaine*) of 2003, the attraction of private investment into projects concerned with the *grands ensembles* has become a key objective of regeneration policy (Mejean, 2003). With the creation of the Agence National pour la Renovation Urbaine (ANRU) by the Borloo law in 2003, the delivery of state subsidies was reformed accordingly. This type of urban regeneration is supported financially by the central state through ANRU, whose function is to fund regeneration projects initiated at the local level. ANRU allocates its funding on the basis of a number of criteria that focus on demolition and reconstruction, social and functional mix and financial viability.

The eligibility criteria for regeneration projects for central state subsidies now include the provision of market housing through the demolition and reconstruction of existing social housing. They also require the budget of the entire project to estimate the revenue expected from the sale of land for economically viable functions (market housing, economic activities) alongside the income from central and local government funding. Revenues generated by the sale of land in such projects should be used to finance the project, thus attracting private investment into regeneration areas became a key objective of initiatives for large high-rise areas.

It is worth noting here that in France, apart from direct central government and local authority funding, such projects can receive loans from the CDC, which manages public funds (i.e. public service pension contributions etc.) independently of the government and its funding streams (see Fraser, 2003b). In addition, when the state assumes the role of land developer, the development process is often managed by the Sociétés d'Economie Mixte (SEM) and the Etablissements Publics Foncières (EPF). These are publicly owned organisations that operate as private businesses and are in charge of the land assembly and land development of regeneration areas, under the close supervision of local authorities (see Trache *et al.*, 2007). The legal framework also predefines specific tools and procedures that the state can use to manage different aspects of the development process. The Zone d'Aménagement Concerté (ZAC) and the Programme d'Aménagement d'Ensemble (PAE) will be discussed further in the chapter of French case studies.

The French public sector is involved in the provision and management of non-market housing mainly through financial tools, whereas rental is the dominant form of tenure so far as social housing is concerned. Different categories of central state subsidies exist that aim at financing non-market housing. These subsidies are linked to the rent level, which in turn is linked to the revenues of the occupant. Subsidies are in principle granted by the central government, unless the local authority has elaborated its housing policy in a PLH (one of the several components of the SCOT).

Three broad types of subsidies exist. They take the shape of subsidised loans: Prêt Locatif Aidé d'Intégration (PLAI), Prêt Locatif à Usage Social (PLUS) and Prêt Locatif Social (PLS). The first aims at the lowest income groups and hence offers the highest level of subsidy in order to compensate for low rent levels. In the same logic, PLUS and PLS aim at higher-income classes, and in consequence offer lower subsidy levels.

Nearly 70 per cent of the French population has a right to benefit from these subsidies. In practice, the existing housing stock cannot accommodate such a large part of the population, since only 18.5 per cent of the total French housing stock is social rental housing in the strict sense. Even though private housebuilders can also receive PLS, the subsidised loans are generally granted to *bailleurs sociaux*, public bodies that build and manage social housing. As we will see in the next section, these bodies also benefit from local government support of various kinds. This support is often referred to as *aide à la pierre* ('support for bricks'), as opposed to *aide à la personne* ('support for persons'), which is support for households to enable them to cover their housing costs. This latter type is linked directly to the income of the households and can be used to finance both rental and owner-occupied housing, within nationally applicable limits concerning the rent level.

In addition to the traditional mechanisms above, an increasing part of the provision of what could be termed 'affordable housing' is financed using tax reliefs. The objective of these tax reliefs is to provide an incentive for private investors to invest in housing that for a certain period (nine years) has to be let at a maximum rent level, corresponding to the level of the PLS. These tax reliefs increase supply in the market for rental housing, but their effects on the provision of social housing are sometimes criticised. The maximum rent level below which dwellings become eligible is fairly high and therefore these tax reliefs have provided an incentive for private investment in real estate, as they increase the attractiveness of investment in (rental) property.

The concept of affordable housing has gained in popularity in France during the 2000s. The term is not explicitly used, but there is a tendency for the public sector to promote the production of dwellings that are sold or rented below market prices. This has become a preoccupation of local governments, due to the significant housing price increases during the period 1997–2007. As a consequence, access to housing became a problem not only for lower income groups but also for middle income groups. Affordable housing is aimed at providing an alternative for these groups other than (rental) social housing and market housing.

This is linked to government policy, which supports homeownerhip by lower- and middle-income households, and also to wider concerns about social cohesion. For example the Loi l'Orientation pour la Ville of 1991 introduced social housing quotas per local authority with the goal of social mixity, a requirement that was carried forward in subsequent laws, like the SRU. For ideological reasons, right-wing governments traditionally favour private sector housing provision rather than provision through the social rental sector. The usual means employed in order to make access to homeownership possible for a larger number of people are tax reliefs and the provision of loans under very favourable conditions (*prêt à taux zero* – zero-interest loans, available under certain income conditions).

In order to integrate national policies for social and affordable housing into a coherent policy at the local level, local planning authorities should elaborate a PLH as part of their SCOT. The PLH sets out the framework for interventions by the local planning authority so far as the provision of housing is concerned. These interventions revolve to an important extent around projects of urban regeneration. The PLH was first introduced in 1983, with the objective of allowing municipalities to define their priorities in the field of housing (until then, housing policies were elaborated at the level of the central state). The first PLHs were limited in scope and in effect – in particular because no financial means were attached. Over the years, the PLH has gained importance, and in 2006 it became a document presenting a territorialised programme for the production of housing. Since 2004 the PLH has to be elaborated by an inter-municipal cooperation structure,[1] and since 2006 it is obligatory for larger agglomerations (over 50,000 inhabitants) to have a PLH. Its objective is to provide an action programme for a period of five years, in which the objectives of housing policy are linked to policies and projects of urban planning. The link with urban planning is assured because the PLH has to be compatible with the strategic planning document (SCOT) for the same territory.

The national-level strategies guide the overall policy objectives of the PLH, which include: satisfying housing need, stimulating urban renewal and social mix, improving the accessibility of the built environment for disabled people and assuring a balanced and diversified supply of housing throughout the territory of the local planning authority. The PLH is also an important tool in the realisation of the objective of the SRU law (article 55) of a minimum of 20 per cent of social housing in all municipalities.

A fine per missing dwelling per year is imposed on the municipalities that have not reached the required minimum. Local planning authorities of conurbations with a population of less than 50,000 inhabitants are not obliged to have a PLH. However, in order to incentivise local authorities to develop a PLH the central government transfers responsibility for disbursing the *aide à la pierre* to local authorities that have an updated PLH.

The PLH is underpinned by a logic of state involvement in the markets that reflects the republican discourse previously mentioned. In order to explain and support its programme of action, the PLH usually contains an overview of the current state of the housing market and considers the issue of social and affordable housing in relation to the market in general. The programme of action focuses mainly on the provision of social and affordable housing, since these are the forms of housing that the market is supposedly unable to produce without government support. However, the PLH contains an analysis of the supply of and demand for housing and of the imbalances between the two, as well as an analysis of the social problems that are related to these imbalances. It also contains an analysis of the policy measures that have been deployed in order to resolve the imbalances between supply and demand. These analyses inform the general orientation of housing policies at the local level and therefore also affect the programme of action emanating from these policies. The programme of action indicates numbers and localities of housing projects, in their various forms (regeneration, extension, refurbishment of existing stock etc.).

Housing and urban regeneration

In France, social housing is typified by the large-scale, high-rise social housing areas known as the *grands ensembles*, built between the second half of the 1950s and the second half of the 1970s. During that period, demand for housing in the urban areas of France was very strong, mainly because of migration from rural areas and from former colonies. The state, with its significant juridical, technical and financial power, considered it its duty to provide sufficient housing to meet those needs. The combination of the strong demand for housing, the dominance of one actor – the state – in housing provision and the architectural ideas and building techniques of the time led to the construction of large-scale, high-rise social housing estates in the peripheral areas of almost all French cities. Following the economic decline of the 1970s these estates rapidly became problem areas where only lower-income households remained because they could not afford to move anywhere else. This concentration of 'captive' populations in social housing areas and the problems that are linked to it are not unique to France, but the scale of the social housing areas, ranging from several hundred to several thousands of dwellings, gives these problems a particular urgency.

For that reason, from the beginning of the 1980s these areas have been subject to several urban regeneration policies. Their decline, which was judged to be very difficult to counter without substantial public intervention, has designated them as areas of primary concern calling for public sector, especially central government, involvement. As Bonneville (2005) argues, the SRU law seemed to enlarge the scope of *renovation urbaine* to cover all run-down areas that do not directly attract private investors. The introduction of the term *renovation urbaine* has not really been accompanied by a clarification of its content; it is, however a close, equivalent to urban regeneration, especially if one considers the way it has been implemented in practice. As mentioned earlier in this chapter, current approaches can broadly be divided into two ideal types that exist alongside each other.

The first approach is to be found in areas of degraded social housing, very often in large high-rise housing estates. This approach is in continuity with earlier interventions under the *politique de la ville*, which promoted a social approach to urban regeneration. In programmes of this type, the public sector intervenes radically and assumes all costs in an effort to give the areas concerned the opportunity to make a 'new start'. Diversification of functions and reinsertion of the areas into the urban real estate market are of secondary importance in this respect.

This approach was reinforced in 2003 by the Borloo law, which promotes higher ratios of demolitions and restructuring of the urban fabric. Demolition is seen as preferable, as there is a growing consensus that refurbishing, even on a large scale, of the existing buildings and public spaces has not produced the expected results. The Borloo law contained an ambitious programme of demolition and reconstruction of social housing: in the period 2004–11, 250,000 dwellings were to be demolished and reconstructed and another 400,000 dwellings were to be refurbished (*rehabilitées*).[2]

This policy underlines the historical role that the state has played in these areas. From the time they were built, they have been subject to direct intervention by the state in its various guises. Central government and its agencies, together with the local planning authorities, which contributed to social segregation and the concentration of deprivation by creating these areas of large-scale, high-rise social housing areas, are now trying to deal with the problems of those areas by proposing yet another special regime for them.

The second approach embraces more property-led forms of urban regeneration and has gradually gained importance in France during the last two decades. This type of regeneration mainly concerns run-down sites and areas in urban centres where there seems to be potential for market-based inversion of the downwards spiral of devalorisation. A key parameter in these cases is the demand for real estate in the (urban) economy. If that demand exists, then public investment, often in improved accessibility, land servicing and the public realm, is used in order to make these areas attractive for private investors and thus to invert the downward spiral of physical degradation and devaluation. This vision of *renovation urbaine* has been introduced in Lille, with the experience of the '*ville renouvelée*' (Roussel, 1997). Generally speaking, local authorities approach urban regeneration along these lines more often than not.

There is a close link between the policies described above and the provision of non-market housing. In France, national policy for the provision of social and affordable housing directly intervenes in both the supply and demand sides of the housing market via subsidies or tax measures. A local authority has three ways to support non-market housing on its territory, if for no other reason than to achieve its long-term legally binding targets. The first means of support is to make sure that housing projects within its boundaries receive central state subsidies. The second is to directly support the provision of social housing, for example by providing land at reduced prices. The third is the use of regulatory tools.

This third option has become increasingly important during the 2000s, due to the urgency of providing affordable housing and because of the growing emphasis on the redevelopment of the existing urban fabric in projects of urban regeneration. The reason for the emphasis on the redevelopment of existing urban land has a lot to do with the attempts to promote sustainable urban development. The efforts to contain urban sprawl, reduce travel distances and use land as a scarce resource have become central objectives of urban policies since the SRU law of 2000. Urban regeneration is a means to achieve those objectives. As a consequence, public authorities are increasingly directing their urban development efforts towards regeneration projects.

The UK: the practice of property-based regeneration

Urban regeneration in the UK is steeped in a "pragmatic, supply-side oriented, partnership based logic" (Hall and Hickman, 2002, p. 695), mainly focused at the local scale (the neighbourhood, the development) and on 'local communities' whose existence is sometimes elusive. Funding initiatives and the legal framework are very much preoccupied with notions of competition (within markets and outside markets) and the efficiencies that it can bring. In addition, the evolution of the UK welfare state since the 1980s has been one of a rather rapid move towards a liberal regime whereby all aspects of welfare provision increasingly operate on a residualist basis, i.e. only as a safety net for the poor (see Esping-Andersen, 1990). Unsurprisingly, the UK rental market can be described as having several of the characteristics of a dualist system (Kemeny, 1995).

It has to be noted here that although central government policy does have an effect throughout the UK, the descriptions and discussions in this chapter and in this book reflect the situation in England more accurately than they do the situation in Scotland, Wales and Northern Ireland. Historically, these constituent countries of the UK had substantial powers devolved to them and their governments have gained even more room for manoeuvre during the 2000s, following the election of local assemblies in all three countries.

In comparison with France and the Netherlands, the involvement of the public sector in urban regeneration in the UK is still significant, the difference lying to a great degree in the way in which the public sector exerts its influence. It plays an important role in the partnership schemes that pursue regeneration, but in most cases the essence of this role is restricted to framing and enabling private sector initiatives. This has consequences for the provision of public goods as well as for non-market housing, especially within the context of the dualist rental market and the undersupply that has typified the UK housing sector since the 1980s. Production levels dropped even lower following the downturn in the property markets in 2008. The notion of partnership, in its broadest sense, is crucial for understanding urban regeneration policies in the UK. It not only concerns the involvement of private developers and financiers in the realisation of public objectives but more generally it describes the cooperation by a wide range of actors.

In similar fashion to other European countries, urban regeneration in the UK emerged in an effort to tackle the social, economic and physical degradation that de-industrialisation or other forms of disinvestment were leaving behind. Until the 1980s, it typically concerned degraded housing areas. During the 1960s and 1970s, large-scale public intervention was deployed in order to renew parts of the cities where living conditions were considered to be poor. The shift to property-led urban regeneration dates back to the beginning of the 1980s, and corresponds to the coming into office of Margaret Thatcher and the Conservatives in 1979.

A heavier reliance on the market mechanism was supposed to counter public sector deficiencies and was supposed to create conditions that would attract private investment into urban regeneration areas. In practice it was combined with greater centralisation of powers, stripping local authorities of a lot of their capacity to act autonomously when dealing with social deprivation. The essence of this approach to urban regeneration is encapsulated by the Urban Development Corporations (UDCs) (Imrie and Thomas, 1999). From then on various regimes came to pass until the mid-1990s, when the Department of the Environment (DoE) began to turn urban policy towards city compaction (see DoE, 1995). In 1997 the Department for the Environment, Transport and the Regions (DETR, the new name for the DoE) outlined the key axes around which regeneration policy was going to be structured (DETR, 1997). These included a strategic view, partnering, resource targeting, competitive and outcome-focused allocation of public funding, value for money and leveraging of funds. As the previous government's Single Regeneration Budget (SRB), which was an effort to defragment and streamline the funding regime, was slowly phased out in the early 2000s, new funding and delivery mechanisms like the Neighbourhood Renewal Fund (NRF) and the New Deal for Communities (NDC) programme came into existence. They were aimed at the improvement of areas whose populations were faced with multiple deprivation. The work of the Social Exclusion Unit (SEU) and of the Social Exclusion Task Force that superseded it was crucial in linking social policy with physical renewal (see SEU, 1998).

Although these initiatives retained certain elements of the past (like the competitive nature of funding and the area-based focus), they shifted urban regeneration policy and practice towards a more strategically informed and comprehensive process. The new orientation was presented in the urban White Paper (ODPM, 2000), which put a greater emphasis on community involvement and focused on the most deprived areas, without neglecting the physical form and design quality of regeneration projects as crucial for their success. This last line was worked out in the Report of the Urban Task Force (UTF), led by Richard Rogers, which made policy proposals as to the way in which an 'urban renaissance' could be achieved (UTF, 1999).

The UTF recognised the need for increased institutional capacity but refrained from suggesting more direct state involvement. It re-introduced the idea of a single-purpose agency concerned with urban regeneration, in the form of the

Urban Regeneration Company (URC). Like the UDCs, the URCs were supposed to take over a local authority task but, unlike in the UDCs, local authorities remained involved as one of the central partners of the partnerships that emerged. Other partners were the Regional Development Agencies (RDAs) and English Partnerships (EP) – the central government's main regeneration agency, later merged with the Homes and Communities Agency (HCA).

These policy initiatives, including the creation of the URCs and the RDAs, aimed at changing the quality of the processes of urban regeneration by emphasising a strategic perspective, linking economic and physical approaches with 'soft' issues such as stakeholder engagement, partnership formation, leadership development and knowledge creation and learning. This expresses a shift in the understanding of what the tools and objectives of urban regeneration should be (de Magalhães, 2004). Although these developments showed a refined managerial understanding of the processes at work, they arguably did not alter the property-dependent character of regeneration. Private developers continued to play a crucial role in urban regeneration in the UK, but whereas the UDCs tackled their task through a centralisation and streamlining of the planning process, the URCs have tried to tackle theirs through capacity building and trust. The URCs could not directly engage in land development via landownership and land preparation, something that UDCs were able to do. Instead, they served a coordinating function between the actors engaging in the development process, a role somewhat similar to the French 'Missions' or the Dutch 'Project Offices' that will be discussed in the case study chapters.

The 2010 elections brought the Conservative–Liberal Democrat coalition into government and with it the ideas of localism and of the 'big society'. It is unclear what these terms mean at the moment, as most policy instruments are still under discussion, but the declared aim of the government is to facilitate economic growth at the local level and to transfer welfare provision (in housing, health, education etc.) into the hands of local communities. The RDAs in England are replaced by voluntary organisations called Local Enterprise Partnerships (LEPs), whose membership comprises local authorities, local businesses and third sector organisations, covering functional rather than strictly defined administrative areas and allowing territorial overlaps by virtue of the potential participation of stakeholders in more than one LEP. However, the devolved administrations of Scotland, Wales and Northern Ireland remain in place, thus increasing the divergence between the governance structures of the UK's constituents. The HCA was scaled back and the URCs saw their funding cut, which meant that several will inevitably be phased out.

Housing and urban regeneration

In general, ever since the reforms of local authority housing provision in the 1980s, the private sector delivers market housing whereas the provision of affordable and intermediary housing remains a residual, almost niche, function performed by Registered Social Landlords (RSLs), who compete with speculative housebuilders for land in the open market. RSLs are independent, not-for-profit organisations that provide affordable housing and related services for people with low incomes and in housing need. They are very similar in their origins and their current objectives to the Dutch housing associations.

Following several years of a property-led approach (see Turok, 1992) in the mid-1990s urban regeneration policy began to shift towards the provision of mixed communities that require a mix of affordable, intermediary[3] and market dwellings in new developments. Affordable housing and other merit and public goods in urban development and regeneration projects come about through state intervention, although the public sector relies most often on RSLs for its delivery, mainly via developers' obligations under Section 106 of the 1990 Town and Country Planning Act and the more recent Community Infrastructure Levy.

Until very recently, the largest proportion of non-market housing in the UK was provided by that route, meaning that the greatest proportion of the amount captured by local authorities through section 106 was allocated to affordable housing (Crook *et al.*, 2006). The idea of allowing local authorities to use part of the new Community Infrastructure Levy (CIL) to deliver non-market housing was also under consideration at the time of writing. Whichever instrument the government may decide to use in the future, the fact of the matter remains that merit and public good provision through this route depends on the overall level of development activity and is perceived by developers as an extra cost, which they attempt to pass on to the consumers of market housing.

Apart from the provision of 'affordable housing', Labour's regeneration policy was linked to housing through the Housing Market Renewal (HMR) programme. This was an initiative specifically aimed at recreating housing markets in urban areas where no demand for housing existed, by actively reshaping those areas. Renovation, new construction and demolition were extensively used in order to make these areas attractive to potential investors, homeowners and RSL tenants, who would move in and thus form mixed communities (at least in terms of tenures and incomes). The results were rather mixed and the programme attracted criticism, especially for subsidising property speculation with public money and thus prioritising regional economic growth aspirations without necessarily addressing local deprivation issues (Cameron, 2006).

On the demand side, housing need is tackled mainly via the welfare benefits system and support is aimed directly at the person. The housing benefit, which in most cases pays the rent of households eligible for local authority or RSL housing, has been capped at 80 per cent of market prices by the Coalition government that came to power in 2010. Since the 1980s all the receipts from either rental of council property or sales of assets such as land or dwellings were channelled back to the central government coffers, thus severely disrupting the capacity of local authorities to engage in housing provision. The first steps to reverse this situation were taken in 2008 by the Labour government, and at the time of writing the intention of the current government was to radically change the way that the Housing Revenue Account worked, in order to allow local authorities to retain the bulk of the receipts.

So far as homeownership is concerned, support is mainly aimed at the person. Various schemes exist that support first-time buyers and/or key workers through capital and interest subsidies as well as joint ownership (part buy, part rent) schemes that aim to make homeownership more accessible. Whitty *et al.* (1994) argue that the systematic undermining of the council housing sector was based on the one hand on initiatives such as the 'right to buy', 'alternative landlords' and cuts in rent subsidies, and on the other hand on the 1988 Housing Act, which facilitated stock transfers from local councils to other types of landlords. This stock transfer, which continues apace until the present day, was combined with siphoning off the receipts from the social rented sector to central government, as mentioned above. Central government used only part of this money to fund RSLs through government agencies (through funding lines from the Housing Corporation, later replaced by the HCA). Thus the production of dwellings for the social rented sector dwindled and the total available stock declined, effectively residualising this form of tenure. Recent cuts in Housing Corporation grants and organisational changes affecting the agency itself also mean that the resources available for the provision of non-market housing are still scarce.

The implications of on-going changes in planning policies brought about by the Conservative–Liberal Democrat coalition government are still uncertain, but current indications are that no changes should be expected that will dramatically raise housing production, or regeneration activity more generally. Although it is unclear what the future of regeneration and of housing provision via regeneration will be, the government's intention is for it to be radically different from what it was in the past.

General trends

The practices of urban regeneration that developed in France, the Netherlands and the UK are in many ways a response to the constant transformations of

Western European economies and cities, as described in Chapter 1. Although in all three countries the evolution of policy followed different trajectories, they all developed mechanisms whereby urban regeneration schemes were utilised in order to achieve government policy objectives at a local level. Notwithstanding the common trends in the evolution of cities in the three countries, there are significant similarities as well as differences between the policy responses that have developed in each country. These are linked to different political traditions and priorities, and also to different physical realities in urban areas. As a consequence, the areas that are primarily the focus of urban regeneration initiatives in the 1990s and 2000s are not exactly of the same type between countries although, for example, a system of area-focused measurement of deprivation has been used in all three of them.

Since the early 1980s, urban regeneration initiatives in the UK relied heavily on property markets and were aimed at urban quarters with high concentrations of dereliction and/or deprivation. Urban regeneration in France takes both local and city-wide aspects into account and has two facets that are becoming more integrated with time: one is the rather centralised *politique de la ville*, which in general deals with high-rise social housing areas in the *banlieues*, and the other is local authority regeneration projects in areas with market potential. In the Netherlands, urban regeneration also has a city-wide aspect to it and traditionally focuses on 'problematic' housing areas. As a result, it more often than not involves housing associations as key actors.

Policy changes in the Netherlands in the 1990s placed increased emphasis on the recycling of previously developed land, a trend that UK and French policy also followed at around the same time. All three countries have a common concern for the provision of non-market housing through regeneration projects, albeit in France (but not in the UK) this option is part of a palette of intervention mechanisms available to the state in its effort to address housing market imbalances. In the Netherlands the provision of housing by housing associations was always at the heart of urban interventions and it is only recently that regeneration practices have been adjusted to take into account market actors and the newly introduced market rationale of housing associations.

In the following chapters it will become clear how the introduction of market-driven mechanisms into the policy and the institutional landscape of France and the Netherlands came about in an incremental way and means that the new forms of regeneration interventions that emerged retain elements of the past and take place within an institutional context that has significant redundancy in terms of the mechanisms that can be used. In essence we are talking about a less radical adjustment of the institutional and the ideological landscape. In the UK, however, the influence of the market logic had a much more disruptive effect that led to the residualisation or elimination of pre-existing institutions and implementation/delivery mechanisms. Although the Labour government later attempted to rebuild some of that institutional capacity and to mainstream strategic thinking, the Conservative–Liberal Democrat coalition that succeeded it once again dismantled many of those structures, in favour of decentralised forms and actor self-organisation.

In all three countries there is an observable drift towards more property-centred approaches to urban regeneration. This general tendency can be broken down into three interrelated trends of particular significance for the delivery of merit and public goods through urban regeneration (see also Verhage, 2005a, 2005b):

1 the emergence of a project-led approach, addressing the diversity of issues (social, economic, environmental, mobility) in a comprehensive way;
2 the reconsideration of the modes of financing of urban regeneration, resulting in less direct state investment and an increasing emphasis on leveraging private sector investment;
3 an emphasis on collaboration with private actors and landowners, which is necessary to cope with the mutual dependence between the public and private sectors for the realisation of their objectives.

As the following chapter will discuss, uncertainty and risk in urban regeneration can be examined at three analytical levels, which are linked to each other: the systemic-contextual, the scheme and the project levels. Insofar as the systemic-contextual level is concerned, policy stability and institutional thickness appear to be (*ceteris paribus*) crucial in affecting the behaviour of agents operating at the scheme and project levels. In both France and the Netherlands housing and regeneration policy are intertwined and combine a range of measures and incentives aimed at both the supply and demand sides. In all three countries central government is a major funder of regeneration; however, in France and the Netherlands, funding is also available through specialist public financial institutions that are not under direct government control, as well as from receipts from land development.

In those two countries, planning and regeneration powers have been devolved to the regional and local level, and regional and local authorities have a strong tradition of collaboration between them and with central government, often formalised through contracts or covenants. For the UK, the picture is more complicated: the significant powers that have been devolved to Scotland, Wales and Northern Ireland have not been revoked, but the English RDAs have been axed. Apart from European Union programmes very few alternatives to central government funding exist, while the capacity of local authorities to raise and keep funds from land development or asset management is very limited. There are no equivalents to the CDC or the BNG, although, in a strange twist of fate, much of the UK banking sector is now state owned.

In the Netherlands, housing associations are key players in the provision of housing in regeneration schemes and more generally. They have indeed adopted a logic of fiscal balancing and are under pressure to reduce their involvement in housing provision but at the same time to engage in regeneration initiatives. Their lending is guaranteed by the state and the institutional framework pushes them to operate with social benefit in mind. The role of housing associations in the UK is relatively important at the scheme and project level but, more widely speaking, the housing associations are not key to regeneration schemes in the way that they are in the Netherlands. This reflects their residualised role in the UK housing system, where private housebuilding and homeownership are given paramount importance. This attitude reflects the belief that the market will solve the mismatch between supply and demand by itself, which has led to measures that have substantively weakened the capacity of local authorities and housing associations to perform a more active role (siphoning off capital and rental receipts is the most characteristic of these measures). Housing associations in the UK now find themselves outpriced in most cases, and thus their participation in regeneration projects on the back of section 106 agreements – and therefore on the back of market housing production – is more often than not their only opportunity to stay in business. The French approach of comprehensively dealing with the housing market through policy instruments like the PLH accepts that it is the government's responsibility to intervene in the housing market in order to address issues that the market cannot address by itself. The same rationale underlies the Dutch emphasis on housing associations' involvement in urban regeneration.

In all three countries there is a policy imperative to create partnerships between private, third sector and public bodies. The objectives of the various actors in the processes of urban regeneration diverge. At the same time, in a context of mutual dependence, the success of the projects has depended on the involvement of all the actors. In order to assure this involvement, the real-estate programme that is to be developed has needed to be sufficiently diverse for all the actors to have an interest in participating in the project. As will be discussed in the following chapters, this has resulted in a mix of uses, housing types and tenures, allowing private developers to develop market housing, while at the same time objectives concerning social and affordable housing or social goods more generally are realised through state involvement. Moreover, the fact that urban regeneration projects are, by definition, situated within the existing urban fabric, results in a great diversity of claims concerning the uses to be integrated in the project.

At the project level, barring direct provision, four types of intervention are available to the public sector: price instruments (taxation, subsidies), regulation (planning, incentives), infrastructure provision and land preparation. From a risk/return point of view these types of intervention address a variety of eventualities and thus alleviate risks and reduce uncertainties. These tools are being used to improve the attractiveness of areas of the city to private investors and are often part of a larger development and communication strategy. This aspect of urban regeneration is also elaborated further in the following chapter.

Notes

1 France has a very large number (over 36,000) of municipalities, which often have only a few hundred inhabitants. As a result, all larger agglomerations comprise several municipalities. In order to stimulate the elaboration of local housing policy at a level that corresponds better to the territorial reality, the competency of elaborating the PLH was transferred to the level of the inter-municipal cooperation structures in 2004. Since 2006 the elaboration of a PLH is obligatory for the inter-municipal cooperation structures that have been created in larger agglomerations, i.e. the *communautés d'agglomération* for agglomerations of 50,000–500,000 inhabitants, and the *communautés urbaines* for agglomerations with over 500,000 inhabitants.
2 The objective of this ambitious programme of demolition and reconstruction is to favour 'social mix' without reducing the public housing stock. The idea is that a portion of these demolished social dwellings are replaced by market housing on the site of demolition and that social housing is rebuilt somewhere else, preferably in an area where it will not reach the threshold of 20 per cent social housing.
3 Also called 'part buy–part rent' housing, aimed at households with a stable income that nonetheless is not sufficient to enable them to own a property outright.

Chapter 3

Actor strategies, risks and uncertainty in regeneration projects

Introduction

As discussed in Chapters 1 and 2, during the 1990s and 2000s urban regeneration became a central theme of urban policies, due to an increased emphasis on environmental, social and economic factors. Until the onset of the 2007 credit crisis, policy makers and planning authorities were formulating ambitious objectives concerning urban development, focused on social and land-use mix and environmental quality. The bulk of these proposals concerned interventions in areas that had been previously developed, usually parts of the existing urban fabric. Although both policy and the development industry are currently in flux, it is highly probable that future policies and subsequent plans will continue to affect the cities' already built-up core using some form of regeneration initiatives. As argued earlier in this book, private investment in these initiatives was a key factor, and indeed a major contributor to housing supply, especially for non-market housing.

This chapter elaborates the analytical framework that will be used to study the way in which the tensions between the context, the content and the organisation of urban regeneration projects were dealt with in the case studies. The inter-dependence of these three factors and the coupling between state and market rationalities mean that actors in the public and private sectors have to implement elaborate plans and procedures in order to manage the risks and uncertainties involved in developing these projects.

According to Albrechts (2009, pp. 215–216), the roots of the trends currently underpinning urban policy and regeneration can be traced back to

the 1980s when the neo-liberal paradigm replaced the Keynesian-Fordist one and when public intervention retrenches in all domains (Martinelli, 2005). Europe witnessed a retreat from strategic spatial planning fuelled not only by the neo-conservative disdain for planning, but also by postmodernist scepticism, both of which tend to view progress as something which, if it happens, cannot be planned (Healey, 1997b). Instead the focus of urban and regional planning practices shifted to projects (Secchi, 1986; Motte, 1994; Rodriguez and

Martinez, 2003), especially for the revival of rundown parts of cities and regions, and on land use regulations.

This emphasis on projects was the socio-spatial expression of a new model of delivery that emerged following the retrenchment (in France or the Netherlands) or the residualisation (in the UK) of the welfare state. Indeed, Oakley and Williams (1994) note that during the 1980s and early 1990s welfare provision in the UK was reshaped towards a model of devolved decision making within a context of quasi-markets. Their argument continues that the resulting transfer of decision-making powers to local managers and users served to mask the pre-eminent role that government still plays in shaping the context within which these decisions are made.

One of the interesting aspects of this process of transformation in welfare provision is the linking up of the private sector developers and public sector agencies in the provision of infrastructure and services as part of regeneration and property development schemes. Thus, the planning system and its mechanisms are increasingly called upon to deliver social policy goals.

It is, however, debatable whether area-based regeneration initiatives should be expected to deliver broad social policy goals as effectively and efficiently as initiatives and measures aimed directly at households and individuals. The production of public goods that serve wider policy goals, such as affordable housing or other social infrastructure, as part of property development projects has been criticised as a cross-subsidy whose efficiency and equitability as well as its capacity to deliver the quantities required by wider social need is debatable (for example see Crook and Whitehead, 2002; Crook et al., 2002; Crook et al., 2006).

Other than the efficiency, effectiveness and equitability arguments for and against the link-up between social policy, the planning system and property development, one has to consider the limitations and risks to which such a model exposes welfare provision, and thus the legitimacy of the state itself in the eyes of its citizens. This conflation of social policy with property markets via the planning system is in itself an indication of a society's understanding of the role of the state. It also reflects the willingness or the financial and organisational ability of governments to perform a redistributive role and to manage the conflictual nature of that role.

In the UK, planning obligations and, by extension, the planning system itself became a key tool for delivering non-market housing and community-level social infrastructure (see Crook et al., 2002; Crook et al., 2006; Henneberry et al., 2008). This approach has mainly financial short-term benefits for the state and it is an interesting attempt to couple the provision of public and private goods. At the same time it also increases the risk of delivery for whichever aims the public sector may have set: depending on the role that the state plays such arrangements can make the delivery of merit and public goods conditional on the delivery of private goods via the market mechanism. Iglesias (2009) supports the idea of partnering for the joint delivery of public and private goods, as he recognises that such partnerships between the public and private sectors could potentially lead to outcomes "greater than the sum of the parts" (p. 29). At the same time he points out the reputational and political risks that such partnerships are exposed to, which may have devastating outcomes both for the idea itself and for whatever it aims to deliver.

As noted in Chapter 2, in France and the Netherlands similar planning system-based, property market-related mechanisms took their place amongst a wider array of available mechanisms upon which the state (or the partnerships in which it was involved) could call, depending on the circumstances. Key to those mechanisms is the capture of the value accrued to land during the development process. In these two countries the state retained a multifaceted role in both social policy and urban development and still considers it as part of its role to get involved with public and private good provision both in strategic terms (housing policy, strategic urban planning etc.) and also at the operational level (land assembly, organisation of the development process etc.), as will become evident from the case studies.

It is necessary at this point to make a brief but important diversion to discuss risk and uncertainty. The book will not get into an elaborate discussion of the different schools of thought that try to define risk and uncertainty – seminal contributions to that topic are John Adams's (Adams, 1995) and Carlo Jaeger's (Jaeger *et al.*, 2001) work. The framework used in this book reflects an understanding of both risk and uncertainty as cultural constructs. Thus, risk and uncertainty are approached as concepts whose existence (and in the case of risk, its measurement) is greatly affected by the previous experiences of actors, the biases inherent in their mental frames that affect their perceptions and the actions these actors take (see, for example, Adams, 2007; Beck, 1992; Wildavsky, 1988). This approach focuses the attention not only on efforts to measure risk but also on efforts to deal with both risk and uncertainty within the cultural context in which they manifest themselves. Following Adams (1999, 2007), risks can be grouped into three overlapping categories as outlined in Figure 3.1.

Adams (2007, p. 10) argues that when

> the science is inconclusive we are thrown back on judgement. We are in the realm of virtual
> risk. These risks are culturally constructed – when the science is inconclusive people are

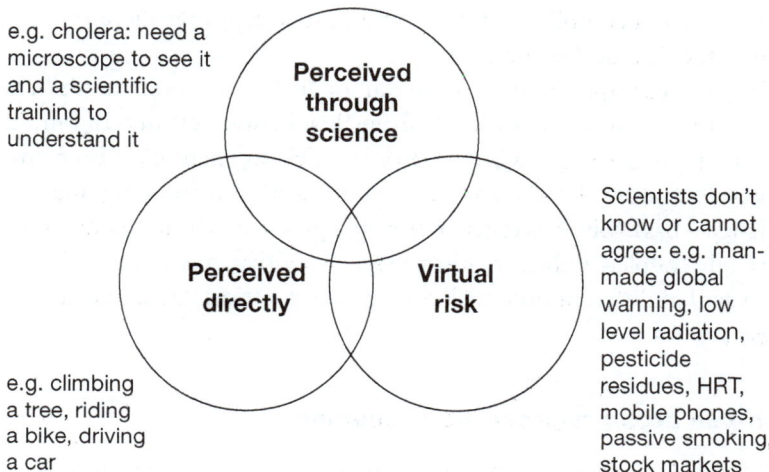

Figure 3.1 The three kinds of risk (John Adams. Used with permission)

liberated to argue from, and act upon, pre-established beliefs, convictions, prejudices and superstitions. Such risks may or may not be real but they have real consequences. In the presence of virtual risk what we believe depends on whom we believe, and whom we believe depends on whom we trust.

Eiser (2004) reiterates this view in his thorough discussion of the "cognitive heuristics" and the "social amplification" processes that underpin decision making under uncertainty. Thus, given the importance of contextual and cultural factors in the perception and attenuation of risk, institutions and governance mechanisms and their capacity to cope with future events appear to be of paramount importance even though actors may not know these events are possible (i.e. 'Black Swans', see Taleb, 2007), or when such events are known to be possible, and the probability of their happening and the impact of their consequences may be unknown, difficult to compute, biased by errors in the data etc.

If one accepts that social and physical reality are continuously under construction (as our understanding of property development and urban regeneration implies), then one can plausibly claim that it is near impossible to estimate the probabilities of a specific regeneration scheme and/or project trajectory materialising or not. In the realm of perceived and virtual risks, developers, financiers, local authorities and all other actors have to make crucial decisions based on their pre-existing beliefs and on educated guesses or gut feelings. It is one thing to say, however, that such trajectories are difficult if not impossible to attach probabilities to, and a completely different thing to accept that there is nothing one can do in the face of the unknown.

Taleb, for example, argues in favour of 'robustification' as the choice of strategies that protect against losses from 'Black Swan' events. In our view, this is a method that actors engaging in property development have been employing for some time now. That know-how – both a way of thinking and a body of knowledge – has evolved as regeneration and property development have become increasingly coupled with each other. Evidence of that evolution can be witnessed in the way that different potentialities have been anticipated and dealt with in all the case studies.

Mixed-use urban regeneration schemes

In all three countries, the move towards merit and public goods provision through project-based regeneration initiatives where the role of the private sector was increasing in significance meant that novel spatial configurations emerged, herein called the Mixed Use Urban Regeneration Scheme or MUURS, to accommodate the new arrangements between actors.

Several authors have looked into the links between the type of actors engaging in large-scale development projects, their roles and the spatial outcomes. Louw and Bruinsma (2006) point out that the perceived benefits of mixed use, from a planning perspective, are the reduced need to travel and the increase in vitality and diversity. Henderson (2010, p. 166) summarises some of the key findings of research looking into the effects that the prominent role of private developers in site-oriented development may have:

> The implication for individual development sites is that these are frequently approached with an inward-looking mindset. As a result, the tendency in terms of the built environment is to ignore or to turn one's back on the local context in which development opportunities are situated. Ground-level implications of this discrete, site-orientated approach can include inadequate attention to future resident/occupier needs and limited consideration of wider public goods, such as open spaces or area connectivity.

According to Henderson (2010) these implications can be tackled through some form of actor collaboration and larger scale planning, which usually requires state involvement in what Henderson refers to as 'comprehensive planning'. CABE (the Commission for Architecture and the Built Environment) and DETR (2001) focus on the advantages of such an approach for urban design quality, whereas Rodney and Clark (2000) highlight the potential advantages of collective action when it comes to minimising risks attached to the provision of merit and public goods.

Since urban regeneration schemes are situated within the existing urban fabric, their promoters have to deal with a great diversity of claims concerning land use. These types of regeneration scheme needed to have a sufficiently diverse content to reflect the interests of all participating actors in order to facilitate actor involvement, which is crucial to the success of any partnership arrangement. By the same token, the need to deliver a variety of diverse outputs was deemed to be better served through the involvement of an equally diverse array of actors. Other than the significant advantages in terms of governance, the increased emphasis on partnering and mixity equipped actors with significant tools that helped them alleviate the risks and attenuate the uncertainties surrounding property development and regeneration.

This new approach therefore resulted in the production of urban environ-ments with a mix of uses and, in the case of housing, a mix of types and tenures that allowed private developers and state agencies to pursue their objectives simultaneously whilst achieving market-leading returns on investment (FDP Savills, 2003; IPD, 2008). It should not come as a surprise that this urban form, the MUURS, which has the delivery of non-market housing (and merit and public goods more broadly) as one of its core aims, is not a totally new concept. It evolved out of pre-existing forms which the Urban Land Institute (ULI) defined in 1976 as "Mixed-Use Developments/Town Centres/Districts" (MXDs), to be distinguished from "multiuse developments". According to the ULI (2003), MXDs are schemes that have:

- "Three or more significant revenue-producing uses . . . that in well planned projects are mutually supported";
- "Significant physical and functional integration of project components . . . including uninterrupted pedestrian connections";
- "Development in conformance with a coherent plan".

The difference between the MUURS and the MXD, however, is that a MUURS adds social policy objectives and the provision of merit and public goods to these three main elements of an MXD within the context of urban regeneration programmes. Thus the MUURS includes both 'hard' and 'soft' measures, aiming at a distribution of social, economic and environmental resources that is different to what this distribution would have been if it had been entirely left to market forces, in what Henderson (2010) calls "site-focused development approaches". A MUURS can therefore be seen as a reflection of a policy regime that aims at embedding merit and public goods provision into market-based property development schemes. It is influenced to a great extent by the strategies, goals and objectives of more than the market actors engaged in it, but the public actors engaged in it have to make similar adjustments too.

The involvement of the state in MUURSs gives it the opportunity to simultaneously implement redistributive policies and minimise capital expenditure by transferring much of the cost of redistribution from the state coffers to the land-development circuit: developers, landowners, investors and financiers, house buyers and sellers. Therefore, the objectives of any MUURSs are a compromise that reflects the extent to which the objectives of private, public and third sector actors are pursued in the project under the influence of state policy, market conditions etc. So far as the public sector is concerned, the outcome of a MUURS is influenced directly through participation in development/regeneration partnerships or indirectly through policy (on tax, planning, housing, the environment etc.).

As with any partnership between public and private actors, it is crucial to understand how the partnership arrangements attenuate or amplify uncertainty and how they distribute risks and returns between the partners. Becker and Patterson (2005, p. 126) stress that there are two parameters that need to be in place whenever such partnerships are formed: "first a strong positive association . . . between risks and rewards for the private partner . . . second a strong positive association between risk and the degree of involvement of the private partner in developments, operations and ownership".

The difficulty of attaching prices to the public goods delivered through regeneration is a well-known issue (see Roberts, 2000), whereas the value of the marketable elements can presumably be estimated in advance with a greater degree of accuracy. According to Becker and Patterson (2005, p. 135), in neighbourhood revitalisation schemes "the general statement can be that the risk to the private partner would be unacceptably high in these situations without the socialisation of most (but not all) of the risk". In their discussion about waterfront regeneration Medda and Nijkamp (1997) readily recognise that the public sector's role is crucial in reducing financial risk, and also in reducing private actor conflicts and in providing a policy framework and infrastructure.

Due to these characteristics, the negotiation between public and private partners becomes fraught with difficulty so far as the alleviation of uncertainty and the allocation of risks and returns in urban regeneration projects are concerned. Under these conditions, flexibility (of plans, contracts etc.) and trust become necessary attributes of any MUURS.

Content, context and organisation: an analytical framework

Three key observations are at the core of the analytical framework used in this book:

1 MUURSs require the mobilisation of several actors and material resources. Each actor has their own objectives and strategies. Some form of coordination is usually required in order to bring resource constraints, the objectives of the various actors and their spatial expressions into alignment, thus forging the *content* of the project.
2 The process of creating MUURSs is greatly influenced by the wider *context*, the external business and social environment, outside the immediate bounds of a given regeneration scheme. Urban regeneration takes place in a physical, economic, social and institutional context that is particular to each site. The characteristics of the site and the context influence both each other and the regeneration process.
3 Even if the influence of the context and content characteristics is prevalent, the regeneration process does not depend only on these. The influence of the mobilised actors on the content, the objectives that are agreed upon, the interventions realised and the interactions that take place depend on the *organisation* of the project.

The argument in this book is that the outcomes of regeneration projects emerge from the interactions of all three elements. These three elements are themselves affected to a large extent by the uncertainties, anticipated risks and returns that the various actors engaging in the process perceive as relevant to their involvement in the development process for a specific site. This means that actors will base their assessment of potential objectives and strategies on their understanding of the development potential of a site, and also depending on the behaviours of other actors.

If a private developer believes that site contamination is a significant uncertainty, then they may commission surveys, proceed with decontamination or seek the support of the state. The state, on the other hand, may be willing to commission the surveys, fund the decontamination or enter into an agreement with the developers that would tackle some of the costs or allow for a better calculation of the potential costs. Figure 3.2 is a schematic summary of the observations above. It distinguishes three central aspects of development processes embedded in regeneration schemes: the *content*, the *context* and the *organisation*.

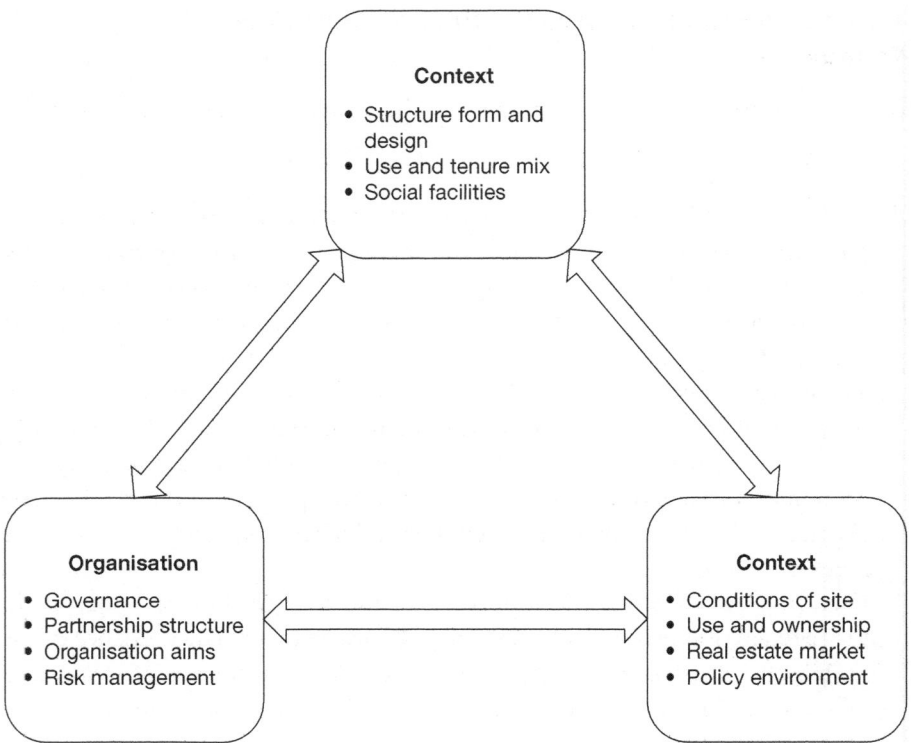

Figure 3.2 The three core aspects of a MUURS

The context, the organisation and the content of the MUURS evolve simultaneously during the development process and hence need to be considered together during the analysis. This view of regeneration schemes coincides with theories emphasising the relation between structure and agency (Giddens, 1984) and the socially constructed nature of property development (Doak and Karadimitriou, 2007; Henneberry *et al.*, 2002; Majoor, 2006). Arguably, this approach tackles the relationships between content, context and organisation and goes a long way to describing and explaining the risk and uncertainty considerations underlying the process. In order to develop this argument, it is necessary to first elaborate on the relation between the three elements.

Property development and the context, content and organisation of urban regeneration processes

The 'recycling' of urban land through MUURSs has been an important objective of current public policies throughout Europe (Trache *et al.*, 2007; Couch *et al.*, 2003) for several years now, although these imperatives are now being tested in a 'post-credit crunch' market context. As discussed previously, a key idea that guides many urban regeneration operations (albeit to different degrees, depending on the country) is that the areas concerned are not immediately interesting to market actors. These areas typically have depressed property markets, indeed in some cases no property markets at all. As a consequence, the argument goes, these areas do not attract the investment necessary to renew them.

To attract the required investment, this line of argument continues, these areas have to be reinserted into the real estate market. A buoyant property market is therefore deemed to be an essential element in reversing the downward spiral of devaluation–disinvestment (Comby, 2001; Guy *et al.*, 2002; Piron, 2002). This line of thinking draws on the 'market failure' approach that, in principle, justifies state involvement to address inefficient and/or inequitable socio-spatial outcomes where the market on its own produces a suboptimal allocation of resources and outputs. Accepting this point of view has important consequences for the legitimation of the role of public actors and state action. State interventions following the market failure argument are aimed at making depressed areas attractive for private investors by addressing the reasons behind the market failure.

Trache *et al.* (2007) mention several points that are important in this respect: the need for a 'critical mass'; the leadership role of public investment; the certainty offered by the planning framework; the location of the site concerned; direct access to decision makers; good phasing of different projects. These interventions aim at tackling informational asymmetries, reducing transaction costs, correcting imperfect competition, resolving agency problems, internalising or alleviating negative externalities and creating positive externalities.

Notwithstanding the equally forceful 'government failure' discussion, the argument already mentioned in this book is that property development projects can be (and are) delivered by various configurations of public and private actors and that the project outputs and outcomes vary depending on the roles that these actors assume. Consequently, the outputs and outcomes of urban regeneration schemes with a property development dimension will be affected by the configurations of actors engaging in property development as part of those schemes.

MUURSs have medium- to long-term completion periods and occur on sites with various levels of infrastructure, often fragmented ownership and frequently unknown environmental conditions. By their very nature, then, these initiatives involve a multitude of actors with interests vested in the past, the present and the future of those areas: landowners, various tiers of government, property developers, local communities and communities of interest,[1] investors, planners, professional bodies, present and future users, just to name a few. The multitude of actors adds to the complexity of the schemes as these actors configure and reconfigure the relationships between themselves with the passing of time. Doak and Karadimitriou (2007) have examined and theorised the ways in which these network-creation processes operate, leading to constant change in the socio-spatial composition of a scheme and thus to its possible futures.

The key driver of these reconfigurations is then the attempt of such networks of actors to pursue strategies and achieve their goals within the social and spatial context of each scheme. The degree to which a scheme can be realised depends to a large extent on the cooperation of the actors involved in the regeneration process and on the economic situation (land and real estate market) within which projects are being developed. The divergence between the motives, goals and strategies of the multitude of actors and the influence exerted on them by market conditions is the main dynamic underlying a process of structuration (after Giddens, 1984) between actors' objectives, market context and project organisation. Majoor (2006) discusses multiple-use development along similar lines and emphasises the role of social norms as structuring factors of behaviour that are, however, constantly "formed, reinterpreted and reconfirmed in practices of interaction wherein multiple actors participate" (p. 18).

As mentioned earlier, uncertainty and risk can be amplified and attenuated by the institutional context. Therefore, a crucial factor affecting the ability of any governance configuration to function is the capacity of institutions (be they frameworks or organisations) to deal with a variety of circumstances, as well as the capability of actors to build up capacity or to reconfigure their relations and the frameworks structuring those relations in response to unforeseen circumstances. At the level of the institutional framework, the tools and mechanisms capable of addressing the failure of parts of the framework itself appear either in the form of contingency arrangements or in the form of redundancy (i.e. in the existence of parallel mechanisms that can be relied upon to keep the system functional). This is where the role of the state is paramount both in setting up such institutional frameworks and also in acting as underwriter of financial and market risks, in effect operating as a 'lender of last resort'.

Finally, an important dimension of any regeneration scheme is time. The notion of 'path dependency' implies that projects develop in trajectories formulated by the realignment of actors' pursuit of their objectives in response to their changing environment (see Henderson *et al.*, 2007; Raco and Henderson, 2009). As discussed later in this chapter, these trajectories are aptly reflected in spatial configurations that in turn affect the future governance structure and form of a scheme. Still, time is not only a backdrop against which these processes unfold, it is also a key constituent element of the processes themselves. The passing of time inevitably affects the relationship between the scheme and its external environment, by virtue of the constant evolution of factors such as markets, economies, policies and technologies over which the immediately concerned actors have little or no influence at all. Thus, time and mastering the contingencies emerging as a project unfolds become crucial parameters affecting the strategies of each actor, from property developers to policy makers. This adds further to the complexity of the scheme, even by the mere virtue of prolonging the process. To put it a different way, the requirement for more time in order for differences to be ironed out and for alliances to be formed can become a positive feedback loop where a need for more time is constantly accentuated, requiring even more time.

The approach used in this book (Figure 3.2) focuses on dynamics, on the interplay between structure and agency and on the relation between the content/objectives of the project, its context and its organisation. Crucially, in an era when property development has been a major driver behind regeneration initiatives, the uncertainty and risk embedded in the property development process will be a key underlying factor behind the strategies of the actors engaging in regeneration schemes.

The relation between processes of urban regeneration and the economic, geographic, social and institutional contexts within which any form of organised activity occurs largely influences its chances of success. An organisation, be it a development corporation, a partnership or a property development firm will not survive within a specific context (or environment) if it is not suitably adapted to that environment. Seen from another angle, any form of organised human endeavour is a product of its time, created to fit certain circumstances and tackle era-specific issues in ways specific to the socio-economic environment of that era. As the issues and the institutional structures within which actors operate change with time, so the focus of an organisation needs to change in order to survive and thrive (Meyer and Davis, 2003).

Regeneration is influenced by a variety of policy discourses and frameworks at the international, national and local levels that influence the regulatory aspect of state intervention and private or third sector involvement and eventually translate into socio-spatial configurations. In most societies policy frameworks are the outcome of a negotiation process involving a variety of stakeholders such as investors, developers, planners, politicians and local communities, to name a few, each with their own interests to promote. When these frameworks are then applied in concrete local situations they are renegotiated and re-interpreted by the actors directly involved with local polity (Henderson *et al.*, 2007).

Since the 1990s, if not earlier, policies throughout Western Europe have promoted the production of MUURSs emphasising mixity, environmental considerations and the provision of non-market housing. These requirements have been shaped in a rather top-down fashion and have been justified as necessary for achieving sustainability. Yet they also are or have become crucial elements of the norms and routines developed by the state, investors and real estate developers in order to manage the risks associated with MUURSs. This is one important way in which the context has affected the organisation and the content of those schemes.

So far as the state is concerned, apart from any risks assumed when public sector actors become involved in land preparation or development (as outlined below), the main risk associated with MUURSs is political. As Sagalyn (2011) points out, these risks can be tremendous, inasmuch as citizens' expectations are for the state to provide merit and public goods or guarantee their provision.

The Investment Property Forum (2006, pp. 12–14) discusses regeneration from an investor's point of view and conceptualises the regeneration process in three stages: remediation/infrastructure, development and investment. It argues that

> regeneration proceeds from one end of the spectrum, namely the remediation/ infrastructure phase characterised by high levels of risk but with opportunities for high returns, to the investment phase at the other end characterised by lower risk and corresponding lower levels of return, but secure revenue streams and more predictable capital values resulting from the occupied development entering the property market. The intermediate points reflect the potential risk of the unfinished building through to the completed product remaining unlet, lacking an income stream, having uncertain capital values and not entering the investment market. (ibid., p. 14)

So far as the developer's perspective is concerned, Byrne (1996, p. 3) describes the following six tasks for any given development project, each task associated with risks and uncertainties influencing its successful completion:

1 "the perception and estimation of demand for new buildings of different types";
2 "the identification and securing of sites suitable for construction of buildings to satisfy that demand";
3 "the design of accommodation to the demand on the sites identified";
4 "the arrangement of short and long term finance to fund site acquisition and construction";
5 "the management of design and construction";
6 "the letting and management of the completed buildings".

Byrne (1996) elaborates that poor performance in any of these tasks can adversely influence the trajectory of any given project. In any type of land development, Byrne continues, there are certain tasks involved: future demand has to be estimated in terms of quantity and quality/type, sites have to be identified and secured to satisfy this demand, the same sites have to be designed and planned to meet this demand, finance has to be found in order to fund acquisitions and construction, the whole process of design and construction has to be coordinated and managed and the end product has to be sold or let and managed/maintained after that. He thereafter separates development into four stages: appraisal, acquisition, production/construction and disposal. Although this list is very close to the approach followed by authors who highlight the institutional aspects of development (de Magalhães, 1999a, 1999b), Byrne's contribution emphasises and identifies the risks and uncertainties inherent in these processes.

Byrne argues that sources of uncertainty in the appraisal stage have to do with changes or lack of clarity in the project's specifications or other parameters, unrealistic assumptions about aspects of the project and of the market and not clearly specified objectives and design characteristics. In acquisition, a major source of uncertainty is the potential response of the planning authority to the requests of the developer and of stakeholders more generally. It is worth noting that a lot of that uncertainty depends on how a planning system approaches discretion. During production, uncertainty arises around the project's characteristics and relates to both planning and project management. Therefore a project whose details have been finalised is less uncertain and thus easier to produce on time and within budget. Finally, when the end product hits the market and the original assumptions are tested, it is rents, prices and investment yields that are the biggest source of uncertainty.

Wellings (2006) referred to housebuilding in particular as an activity combining two 'functions': the development/wholesaling function and the construction function. This distinction, however, can be applied to the development of all types of property, as it is directly linked to the allocation of development rights (bear in mind that in the UK development rights are nationalised, which is not the case in France or the Netherlands). It is through the development/wholesale function that the higher margins are achieved in the industry. Construction, on the other hand, is a lower-margin activity than can be disassociated from development. Developers are not primarily construction companies and indeed, as Wellings shows (ibid.), mergers between construction companies and housebuilders are rarely successful.

With that in mind, delivery of the ambitious objectives of the MUURS is also faced with extra risks and uncertainties induced because:

- Larger numbers of actors result in greater variety in goals and in the strategies that these actors follow to achieve those goals.

- Sustainability and regeneration do not mean the same thing to everyone and are definitely not within every actor's scope in the same way.
- As the number of involved actors increases, so does the number of potential interactions between them. This results in exponential growth in the complexity of the types and scope of relationships that emerge between actors. Discursive complexity increases as well, as the volume and diversity of communications increase.
- The management of such complex interactions between actors requires suitable institutional frameworks, skills and resources, as well as sufficient levels of trust. The availability of these elements in any given locale at any given time period may vary and the required institutional capacity may have to be built from scratch.

When seen in this light the links between risk, uncertainty and concepts such as mixity, partnership etc. become clearer. Childs *et al.* (1996) have examined the potential of mixed-use schemes and concluded that they can be used to reduce risks when markets for different uses are not highly correlated, and to add economic value when increases in supply for a particular use lead to declines in marginal revenues. Similarly, when Lai *et al.* (2004) examine ways of reducing the uncertainties arising from future demand predictions they argue that pre-sales are not only a tool to tackle the uncertainty of future demand but can also prove effective in cutting down the cost of inventory, thus substantially affecting the profitability of large projects.

Within such a context, uncertainty in MUURSs could be revisited in view of the six tasks identified by Byrne:

1 Future demand must be estimated, given the time span, the particularities of each location, the relative novelty of MUURSs and the complexity of such schemes.
2 Identification of sites is restricted by planning policy regulating the type of land available. Although this clarity increases certainty at the policy level, securing such sites may become more uncertain for developers, due to increased competition and the complexities of acquiring urban land.
3 The set of skills required in order to develop property in such schemes is radically different to those required for low-density greenfield development. This imposes new uncertainties, to the extent that a wide variety of actors need to build up their capacity and their understanding in order to produce those schemes.
4 Even before the financial crisis occurred, the 'non-standard' and unusual nature of regeneration schemes affected the risk/return considerations of

financiers (work by Adair *et al.*, 2000; Nappi-Choulet, 2006). It took several years of research and experience to convince the market that regeneration schemes may well offer attractive risk/return profiles (FDP Savills, 2003; IPD, 2008).

5 Managing the design and construction of long-term, high-density mixed use schemes like MUURSs requires a set of methods and skills that in many cases have to be developed afresh.

6 Managing the mix of uses and tenants in MUURSs efficiently and effectively requires adjustments to the existing legal and institutional arrangements regulating property rights and facilities management.

To these one should add the risks and uncertainties that are generated and attenuated by the institutional and cultural context both (7) in itself and also (8) in the way it affects the organisational structure of the project. This context includes the tools available to public and private partners that allow them to perform certain operations in specified ways with low transaction costs. For example, it includes standardised mechanisms through which public and private resources and expertise can be pooled together to provide capital, underwrite risks, assemble and service land and generally make investment in regeneration an attractive proposition for public and private investors alike.

The trajectories of urban regeneration processes

The importance of initial conditions is paramount to the evolution of MUURSs. It is the parameters affecting the configuration of the project at the initial stages that create the path upon which the future stages of the projects will be based. From the variety of initial conditions we isolate three key aspects: development potential, the distribution of rights/landownership and finance. Some ways in which they affect the possible futures of a MUURS are detailed below.

Development potential

The development potential of a site, the likelihood of it attracting development, depends on parameters drawn from content, context and organisation. Firstly, as we have previously argued, one of the key functions that the state performs in MUURSs is to increase the potential for value generation by attenuating the uncertainties and the risks associated with the scheme and the projects therein. Apart from attributes such as good infrastructure, transport links or a beautiful waterfront (which, incidentally, can be improved), projects also seem to benefit when located within larger designated regeneration areas (Adair *et al.*, 2003;

Nappi-Choulet, 2006). This designation reinforces investment attractiveness by alleviating uncertainties affecting the risk/return profile of investments in the area – in essence it is a confidence-building exercise.

Secondly, 'development potential' is affected by the strategic guidance relating to the development of the site, again a confidence-building exercise. Combined with a political tendency to pull back from (too) costly national redistributional arrangements, the introduction of elements of competition between cities has incentivised city authorities to formulate new development strategies, sometimes independently of national policies (Le Galès, 2003). By creating an attractive urban image and a business-friendly spatial strategy, cities attempt to meet the needs and priorities of the users whom they wish to attract. Regeneration projects are often related to such efforts, which, apart from anything else, reduce market uncertainty and reassure stakeholders about the support from the state (policy, regulations, incentives etc.) that, as the case studies will demonstrate, is necessary for long-term schemes.

Thirdly, and finally, the supra-local (national or even international) institutional and policy context is crucial, not only in the way it addresses development rights but also in the way it frames the state interest and stake in the development process. This affects the agenda that the state agencies dealing with the project will pursue. Policy emphasis on non-market housing provision, for example, influences the mix of uses and the social character of the development and thus the profit potential of the scheme. It also affects the possibilities of stakeholder coalitions, as it may or may not reflect the needs and aspirations of local communities or state agencies that could potentially engage in the process.

Allocation of property rights/landownership

Allocation of property rights, most often tied to landownership, is a key factor affecting the path that a development could follow, as it exerts significant leverage in the structuration process during the early days of every project and also affects the distribution of the returns from the investment. Depending on the form and distribution of property rights, landowners may find themselves possessing monopolistic or oligopolistic power in the early stages of a MUURS.

Thus, in some cases, complex landownership situations may hamper regeneration schemes. Problems of coordination may arise between the landowners, the local state and the developers, due to their divergent interests or even due to lack of effective communication and negotiation mechanisms. Often, the coordination challenges are more intense in previously used urban sites, as they tend to comprise a large number of different plots of different sizes and with varying preparation needs, involving many landowners. In cases where a convergence of interests fails to materialise, the state can intervene in order to reconfigure the allocation of property rights via expropriation/compulsory purchase (as is the case in France, the UK and the Netherlands) or by intermediate ownership and pre-emption rights (in the Netherlands and France).

The predominant landowner can greatly influence the speed and effectiveness of the regeneration process, yet arguably the type of landowner in itself (public, private, community etc.) is not a reason why MUURSs would not proceed, especially given the role that partnerships play in regeneration. It would be verging on the trivial to say that a private landowner is much more concerned with private goods production, whereas, in principle, public or communal land-ownership may be advantageous for planning and design as well as for extracting social benefits. All types of landowners are subject to their own biases and limitations, some of which can be overcome through partnering; the key aspect so far as public policy is concerned is the leverage that landownership gives in negotiations relating to the extraction and allocation of value.

Funding

Similarly, although landowners have the potential to exert monopoly or oligopoly power, funders also exert significant influence during early negotiations, and even more so at later stages in the project, when landownership's power declines. Issues like interest rates, market cycles, availability of finance, the economic climate and the situation in the user and investor markets greatly affect the attractiveness of an investment in a specific site in the eyes of investors and developers. Again, increased market volatility or unpredictability as well as self-fulfilling beliefs about the prospects of a market greatly affect the appetite of investors and developers to undertake projects.

In general, MUURSs require significant upfront investment in order to improve the development potential and/or to re-structure landownership. Thereafter, significant medium and long-term capital is required to sustain the momentum of regeneration especially given the cyclicality inherent in property markets. This capital is unlikely to come exclusively from public or private sources, there are enormous risks attached that incentivise actors to diversify. In addition, by its very nature property development tends to create a rather unbalanced cash flow for the developer, although there are several ways through which developers try to rebalance it (like off plan sales or pre-tenanted com-mercial schemes).

In a fashion similar to landownership, and often directly linked to it, the way a project is financed at the early stages can significantly affect its risk/return profile and the capacity of actors to extract value. The Investment Property

Forum (2006) makes several suggestions as to the types of funding vehicles and investment products that could be used to fund regeneration. Usually, up-front investment and investment during a downturn are the most difficult to come by because of the uncertainty and the negative mental biases prevailing during such periods. Thus, the importance of funding mechanisms that could act counter-cyclically is paramount for MUURSs not only from a social benefit point of view but also from the point of view of private investors who seek medium- or long-term capital security and rates of return that do not fluctuate dramatically during the time-frame of their investment.

Trajectories

The idea of trajectories of urban regeneration projects unifies the three elements of our analytical framework (context, content and organisation) and highlights their interconnections. National policy and legislation outline the limits of potential trajectories and often structure the possible 'ways of doing things'. The initial site characteristics, such as environmental conditions, existing buildings or the terrain/geomorphology, affect the viability and the risk profile of the invest-ment in many ways, and thus they affect the type of actors and the type of finance arrangements required in order to exploit the development potential of the site.

Another crucial factor is the role of the key public and private sector actors. That role reflects local and central planning or related policies, market conditions (interest rates, yields, rental incomes) and the distribution of property rights between public and private sectors. The number of actors to whom property rights are distributed and the type of those rights affect the leverage that each party has in achieving its goals in the early stages of the development process and dramatically influences the subsequent organisation of the regeneration process (Needham, 2006). Notwithstanding the role of innovation, the route of future partnerships and alliance building is influenced by pre-existing alliances and relationships between actors, by the business practices of developers and investors and by pre-existing contractual building or letting arrangements.

Depending on those interconnected factors, the project will pass through different trajectories, with alternating state and private interventions mainly focused around the management of risk, the attenuation of uncertainties and value generation at each stage. The management of risk is a common thread underlying the interaction between context, content and organisation, and it becomes our window for looking into the structuration processes previously mentioned.

The unique characteristic of MUURSs is the combination of market impera-tives with state-induced equitability concerns. All actors operating within such a context are faced with a unique set of challenges. Due to their long-term horizon, their internal variety and planning requirements, MUURSs carry with them a unique set of risks and uncertainties. Managing those risks and tackling those uncertainties requires actors involved in MUURSs to develop specific strategies and practices in order to cope with the risks and the uncertainties attached to that particular kind of development process. As discussed already, some of those strategies have been explored to some extent by Lai *et al.* (2004) and Childs *et al.* (1996).

Conclusions

During the last 30 years the readjustment of the role of the state in the financing and development functions of urban regeneration processes has frequently elevated the participation of private sector actors to a structurally necessary condition. Whereas, generally speaking, a project could take place in the absence of community participation or state-led planning, it cannot materialise without funding and development know-how. Therefore, with the reduced involvement of the state in funding and developing increasingly physical regeneration schemes, the role of private developers and investors in urban regeneration has been enhanced. This change in the distribution of roles between public and private actors also signified the coupling between the delivery of merit and public goods and the delivery of private goods through MUURSs, and thus tied social policy to market cycles and property development to social policy.

Faced with the need to finance and organise the transformation of urban space through urban regeneration, private, public and third sector actors have developed their strategies and practices in ways that allow them to manage the risks and uncertainties emerging from their newly found roles within an equally new operational environment. The MUURS can be viewed as a configuration, a format, through which the outcomes of the negotiation of the variety of interests, strategies and risk considerations that these actors bring with them can be expressed.

This book proposes an analytical framework through which the processes of spatial transformation in MUURSs can be looked into. It conceptualises the process of regeneration as an outcome of a wide array of actor interactions that create feedback loops between the content, context and organisation of MUURSs. The book will also emphasise the trajectory dimension, in essence the path-dependent character of any MUURS, which relies to a large extent on initial conditions and on the outcome of negotiations in the very early stages of the project. Thus, from the variety of factors that can influence that trajectory, the book will put more emphasis on the development potential of the site, the landownership and the funding arrangements.

When the effects of the financial crisis on regeneration schemes became apparent the whole model of merit and public goods delivery through regeneration came under threat, with potentially devastating consequences for the legitimation of the state in the eyes of its citizens. The examination of the state's response to the financial crisis in terms of its emergency involvement in regeneration schemes reveals a great deal about the policy situation and the institutional capacity in each country and can offer insights into the direction that future policy making could take.

Note

1 This refers to networks/communities that may not have a local link in terms of residence or legal rights but may wish to have a say, due to the particular importance of these areas for the specific thematic interest of those networks, e.g. nature conservation, heritage etc.

Chapter 4
Dutch case studies

Introduction

The first two case studies explored in this book come from the Netherlands and, given the character of regeneration in that country, they include housing as a key component. In IJoevers (in central Amsterdam) the challenge was to attract investment into an area that had been largely abandoned by the private sector following the shifts in goods transportation technology and their effect on ports. The role of local government increased in significance following a failed attempt to launch a scheme based on a private sector-led partnership. Hoogvliet (in the periphery of Rotterdam), on the other hand, is a case of a public sector-led intervention aiming to turn around an area with large social housing estates, a product of public sector housing provision that had turned into a pocket of social deprivation.

In both case studies the Dutch state played a crucial role in coordinating development, attracting investors, providing infrastructure and underwriting risks whilst reducing uncertainty through long-term commitment to the future of the area. The purpose of this involvement was to increase long-term control over the value chain and its outputs in order to provide merit and public goods (non-market housing, infrastructure, public realm etc.) and achieve policy objectives. Private investment and the participation of private developers were crucial in both schemes, especially in terms of know-how about satisfying market demand. From the public sector, it was the local authorities that were directly engaging in the regeneration activities, while central government was at least one step removed. The role of housing associations, which operate with a market rationale but pursue a social purpose, was also quite important in both schemes. The collaborative relations between housing associations and private developers increased even further their capacity to address market circumstances.

In both cases the land was or came under public ownership for all or part of the process. It is therefore crucial to note the competencies that local authorities have developed, and especially the importance of institutional mechanisms that allow profitable land servicing and trading on the part of the state as well as a capacity to operate anti-cyclically and thus dampen the efforts of market volatility.

IJoevers, Amsterdam

Context

Site conditions

The IJoevers project is located on the south bank of the IJ, in an area occupied in the past by the port of Amsterdam. The project, which started in the late 1990s and was planned to be finished by mid-2015 at the time this research was undertaken, is divided into six relatively separate development schemes. When completed it will comprise 300,000 m² of office space, 240,000 m² of public facilities (including a library and a concert hall) and 2,400 dwellings, 30 per cent of them social housing.

The project encompasses multiple sites on the left bank of the IJ that were formerly occupied by port-related activities and port-related transport infrastructure (Figure 4.1). Many parts of the site were the product of land reclamation interventions in the past. A number of buildings had been built at the edge of the river and there were problems with submerged foundations that needed to be removed.

Figure 4.1 The location of IJoevers (Centraal Bureau voor de Statistiek. Used with permission)

Accessibility to parts of the site, especially vehicular access, was difficult to the point that many property market players preferred an alternative area for development (the Zuidas, to the south of central Amsterdam) that was far more accessible. A study of the infrastructure in the 1990s confirmed the accessibility problems, both on the site itself and in terms of the connections between the site and the city centre.

Evolution of the use and ownership of the site

Amsterdam first grew to prominence in the seventeenth century as the commercial centre of a maritime empire. Though the Dutch Empire waned, the role of Amsterdam as a major port did not. From 1870, areas of the IJ were filled in to accommodate docks, wharves, warehouses and other commercial installations. In 1876, port traffic grew with the completion of a canal connecting Amsterdam to the North Sea. At the turn of the century, several islands were created in the IJ to the east of the harbour so that additional port facilities could be built. At the same time, and with some controversy, three islands were created at the mouth of the Amstel to build Amsterdam's main railway station, Amsterdam Centraal, and thus the city was cut off from the waterfront.

After the Second World War the port of Amsterdam began to decline. The harbour was unable to handle longer and wider ships and could not accommodate the requirements of containerisation. New port facilities were built in the IJ polders to the west of the city; by 1980, many docks and warehouses on the southern embankments and the eastern islands of the IJ (the old port) were derelict and abandoned. As a function of its previous use, much of the land along the IJ was owned by the national railway companies. After the port activities declined, during the 1980s the municipality decided to buy the land in order to use it for its own projects.

Many of the sites in and around IJoevers were derelict or empty when the regeneration project started in the 1990s. However, some were still used by a few remaining port-related activities (transport, warehousing) that were not themselves in decline. These businesses fought against any changes in the general character of the area that could affect them. Some of these firms were branches of multinational corporations that did not welcome the introduction of a mix of uses into the area, especially housing. They hired top lawyers to fight the project and led the promoters to a compromise that accommodated their interests.

Amsterdam is a rather unique city in that the municipality owns a lot of land and operates a system of leases. The land in IJoevers has been leased out by the municipality to the project's development partners. This follows a well-established practice of land leasing by the municipality of Amsterdam to private developers. For the first 70 years after they were established in 1896, municipal land leases incurred a fixed rate of payment from private lessees. Since the 1970s, payments have been linked to an inflation rate that is adjusted every five years. Most leases are for 50 years but there are also contracts of 75 or 99 years, although after 50 years the contract is renegotiated. Payment can be either a small annual sum or an advance payment of the whole sum for the duration of the lease. On expiry of the lease, the land and buildings revert to the municipality for free. Since the early 2000s a compensation mechanism for leaseholders has been introduced.

Property and financial market conditions

The development of IJoevers has been carried out over two decades amidst a volatile Amsterdam property market. From the late 1990s through to 2000, the property market was quite healthy. It then declined for a number of years and reached a low in 2003–04, following which Amsterdam experienced a property market boom until 2008. In 2008 property markets turned down once again, due to the global financial crisis and have been in a precarious state ever since. The expectation was that IJoevers should be completed by 2015. Due to the market situation it is uncertain whether this will be the case.

The variation in market conditions led to some conflicts between private developers and the municipality, with the former trying to adapt the project so as to retain their desired levels of profitability and the latter trying to keep to the original plans. Developers who were forced by the municipality to rethink their projects in 2003–04 when the market was weak found that the property market had recovered by the time the projects were completed between 2006 and 2008 and therefore were not terribly excited by the prospect of further intervention by the municipality. However, in view of the role of the local authority and the prominence of housing associations, developers will often form consortia with them in order to undertake development together.

Policy environment

Similarly to France, Dutch urban policy witnessed a turn towards 'mixity' during the 1990s. As mentioned earlier, housing policy liberalisation had begun in the late 1980s and shortly afterwards urban policy began to shift from 'Building for the Neighbourhood' to urban renewal and the 'Big City Policy', leading to the Urban Regeneration Act of 2000. The trend towards greater involvement and reliance on market actors in housing provision was very influential, especially following the 'grossing' of 1995. Until that date the housing associations played a central role in spatially transforming areas so as to pursue a welfarist agenda, but thereafter they had to be able to balance their books and compete directly with private housebuilders in the open market. Apart from a wave of mergers, this fundamental change in scope had a dramatic effect on the types of projects that housing associations were willing to pursue and increased their willingness to form partnerships with private sector developers.

At the beginning of the project a coalition of the centre/centre right was in government. It was keen to promote homeownership and more middle-class housing in urban development. Central government can greatly influence the policy direction at the local level because municipal government needs central government finance. Amsterdam was and still is run by political parties that are not in favour of more market housing; however, it had to shift its position, due to government pressure that was also expressed through changes in the funding regime. The IJoevers scheme was one of the first schemes on such a scale to take place under the new, more integrated 'urban regeneration' regime.

Content

Project structure, form and design

According to the current plans, the IJoever development will provide 2,500 apartments with a density from 100 to 200 dwellings per hectare, 330,000 m² of office space, 130,000 m² of retail space, including six hotels, and 105,000 m² of cultural facilities, including a library and a music conservatory. The development will also include 5,000 car parking spaces, 7,500 cycle parking spaces, two marinas and several houseboat jetties as well as seven bridges, a mass-transit metro line, a tram line, a bus terminal and a road tunnel. The total investment in IJoevers is €3.6 billion with €1.1 billion of public funds and €2.5 billion from the private sector. This total excludes the cost of the new metro line.

The whole development comprises seven separate schemes: Silodam, Western Dock Island, IJDock, Western Station Island, Central Station Island, Eastern Dock Island and Eastern Commercial Quayside (Figure 4.2). Each scheme comprises a number of individual development sites.

SILODAM

Silodam is a mixed-use project located on a pier along the IJ (Figure 4.3). Between 1999 and 2002 two old silos were converted and one new building was constructed to contain 245 luxury apartments, 99 social housing apartments and 6,700 m² of office space. The project also includes an automated mechanical car park with 214 parking places.

WESTERN DOCK ISLAND

Western Dock Island was once a Dutch Railways yard as well as the site of Dutch customs warehouses and is now a high-density residential area of around

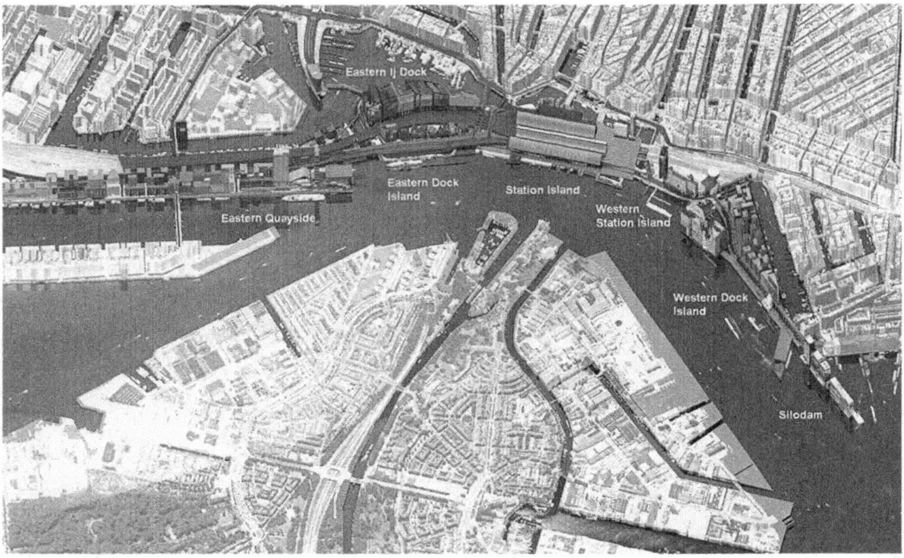

Figure 4.2 Plan of the IJoevers regeneration scheme (Projectbureau Zuidelijke IJoever. Used with permission)

Figure 4.3 The Silodam site in 1990 before redevelopment (Joost J. Bakker, IJmuiden. Used with permission)

Figure 4.4 New housing in Western Dock Island in 2010

200 dwellings per hectare (Figure 4.4). The warehouses were demolished in 2003 and construction started in 2004. Three developers worked together to build four blocks with a total of 900 apartments. Thirty per cent of the apartments are social housing, 11 per cent are affordable private housing, 20 per cent are available for market rent and 50 per cent are owner-occupied housing. The blocks also include some commercial and retail space as well as public facilities. The project was completed in mid-2009.

IJDOCK
IJDock is mostly a commercial complex that is located on the IJ in a former harbour. The harbour was first built for inland navigation vessels but was later used by houseboats that were relocated so as to accommodate the new building. At the time the research was undertaken the IJDock was planned to comprise a hotel, a marina, 60,000 m² of office and retail space including the Palace of Justice and a station for the Harbour Police as well as 55 luxury apartments. Construction of IJDock started in 2008.

WESTERN STATION ISLAND

Western Station Island is planned for commercial use, due to its existing office buildings and its proximity to Amsterdam Centraal train station. The municipality would like to see the existing office buildings renovated and have some new commercial buildings to house a mixture of hotels and other small businesses. Due to the poor demand for commercial space in 2010, the development of Western Station Island has halted and awaits a new plan from the landowners, the Dutch railway companies NS and ProRail.

CENTRAL STATION ISLAND

The redevelopment of Central Station Island is the most complex part of the IJoevers scheme. Each day 300,000 passengers travel to and from the Central Station by train, bus, tram, ferry and bicycle. The redevelopment, planned to be completed by 2014, includes the construction of the North–South metro line, the IJ tramway, a new waterfront bus station, as well as a 300 m road tunnel.

EASTERN DOCK ISLAND

The development of Eastern Dock Island, located east of Amsterdam Centraal, is a joint venture between a private developer and the municipality. Following the demolition of a postal distribution centre in 2003, the developers planned to construct a new central public library, the Conservatory of Amsterdam, a top-end 530-bed hotel and congress centre, as well as to include commercial and retail space, some non-market apartments and private housing. The development will also have 1,500 car parking places and 2,500 cycle parking places, both underground. The library opened in 2007, the conservatory opened in 2008 and much of the rest of the development was under construction at the time the research was undertaken.

EASTERN COMMERCIAL QUAYSIDE

Eastern Commercial Quayside is a mixed-use development with 825 residential units, 125,000 m² of commercial space and 52,000 m² of public facilities. The most prominent public facility is the music centre, 'Muziekgebouw het IJ', which was completed in 2005. At the time the research was undertaken the development was largely complete, with only one residential project (330 units) and one commercial project (28,000 m² with a bus station) remaining to be built.

These schemes are not the same as those envisaged at the beginning of the project. They are the result of changes in factors internal and external to the development over almost two decades. The development of the southern embankments of the IJ and the Eastern Islands was first discussed in the early

1980s. At that time, the municipality of Amsterdam proposed a high-density, medium-rise development with housing as a major component. The tenure mix was to be 70 per cent non-market housing. Accordingly, in 1984 a design competition was held and the municipality selected the 'IJ Boulevard' masterplan by Rem Koolhaas for the waterfront.

As the municipality did not have the resources to undertake the development on its own, it decided to partner with the private sector to implement the masterplan for the whole embankment, including the eastern harbour. In the late 1980s the municipality became involved with an investor group led by the director of ING. A committee led by ING was in charge of organising private finance and setting up an organisation not only for the development of the buildings but also for new infrastructure, roads and railway etc. This committee concluded that one public–private partnership (PPP) for the entire IJoevers development, including infrastructure, was too large and too risky and that there would be a low return on investment. Eventually, in the early 1990s, after proposing to break the development into pieces, the municipality finally entered into a PPP agreement with ING and the property developer NMB. The private sector partners set up their own financing and development company, Amsterdam Waterfront Finance (AWF), and started work on a masterplan that mostly comprised commercial space. This special body received €13 million to study the area and to make both a physical and a business plan.

At this stage, the municipality changed the tenure mix of the masterplan to be only 30 per cent non-market housing, with the view that there would be too many small housing units and not enough larger houses to accommodate the growing number of wealthier households. Also, the municipality allowed for more office space so as to stem the flow of businesses away from Amsterdam's city centre to the new Zuidas commercial development to the south of the city.

The first actual developments were south of the railway yard in the Eastern Dock area. The idea was that the whole project should create enough income to pay for non-income-generating facilities. The project team also realised that public space, together with infrastructure, would bring cohesion between the different areas of the project through a public space masterplan. Public facilities and spaces were among the first interventions to be initiated, with the expectation that they would be followed by profit-making development in the prime office locations. However, the office market in the early 1990s was not particularly buoyant and competition from Zuidas was stiff. As a result, no significant office development took place in IJoevers for a few years. Similarly, in the early 1990s a housing association bought the warehouses by the river, demolished them and built apartments that were too expensive for that location at that time. None was sold and they had to be converted into flats for rental.

In 1994 ING pulled out of the deal, effectively killing off the partnership agreement. Its decision to abandon the project was the culmination of a number of factors that worked against the PPP. The AWF masterplan was primarily focused on providing office space and was therefore highly susceptible to the collapse in the commercial property market at that time. ING had preferred to make the area more accessible by car, yet it was uncertain who would pay for the costs of infrastructure. In addition, some residents of Amsterdam believed that the planned IJoevers development scheme resembled Manhattan and thus did not belong to their city. All these factors were compounded by the length of the commitment required to a development of that size, resulting in stakes that were too high for too low a return on investment.

Meanwhile, in the early 1990s a Green/Social Democrat coalition had presented an alternative to the AWF proposals in terms of separation of uses, the number of organisations that should be involved and whether or not all of the area should be treated as a single project. In 1995 the municipality of Amsterdam adopted a similar approach to the development following the collapse of the IJoever partnership with ING. As outlined in the memorandum "Anchors of the IJ", the municipality would adopt plans for mixed-use peninsulas instead of single-use; would involve many smaller organisations instead of one larger organisation; and would devise many smaller projects instead of one big project.

The municipality realised that it would be organisationally difficult to redevelop the area in one go and that financing for schemes of that magnitude would be hard to come by. The 'Anchors' approach to developing IJoever sought out a mix of different types of investors and developers working on smaller plots with smaller stakes. It allowed the municipality to focus its efforts and resources on more manageable areas and to take back control over the development. As an academic commentator put it:

> Then Amsterdam licked its wounds and tried to come up with a new strategy, and this new strategy was much more low-key and very successful because, learning from the previous experience, the municipality took greater control. Because Amsterdam felt that it had lost a bit of control, that it was much more ING. So they took control themselves, and it was very important that Amsterdam owns the land.

The main three goals of the new strategy were to reduce the barrier created by the railways and thus to reunite the city; to create space for facilities that fitted into the city centre (like libraries, music halls etc.); and to create a high-quality residential neighbourhood close to the city centre.

This strategy was described by a planner in the municipality of Amsterdam as a "pearl necklace with all sorts of pearls and the necklace is the public space".

Carefully planned public spaces would make the different parts of the develop-ment work together, whilst every part would have its own strategy, its own function and its own dynamic, its own working. In property market terms, the emphasis on housing recognised that since the early 1990s housing has been more profitable than offices, given the particular attraction of central Amsterdam as a residential location. It is this strategy, with emphasis on housing, public space, central city-type public facilities and several differentiated development parcels that has underpinned the current development as it has evolved since the late 1990s.

This strategy informs the masterplan for the various development parcels and dictates the rather flexible rules that apply to the structure of each parcel. Each parcel is brought forward for development by the municipality, and the developers are selected through a competition in which different proposals for the parcels are compared. Some of the elements of the proposal such as density, amount of social housing, overall costs of development, overall land-use mix are fixed and are reflected in the value of the lease that will be paid by the developers to the municipality. Other elements are variable, and there is scope for variation such as total number and size of housing units, exact location of buildings, architectural styles and precise mix of uses. As described by one developer:

On every spot was a competition on something else . . . And here was a competition, and they asked a couple of questions and we had to consider several topics, like the density – they really want to have a huge density . . . and "what's your opinion about building logistics", "what's your opinion about the market" and "how is your ambition about building around the core", that's the word for courtyard . . . I think – twenty-five consortia sent their views in, then there was a shortlist of – I think – six parties. There was a discussion, a presentation, and there were three parties left.

As put by another developer:

So there are some specifics, such as the maximum height, volumes, density of development and so forth. And programmatic components like so many private properties, so many rental properties, market letting and social housing. The council instructed an architect to draw up the urban development plan. And then we were asked to present our vision of, well, how we see it, how the properties could be realised and what qualities they would have and so forth. A tall building with around 100 homes is quite a challenge, to fit everything in there and follow the plan to the letter. We had one architect and we showed some sketches and proposed a construction schedule. That was in cooperation with Amvest, because with large developments we like to spread the risk a little bit. Back then, our submission was so well received we won first place and we were given the choice of what parts we wanted to develop. We chose the two blocks of residential properties because they had open views to either side.

Use and tenure mix

As already indicated in the previous section, when the first plans for the development of the banks of the IJ emerged in the 1980s, they envisaged a predominantly residential development, 70 per cent of which would be social housing.

However, by the early 1990s the partnership with ING had meant a change in the use and tenure mix towards a dominance of commercial uses, particularly offices, and a much reduced proportion of social housing in relation to market housing. The municipality had identified an oversupply of small social housing units and undersupply of large market housing, not enough to accommodate the growing number of wealthier households. Also, the municipality allowed for more office space, so as to stem the flow of businesses away from Amsterdam's city centre to the new Zuidas commercial development south of Amsterdam. These different uses and tenure forms were also to be separated, as ING was in favour of separation of uses and was resistant to mixing not just luxury and social housing but also housing and non-residential property. Accordingly, in the early 1990s the proportion of social housing to market housing was changed to 50:50 for the Eastern Harbour (8,000 new homes) and later to 30 per cent for the whole development.

With the collapse of the ING-led PPP, the strategy changed to one in which every part of the IJoevers area would be much more mixed in both use and tenures. This represented a move away from a dominance of office buildings and towards creating new high-density residential areas with high living standards as well as creating new space for public facilities. It was hoped that the profitable residential and commercial elements of the project would cross-subsidise the public facilities and social housing.

In terms of housing tenure, the 30 per cent proportion for social housing remains in force. Within a development of 100 apartments, in addition to the 30 apartments for social housing, there must also be: 10 apartments for affordable housing for key workers; 10 apartments for sale for less than €250,000; and 15 apartments for rent at market prices. There are also apartments for young people in some of the blocks, as well as WIBO properties (*Wonen in een Beschermde Omgeving* – living in a sheltered environment), intended for elderly residents, with wide hallways, special bathroom fittings, wide doors etc. and communal shared spaces. Private developers can expect to draw a profit only from the remaining 35 per cent that is intended for sale in the market. The municipality, wary of the desire of private developers to build the more profitable dwelling types, imposes many rules and prescribes the required output with a high level of detail. As the main landowner for IJoevers, the municipality can sell or lease land to developers with conditions that ensure that what is built is as close as possible to what the municipality wants.

Once the contract is signed with one or a combination of developers and the lease is signed, the programme for each site becomes fixed and detailed. This will include architectural detail, building footprints, proportion of one-, two-, three-, four-bedroom units etc. However, not all these project specifications can be enforced, and as a result some of the developments have turned out to be different from the original concept, albeit within the broadly defined guidelines on uses and use mix. The following three quotes reflect the attitude of developers towards this approach.

> I think that's the problem of working in Amsterdam, you're not free to develop whatever you want – there are a lot of rules, a lot of people. So it's quite difficult to make a profit. If you grow up in Amsterdam and develop here all your life you know how to deal with those rules.

Changes were negotiated as the development progressed, market circumstances changed and developers had to adjust to unforeseen constraints or problems. Some were related to the final appearance, use mix or tenure mix of the project, others were related to development strategies:

> Initially, our idea was to develop these two blocks together as a single project. Then we would have contracted to deliver them both at once. Because that market wasn't so buoyant, we then decided we would do it in phases . . . We also contracted different construction companies to realise the two halves of the project. But it was due to the market that we decided to work in phases.

Overall, adherence to some of the details of the masterplan by a multitude of about 40 separate developers was secured by the need to retain the trust of the municipality of Amsterdam in order to have an opportunity to bid for future developments:

> If you haven't done what the municipality said, what sanctions are there, in what way can they impose these constraints? In the end, nothing. But if you're a dedicated developer you want to have a good reputation in Amsterdam. I think people in Amsterdam and the municipality, they know that we didn't bend the rules so there's a sort of trust for new developments.

Whereas the basic infrastructure for IJoevers has been funded by the local and national governments, finance for development has been provided on a site-by-site basis by each development consortium, involving equity capital, forward sales and bank loans. Some of the developers in charge of development parcels are property development companies with an equity interest in the final product, others are construction companies, others are investment institutions, others are housing associations developing both market and social housing, and many are partnerships between two or more of the above. Although all of them will be working along the general lines set by the IJoevers masterplan, they will have different interpretations of that plan, depending on their main long- and short-term interests in the development. As a result, each parcel will reveal a different approach to the combination of uses and tenures within the same overall guidelines. As put by a housing corporation development manager:

> For example, the Zuidblok, that was developed by Bouwfonds in partnership with Smits Bouwbedrijf construction company. And there is no cooperative involved there and so they made different arrangements, so they have a turnkey contract to supply those properties to a cooperative. But there the social housing is clearly located on an inferior site. We prefer not to do that, we are a housing corporation and so we know exactly what we want. And of course we want our social housing there to be good, to be of quality and be in the right places and possibly to have added value in the future.

However, in a development made up of several separate development parcels united by a masterplan the mix will work differently, depending on the project, and some parts of the mix will not come into being until other parcels are fully developed. This means that some blocks will have a mono-functional character until the other blocks with complementary uses are completed, which may take a number of years. As put by the developer of one of the blocks:

> There are hardly any shops in our blocks. That is the council's intention because the local commercial centre is Haarlemmerstraat, Haarlemmerdijk. We did attempt to include a neighbourhood supermarket, of a limited floor area, which would just about comply with the masterplan . . . But we didn't succeed in getting it.

Also:

> It is always in the zoning plan, that determines where you can and cannot operate hospitality businesses. And here in the master plan, it is logical, this is the area for hospitality and catering. But this whole area is still vacant . . . The intention was that the entire south facade would become a fun area for going out. I'm sure it will be one day, when the Justice Ministry and who knows which other businesses move into the offices.

Social facilities and non-market project components

The masterplan envisaged the provision of city centre-type facilities such as libraries and concert halls, which cannot be built in Amsterdam city centre because of a lack of space but fit into IJoevers, which has been planned as a residential extension of the city centre. Moreover, the masterplan is predicated on a series of high-quality public spaces that would secure the spatial and morphological connection between the separate parts of the development and the various development parcels within them.

The funds to build these facilities were to come from the premium that development consortia would pay for purchasing leases on land on which profitable commercial and residential uses were permitted to be developed. However, this did not happen in the first stages of the development. As discussed earlier, the demand for office space in this area of Amsterdam remained weak for most of the history of the project. The demand for private housing, although much stronger, has followed the ups and downs of the property market (strong in the late 1990s and early 2000s, weak in 2003–4, strong in 2006–8 and then weak again after that). As a result, the take-up of sites for development has been slower than predicted, and lease values have had to take into account the volatility and uncertainty of the market. Most of the facilities and infrastructure have been built with public funds, especially those that needed to be in place in the early stages of the development. Over the long term, the expectation is that the public investment will eventually be recovered, in spite of any short-term losses as all the sites will be leased out to developers.

However, the development of market housing for rent or sale is not just an aspiration of private developers. Housing associations, the main providers of non-market housing, also require a percentage of market housing in their developments in order to finance the social housing component. This process of cross-subsidisation operates both within a development and across developments in different sites. As put by the manager of a housing association involved in one of the parcels in IJoevers:

> The redevelopment resulted in 108 apartments, 30 for social rent and 78 for market rent. This amount of private market apartments is there to generate money for building in other areas of Amsterdam where the need for more social housing is greater. Some of these other areas are like ghettoes of social housing and you cannot make money there. We need to ensure that to balance out all non-profit projects, we have this type of profit-making project as well.

Whilst the project is made up primarily of social and market housing, public buildings and some commercial activities, there are also some spaces for creative industries because of the history of squatting in the area by artists, who have a right to come back. These spaces have subsidised rents, partly funded by the municipality, for a limited period of 15 years.

Organisation

Governance arrangements and partnership members
Governance arrangements for the project are quite complex because of the number of parties involved. The project falls under the responsibility of the Central, West and East districts of the municipality of Amsterdam, who are the landowners. The key strategic player in the governance of the IJoevers project is the municipality of Amsterdam (*Gemeente Amsterdam*). As with similar urban projects in the Netherlands, it is managed through a dedicated project director and a project office. This office, the 'Projectbureau Zuidelijke IJoever', is responsible for managing the development of the area and for acting as a contact point for investors, companies and other stakeholders. However, strategic decisions and implementation responsibilities are shared between the municipality of Amsterdam and three of the eight districts (*stadsdelen*) into which the city is divided. Station Island is under the jurisdiction of the central city and thus has its own project coordination office, 'Coördinatie Stationseiland' which coordinates the work and the contracts for it. The districts are responsible for the planning, financing and implementation of the parts of the project under their jurisdiction.

Both the municipality and the districts are elected tiers of local government, and this dual management structure was designed to bring about some balance between more central decisions and local concerns. The project team has members from the various relevant departments of the municipal council, who liaise with their counterparts at district level. There are also separate teams linking the project to the residents. The municipal project team is directly involved in the financing and implementation of much of the public space and infrastructure. Its main source of income for the project is the leases on its land, which vary depending on the use the land is put to.

Organisation aims and their evolution
The buildings have been developed by housing associations and private developers, often in partnership with each other, under a masterplan prepared by the project team with detailed requirements from the district councils. However, some private sector interviewees suggested that it would not be appropriate to refer to this arrangement as a PPP, as there is no real sharing of investment or market risk in their view. As put by a housing developer:

If you think about the development here in terms of PPP, there's a clear distinction between what the municipality does – takes care of the land assembly, the land servicing, selling building plots – and what we do [develop the buildings]. Everything around the buildings is done by the municipality alone. And they tell us how to develop. So then it's not a real PPP because of all the rules that went into the development. Because they aren't involved in risks . . . If it's a combined project there's a risk for all partners in terms of selling the houses.

In Amsterdam, the most important developers of housing are housing associations. They are the main developers of non-market as well as of market housing and own around 50 per cent of the total housing stock in Amsterdam. In 2008, 81 per cent of all new housing developments were undertaken by housing associations or partnerships between housing associations and private developers. Housing associations are also major providers of luxury and mid-range market housing and use the proceeds to cross-subsidise their social housing role. The cross-subsidy can work between buildings within a single development or between developments within a city where housing is sold in one area to finance social housing in another area where market housing cannot sell.

As market housing developers, housing associations compete directly with private, for-profit developers. Because housing associations have large stocks of assets to use as collateral and are perceived as safer borrowers than are private developers, they can get development finance at lower cost. However, the increasing need to cross-subsidise social housing and public facilities with the proceeds from private housing and commercial property has led to more opportunities for private developers. This is reflected in IJoevers, where housing associations and private developers have been involved in the delivery of social and market housing in a variety of partnership arrangements between private developers, housing associations and private investors:

We [private developers] have developed a partnership with an investor, so we are an investor/developer combination with the backing of a housing association who purchased the social housing from us. The social housing, which is rental, was sold to Amhas. They invested in about 60 houses. The development next door was a powerful developer in combination with a housing association, then there was one with just a building company and the middle one was a small developer with a housing association as turnkey buyer of the social housing.

Some of these partnership arrangements have been sale–purchase contracts, some have been real partnerships operating as a single entity and with their own governance arrangements:

It is not as if Amvest [private housing developer and investor] will do the open market properties and Ymere [housing association] does the social housing. We are genuine 50:50 partners in this project, so all the risk, all the profit is shared. And it's not the case that we just divide the project in two and say, this is your half, this is our half, and we are developing alone. Here you can see the plans for these two blocks. This is social housing and that is social housing, these are private, here is private, and then here and there are rental properties by Amvest, they are spread around a lot across the whole complex. It is an association of owners. We develop as a single entity and so we supply private residential properties to individual homebuyers, we supply social housing for renting to Ymere, and rental properties for the open market to Amvest.

Apart from the pooling of the expertise in different sectors of the market that these partnerships represent, they also emerge as a solution to the problem of coordinating a multi-tenure development, in which each component caters for a different segment of the market and has its own dynamics.

Many housing associations have participated in the development of IJoevers through a development subsidiary, Kristal. It acts as an adviser to the housing associations when it comes to making plans for specific locations and also manages the process of making a deal with local authorities when it comes to buying a site.

As explained earlier, the programme for the project is expressed in a masterplan, and discussions about how the masterplan should be translated into individual developments are managed by municipal planners. Each of the seven areas that made up the whole of the IJoevers project has been divided into several development parcels. Consortia of developers have been allocated parcels after a tender process in which they put forward their views on how they would translate the masterplan objectives in their particular sites, how they would operate the site and how they would finance the operation.

Some developers are single, private construction firms, others are consortia made up of one or more housing associations, others are partnerships between a housing association and private developers. Some of these development consortia have complex management structures of their own: one of the sites is developed by a partnership of a housing association (Kristal) and construction firms, employed a third party as a project manager to oversee negotiations with the municipality, the construction process and the commercialisation of the for-profit parts of the development. A senior manager with Kristal describes its role as follows:

Kristal manages the masterplanning and project feasibility studies that happen before the site is negotiated with the municipality. It advises the housing associations. It also manages the contracts and the project. The structural engineers, etc. are all hired by Kristal. Kristal also operates as selling agent for the private apartments, although they do this through a third party. This sale happens before the project can start.

Other consortia are made up of construction/development companies under a contract to sell the buildings upon completion, to private investors (the commercial elements and market housing) and housing associations (the non-market housing). These consortia will have some management structures of their own to supervise and monitor contracts. In some cases the consortia are constituted as independent companies that will then sell the completed residential and commercial units to the parent organisations at market prices. This was described by a consortium manager as follows:

> Hofmakerij [a joint venture between housing association Ymere and private developer/investor Amvest] is another independent company that needs to perform in a particular market situation. Naturally I want Hofmakerij to make a good profit . . . And naturally we won't be selling property to our Ymere partners for less than market value. If I were to do that, then Amvest would have something to say about it, in this type of partnership. So it all works well if you do it that way.

Over the long run, the management of the public facilities, public spaces and infrastructure is a responsibility of the public sector bodies that normally manage those types of facilities and infrastructure. Commercial buildings and private housing will be managed by private facilities managers as in any other commercial building or private residential block. Public facilities are normally provided by national or municipal governments, even if the funding comes from receipts from the lease of land for development. However, more recently there has been pressure on housing associations to produce those facilities themselves, and this has been the case in parts of IJoevers. For social housing, post-completion management will be done by housing associations, both for the stock they themselves have developed and for units they have acquired from others.

Risks and uncertainties
The initial plan for IJoevers covered an area larger than the current scheme and that in itself was identified as a risk by the ING-led PPP. The response was to reduce the scheme's area by excluding the Eastern Harbour and by breaking up the remaining area into smaller components. However, size and length of development time still were perceived as a risk and when ING pulled out of the project in 1994 it cited as its main reasons the long-term commitment that would be required to see the whole project through and a predicted low return on the

investment. This led to a development strategy based on the division of the area into separate projects, with not just one or a few large investors, but several private partners tackling smaller development lots.

In the past, the municipality would have used its own resources in house-building projects, assuming most of the development risks in exchange for much larger degree of control over development outputs. A senior municipal officer recollects:

> Back when I started in Amsterdam, in those days the council housing department would develop plans for social housing rental properties, because there was a budget, we had to subcontract, but it was very much in the council's control. The council even considered the contractors. Well, those days are long gone. The disadvantage, of course, is that . . . the developer is not going to be the property manager. And that is no good, of course. So then plans were developed that made us think: are we able to maintain it properly? And if the market was against us, when subcontracting or something, then there would be cut-backs and then it turned out, in our opinion, that the wrong things had been cut back on. So, we'd better leave these decisions to developers.

The present approach separates the risks and uncertainties associated with the municipality's pursuit of the main aims and objectives of the redevelopment of the whole area from those risks and uncertainties linked to the development of individual land parcels and borne by the various development consortia. For the municipality, which owns the land and has invested in public facilities, the main uncertainty was whether development would take place, and if it would, then that it would lead to the expected outcomes. This has been addressed through an increased local authority role and with variations in the structure of the project to cope with property market volatility and changes in demand (e.g. the different mix of uses of various development plots, and the phasing of those developments over a relatively long period of time). All this within the context of a clear masterplan supported by the long-term public ownership of land and the recycling of receipts from land leasing into provision of public goods. The traditionally strong property market of Amsterdam ensures that sooner or later development of the desired shape and quality will come forward. As put by a developer:

> If I were the municipality I would do exactly the same thing – I would tell people what to do, then I would sit down and watch them struggling. It's the best way for the government to do it. You have to buy land, make a plan, then sell the plan to a building company and then let them struggle. Tell them how to do it. Then again, the municipality can act in this way because they own the land. Maybe because this is the capital of Holland, it's definitely completely different in the other cities.

For the several development consortia that have taken charge of the development parcels, the nature of the risks they have had to face and their risk-reduction strategies are a function of the development mix and specifications, of its timing in relation to property market cycles, of variation in construction costs and of the flexibility of their development strategies. However, the way those risks take shape is affected by the highly prescriptive nature of the contracts that developers have with the municipality.

The following examples are typical of how uncertainties during the construction phase were dealt with. All the IJoevers developments are on the waterfront and every building project had to transport building materials via the same access road. In 2007, just as development was about to start, the authorities discovered the road could not safely accommodate such high levels of heavy goods vehicle traffic. The ensuing delay lasted for a year and cost €1.5 million, but allocating the costs was a matter of complex negotiations between the developers, the housing associations, tenants, residents, other businesses and the municipality, whose task it is to provide infrastructure. The alternative would have been to bring in construction materials by boat, but it would have been very costly and would have resulted in a development time of eight years. Building on a brownfield site close to the water also entailed its own uncertainties. The previous buildings had reinforced foundations that were very difficult and costly to remove and so, eventually, construction methods had to be adjusted to deal with the circumstances of the location. The cost of cleaning up the river-bed was partly covered by the municipality, since it had leased out the land as "clean and without any obstructions to development".

A scheme of the size and complexity of IJoevers will inevitably span different phases of the property cycle. Some parcels will reach completion during periods of high demand, whereas others will not. The strategies that developers have used to cope with this market uncertainty have varied. Housing developers have followed the established practice of trying to sell a substantial number of units off-plan, before the development has started. This approach has the advantage that it reassures potential or existing financiers, who feel more confident with putting money into a scheme. One developer referred to 50 to 70 per cent pre-sale as the desired norm. A flexible approach to tenure composition and unit specification seems to have been part of its uncertainty reduction strategies when substantial pre-sale was not possible. In the words of one of the developers:

> Well, if you can decide for yourself then that's an advantage because then you can go with the flow with the market, so if the market is good you can make huge expensive apartments and if the market is poor you make smaller houses but more.

In a number of developments, changes in demand have led to adaptations to projects and even refurbishment of nearly completed units. Larger flats have been converted into small flats, houses for sale have become rental housing and so on as market conditions and demand have changed. However, this flexibility is limited to the market components of the development, which in the case of housing is limited to less than half the total number of units. Although beneficial, these changes affect the profitability of the development as well as the time-scale of expected returns. Therefore, such changes may well create difficulties for developers who have already negotiated land prices with the municipality and have agreed on the conditions for development finance with banks; both are difficult and costly to change. One of the developers mentioned a contingency fund to cope with the eventuality of a different profile of returns:

> We built the first part of the development because it was mostly cheaper apartments. If they didn't sell we would have made them into rental apartments. That solution would have presented some problems because of all the finance and how we would repay it, but that's relatively easy to deal with in the case of those apartments. The second part of the project was riskier, but we already had success with the first part, and we organised a sort of investment fund in case the apartments weren't sold and we didn't have the income from that. Fortunately, in the end we didn't have to use it.

As mentioned earlier, when some developers faced the prospect of falling demand for the mix of units in their developments they opted for redesigning that mix half-way through the development process to meet changing demand. Other developers saw this option as risk inducing and preferred to stay close to their original plans and make small adjustments as and when necessary:

> If there aren't rules then you have to make your own rules. Otherwise you have to redevelop, redevelop, and then you just finish your redevelopment and you have to start again. You can see that in IJoevers some developers redesigned their buildings in the years 2003–4 when the market was poor, but when they finally finished building the market was good again. I think if they had persisted and hadn't redesigned they would have been much more profitable.

Another approach to reduce risks was the formation of partnerships between developers of different natures to deal with one development lot. These would involve e.g. a housing association developer and a private developer, or a commercial developer and a housing developer, on the basis that these developers would have different business models, differently affected by fluctuations in the property market. Here is how two housing association officers describe this approach:

Although we are social housing developers, we got involved with business premises, this entire block. It was nice that at this stage, phase 1, when the market wasn't so good, we had one partner who understood commercial development and who wanted to purchase all of that office space. Then it is out of your hands, you no longer have the risk.

Or:

For this project we chose Amvest as partners, because Amvest is an investor but it is also a fairly active developer, and engaged in a different market segment, the rental market. So we do always try to work with market players that we know or have experience with, and who complement what we do.

Or again, as put by an officer from a housing association working in partnership with a private developer:

When Nieuw-Argentinië came up the council asked us to find a partner . . . We could have easily done it alone . . . But we decided to seek partners, not just for the risk, but also because they are a partner with ideas about slightly more expensive homes, a more expensive segment, and with the right contacts for that.

The development contracts with the municipality specifying the number and nature of residential units, the use mix and the amount to be paid for the land were perceived by some as a risk to profitability, as market conditions often changed and contracts signed at the peak of the market could be punitive when the market was weak. However, some developers managed to link the payment to the municipality for the land leased to them, to the percentage of market units sold. In that sense, a fixed deal provided certainty and clarity. A consortium manager describes the deal in place for the project he was involved in:

The question is how much of the 50:50 profit made by Hofmakerij, how do we determine under what terms it will be paid out. We sell to Ymere and Amvest on a turnkey contract. But it isn't at the point of completion that we get paid, but it is the same as buying a house; if you move into a new house you pay for the land and the first instalment, and in the course of construction you pay the following and final instalments immediately before completion. That is how our rental properties and business properties were invoiced.

The existence of clear rules coming from the municipality was therefore seen as an uncertainty-reducing factor. Clear rules that apply to everyone in the project were seen by some actors as reducing the damaging competition between developers in different parcels. As those rules are well known and discussed in advance, developers can plan for contingencies and have a clear basis upon which to negotiate changes.

The main source of uncertainty at the time the research was undertaken was the situation in the financial market. Potential buyers have problems in accessing mortgages and housebuilders have problems in finding finance for their projects. Therefore, they are adjusting their production to the level of available finance by delaying many of their projects.

Hoogvliet, Rotterdam

Context

Site conditions

Hoogvliet is located near the port of Rotterdam (Figure 4.5). The site covers a vast area of social housing built in the 1950s and 1960s following a decision by the central and municipal governments to solve the local housing problem by building a new town. According to Crimson Architectural Historians (CAH) and Rottenberg (2007), the authorities at the time got carried away with their utopian vision of building an English 'new town' in order to accommodate the

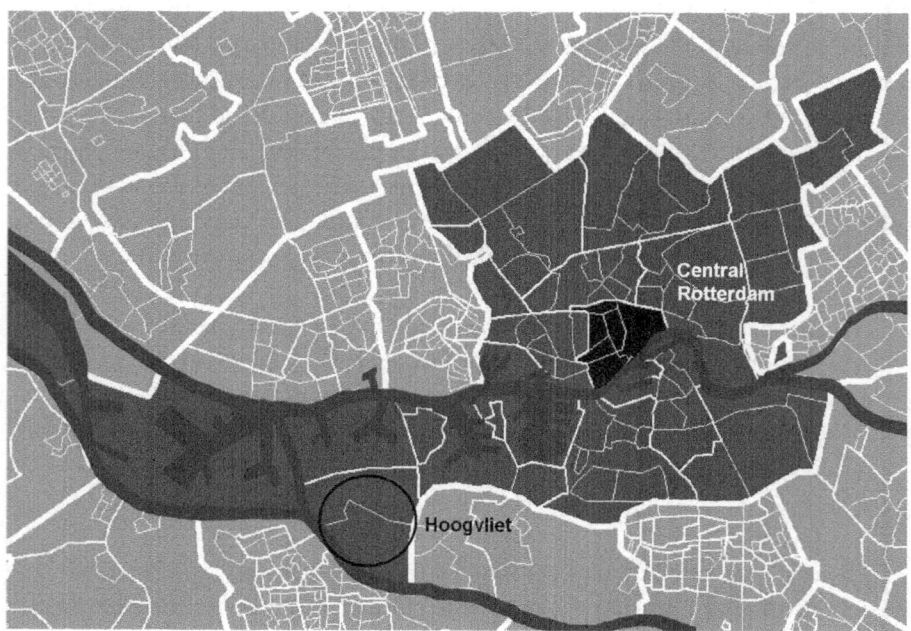

Figure 4.5 The location of Hoogvliet

refinery workers and support the vision of turning Europoort into the biggest port on the planet. Most of the existing housing was in low-cost blocks of flats or gallery flats that were badly maintained and in poor condition. The scheme examined here involves the mass demolition of 4,500 housing units, together with the construction of another 2,000 units and the sale of a comparable amount of housing association stock to private owners.

During the 1970s, health, safety and environmental considerations related to the proximity to the harbour activities and the petrochemical complex at Pernis (where facilities blew up in 1968) forced the city of Rotterdam to change the direction of future development to other areas, to Spijkenisse and Hellevoetsluis. Because of this decision Hoogvliet remained unfinished, in the sense that it never got a real city centre and that small, inexpensive, social rental dwellings and larger maisonettes that were unsuitable for families were overrepresented in the housing stock. Richer residents moved to the newer developments further away, while housing association tenants refused to move in. As a result, much of the stock remained empty, the population fell to 30,000, property prices declined and Hoogvliet gained a reputation as a haven for gang crime and other forms of criminal behaviour. As a local authority officer recalls:

> It attracted criminal behaviour, which Hoogvliet used to have a well-known reputation for. Antillean gangs in estates that the police didn't even dare to go to. Well, it made the national newspapers a lot in the '90s. And then the decision was made: this has to stop. So the redevelopment, the intervention in the built environment is a cause, or a method for social improvement of the whole area . . .

The site is peripheral to Rotterdam city centre but quite accessible. Hoogvliet is linked to the centre of Rotterdam by metro. The area's accessibility by car is assured by the A12 motorway, which connects directly to the Rotterdam Ring Road. Moreover, Hoogvliet is located very near to the harbour area of Rotterdam, which is an important centre of employment.

Evolution of the use and ownership of the site

As discussed in the previous section, Hoogvliet was once a small village on the outskirts of Rotterdam, which in the 1950s and 1960s grew into a town of 40,000 inhabitants. The new town was built to look quite unique from above, in the shape of a flower, with a central area for commercial use and petals for residential areas. Ninety per cent of the housing, mostly small apartments, was speedily built, poorly maintained and soon fell into a bad state of disrepair.

The municipality and the housing associations were the main landowners in Hoogvliet. Most of the housing in Hoogvliet was owned by housing associations.

The housing associations owned the land on which their housing stock was built, whereas the municipality owned all the roads and public spaces. After a wave of mergers in the 1990s, only two housing associations were left in the area: Woonbron and Vestia.

The development agent of the municipality was the Rotterdam Development Company (*Ontwikkelings Bedrijf Rotterdam* – OBR). The OBR became involved as an intermediate landowner and, in effect, mediated all the land transactions in the area. For the housing associations as well as private developers, each building scheme in Hoogvliet began with discussions with the OBR to acquire land for construction. After a scheme was completed, ownership of the public realm (infrastructure and public facilities and amenities) reverted from the developers to the OBR.

Property and financial market conditions

The first developers of Hoogvliet were the housing associations, as there were few incentives for private developers to become involved in an almost exclusively social housing area. The decision by the housing associations in 1998 to demolish and rebuild their stock (Figure 4.6) was taken in the face of great market

Figure 4.6 Hoogvliet: original housing stock

uncertainty, in the sense that demand for housing in the area was very low. It was not at all certain at the start of the project that there would be any demand for the new dwellings when they were completed. Eventually, it was not possible to sustain the expected pace of demolition and reconstruction. Market conditions did not allow sufficiently quick sale of the new dwellings, which meant that work to regenerate Hoogvliet progressed more slowly than had been hoped.

Halfway into the project (ca. 2005) the pace of regeneration was so slow that it would have taken another 20 to 30 years to complete the development plan. Private developers were reluctant to engage in the regeneration of Hoogvliet because of the uncertainty surrounding the sale of housing in the area. The housing associations were supposed to develop around 70 per cent of the new dwellings in Hoogvliet (both social rental and owner occupied) but were unable to realise their plans, due to the poor reputation of the area, which hindered sales. Moreover, they were still fairly inexperienced in operating as market actors, since the grossing operation dated back to only 1995. As a result, their choices as to which type of project to develop were not always well judged and their marketing was not always adequate.

Private developers began to show an interest in the area from the mid-2000s as green space, leisure and education facilities were built. Those private developers wanted to attract higher-income residents to Hoogvliet by building the types of homes that would be attractive to that market segment. The lack of such dwellings had been a problem in the past; residents of Hoogvliet whose income rose very often left the area and if there was a desire to stay there were few opportunities to buy a large family dwelling. It is noteworthy, however, that developers hoped to keep upwardly mobile people in Hoogvliet and were not exclusively aiming to attract new social strata into the area. In addition, Hoogvliet offered private developers an opportunity to create something new and innovative supported by a municipality willing to help. Nevertheless, private developers working in Hoogvliet, and in Rotterdam more generally, were conservative, as market conditions in the city were not easy.

In spite of the difficult local conditions even during the years preceding the latest downturn, Woonbron and Vestia focused on building market housing in Hoogvliet, as it was felt that there were already sufficient stocks of social housing in the area. The financial crisis and the subsequent fall in sales of market housing forced Woonbron and Vestia to consider undertaking non-market housing projects once again. This meant, however, that they, as well as other developers, had to negotiate with the OBR to reduce their expected rates of production in order to adjust to falling demand. Land prices paid to the OBR are normally based on expected production, and so a reduction in expected production meant lower land prices.

Developers had already been exercising caution by phasing projects in cooperation with each other so that not too many projects would be completed at the same time. Even so, projects in Hoogvliet did face difficulties after 2007–8: one project was scrapped; another project was delayed as the developer tried to sell it to another housing association; and the developer of an apartment project tried to sell its project to a housing group for the elderly after having sold only 2 out of 60 units in the open market.

Policy environment

Hoogvliet is a rather typical example of how the shift in Dutch urban policy affected the situation 'on the ground'. The grossing of 1995 put pressure on housing associations to make their assets work harder and to enter the private market. At the same time they were and still are obliged to have a social mission. The urban policy landscape of the time also shifted radically, mixity of uses and tenures became a core element of urban policy, focusing on attracting owner-occupiers (especially when the right-wing populists were in power between 2002 and 2006).

In Rotterdam at the time an 'undivided city' policy applied that aimed at spreading non-market housing more evenly across the city without losing too much of the available stock. The combination of those two forces, mixity and market incentivisation, shifted the remit and scope of local actors and resulted in a scheme that focused on radically altering the social composition of a 'failed' satellite city (by Dutch standards). The first step was taken in 1998 when the local authority, in collaboration with the two biggest housing associations that were active locally, drew up a strategic plan to turn around Hoogvliet Noord and Maasranden.

As mentioned, the suggestion to demolish social housing was taboo until then, and the idea that communities should explicitly be the subject of intervention in order to alter their profile is still rather contestable, although Stouten (2010, p. 17) argues that Rotterdam has "a long tradition of social policies directed at the management and control of population characteristics". Yet one has to recognise that Hoogvliet was already a construct of social engineering, since it was developed as a dormitory town to satisfy the housing needs of one particular social group without necessarily recognising the social variety of Dutch society. In that sense the change in the approach of urban policy is striking, as the following quote from a senior municipality officer shows:

> The population mix was very homogeneous, in terms of socio-economic status, but skin colour as well, ethnicity and so forth. And that was already being discussed a great deal in the Netherlands, about the problem neighbourhoods and places where large concentrations

of particular groups were living, and how to change that. The only means that you had to force the people living there to move was demolition and reconstruction. And by introducing differences in the types of housing and across neighbourhoods and in designs, those estates underwent social improvement.

This quote reflects the general approach of 'urban restructuring', discussed in Chapter 2, that has typified Dutch urban policy of late. That approach has been criticised as sate-promoted gentrification, often at a substantial net financial cost, with the goal of establishing social order – often at the expense of social capital (Uitermark *et al.*, 2007).

In the Netherlands, urban development plans for areas are established at the local and provincial levels in accordance with the Spatial Planning Act. Building plans are also tested in minute detail (including building width, height, etc.) against the provisions of the development plan, but if a building complies, then it can be built. In Hoogvliet, the local council had established an urban development plan for each area and tested developers' proposals against this plan. The two parties then entered into negotiations to discuss what was permitted in relation to the market demand. The urban development plans were quite detailed in terms of building specifications, were legally quite strict and were enforced through systematic visits by building inspectors. However, these plans were not so detailed as to close off development options, and procedures for deviating from the development plans did exist. These procedures could be time consuming, and some stakeholders criticised the delays they have caused.

Content

Project structure, form and design
The regeneration of Hoogvliet is state led and involved the local council as well as the municipality, which coordinated the development and defined its terms, schedule and types of work. The local state had to initiate development in Hoogvliet because private developers would not normally invest in such areas and housing associations did not have the resources and powers to initiate a major regeneration project.

It was the first time in the Netherlands that a regeneration project had involved the demolition of existing dwellings on such a large scale. The Hoogvliet local council was the first in Rotterdam (and in the Netherlands) to propose the mass demolition of social housing – something that had not even been talked about before, let alone done. The proposal was initially refused by the municipality of Rotterdam but eventually the council received permission to knock down the dwellings that were deemed to be in the worst condition.

After several smaller-scale efforts, Wonbroon and Vestia decided in 1998 to participate in a regeneration project involving the demolition of almost 4,500 dwellings, combined with the construction of 2,000 new dwellings and the sale of almost 2,000 other social dwellings to owner-occupiers between 1998 and 2012 and a commitment to allow every Hoogvlieter who wished to remain to do so.

The housing associations considered demolition to be the appropriate way to solve the problems in the area. Refurbishing the existing dwellings would have been very costly, given the condition that the dwellings were in, and demolition had the advantage that it signalled a rupture with the past and thus allowed rebranding of the area in order to make it attractive to investors (either home-owners or institutional investors). The housing associations' decision also had to do with their own position as owners of the property. Since the grossing operation of 1995, Dutch housing associations have become financially independent and no longer receive government subsidies for maintaining and building dwellings. As a result, they have developed new strategies for the management of their housing stock. The long-term development of the value of this stock, through a strategy of asset management, has become crucial for their survival. The combination of the duty of housing associations to operate for the benefit of their tenants and their concern with the long-term value of their stock were the two main motivations behind their decision to intervene drastically in Hoogvliet. In turn, the decision put housing at the centre of the regeneration of Hoogvliet, over and above questions of economic development.

At the start of the regeneration process in 1998 the plan was to improve the built environment of Hoogvliet over the next 12 to 15 years. The interventions in the housing stock were combined with changes in the urban layout and the public space. The intention was to maintain and enhance the green character of Hoogvliet because it would contribute towards its sustainability and liveability. In order to do this, new parks and green areas had to be developed in relation to the important physical changes in the urban structure of the housing areas. As these facilities and amenities were developed, private developers gained confidence in the marketability of the area and began to express their interest in investing in it.

Use and tenure mix

As discussed, the main idea behind the scheme was to achieve social change through improvements in the built environment, therefore the aim of the regeneration effort was to change the proportions of non-market and market housing (from 80/20 to 60/40) as well as the mix of housing in terms of design and tenure, thus changing Hoogvliet's demographics. The assumption, as previously mentioned, was that physical transformation would facilitate social transformation. Despite the social engineering agenda, the municipality was committed to ensuring that those who wished to remain in Hoogvliet could do so.

There was little resistance to the regeneration plans, although local residents' organisations are well organised and can be quite vociferous. The lack of resistance has been attributed to the thorough engagement of the municipality in consultation with residents and to the real benefits that residents saw, says one academic interviewee with long experience of the area:

> although these programmes [social programmes] are not that big, they seem to have to a certain extent some positive effects, in that residents see that some changes are actually improving their situation. And the same applies to many residents who had to move involuntarily, because of demolition they were relocated within Hoogvliet primarily within newly constructed dwellings, so they also experienced progress not just in their housing situation but also in several other ways.

Other interviewees point out that the people in favour were predominantly the older white residents. In the words of a municipality employee, the scheme

> got enormous support at that time from the tenants' organisations. Something to do with neighbourhood change. There was a fairly organised residents' association, tenants' association with mostly older white people with some labour union backgrounds. And they were seeing that the neighbourhood was changing and saying we want to get in on that situation. It was the idea that something had to happen, there was a lot of that.

Indeed, these views reflect earlier findings by Uitermark *et al.* (2007), who also point out that the pressure to improve the living conditions in the area had been building since the early 1990s. Uitermark *et al.* also argue that very often the efforts of local residents (older social tenants and newly arrived homeowners) to maintain and improve their housing and living standards were revanchist towards specific ethnic groups who were viewed as the 'newcomers who ruined the area'.

Hoogvliet was meant to be primarily a residential project, so there was little economic development in the plan, but the maintenance of existing economic functions did receive attention. Existing premises for small businesses were preserved and dwellings that could be used as live-work units (*woon-werk woningen*) were built as part of the new development. Land was set aside for industrial estates and for office buildings near the metro stations. The existing shopping centre was redeveloped with the intention of making it a more attractive destination for residents to meet and socialise. This involved the introduction of restaurants, dwellings and offices into the commercial centre in order to make it more lively at all times of day. The construction of an indoor leisure/sports facility also served an economic and a social function.

The gentrification aspect should not be overestimated. Hoogvliet was limited by its market potential, particularly when the regeneration started; it offered few amenities and was located too close to chemical industries and too far from the city centre. Most buyers for the new homes were expected to come from Hoogvliet itself or neighbouring areas, so development plans did not include many up-market, high-priced developments. Admittedly, however, the housing product mix changed with time, as housing associations and private developers had the opportunity to test the market.

Despite being social housing associations, Woonbron and Vestia built mostly market housing in the years preceding the credit crunch. In Hoogvliet almost all newly built housing was market housing, as it was thought that there were already sufficient stocks of social housing in the area. The credit crunch and subsequent fall in sales of market housing made Woonbron and Vestia consider undertaking social rental projects once again.

Woonbron planned to build high-rise apartments in Hoogvliet. However, around 25 per cent of the apartments in the emblematic Oosterbaken tower (completed in 2007) were not sold (Figure 4.7). The unsold apartments were made available in the private rental market, which was still doing relatively well, as people seemed to prefer to rent apartments in Hoogvliet rather than buy them. As a result Woonbron realised that apartments in high-rise towers were not appropriate for Hoogvliet, although they were selling rather well in more central parts of Rotterdam. The selling points of the area are its green space and its low densities and people in search of these qualities are interested in houses rather than in high-rise apartments. As a consequence, Woonbron shifted its production to single-family residences as well as apartments, with an innovative option for prospective buyers to rent first and buy later at a price that took into account the rent that had been paid.

Without the involvement of private developers, work to regenerate Hoogvliet had been progressing slowly. It had taken several years to build a few dozen dwellings and would take decades for the development to be completed at that rate. The housing cooperatives had the right to develop from 70 to 80 per cent of the properties in Hoogvliet but were unable to realise their plans; they developed the wrong projects, their prices were too high and their marketing was insufficient. As the housing cooperatives built social housing for rent, they also had to bear the added cost of outfitting their houses to a very high standard so as to withstand frequently changing tenants. It was believed that Hoogvliet could benefit from the involvement of private developers, who were thought to be

Figure 4.7 Hoogvliet: renovated tower and new housing (Michiel1972. Used with permission)

better at making profits. The housing associations intended to develop part-nerships with private developers in order to complete schemes where the developer arranged finance, got paid for its work and gave a 10 to 15 per cent share of profits to the housing associations.

Private developers began to show interest in the area from the mid-2000s as amenities and leisure and education facilities were built. Echoing the issues raised about gentrification, private developers wanted to cater for higher-income clients by building in Hoogvliet the types of dwellings that their clients would buy. The lack of houses had been a problem in the past; anyone in Hoogvliet whose income rose left the area immediately, and if there was a desire to stay there were few opportunities to buy a large family house. The Dutch do not usually move between cities or over large distances when moving to a new house, thus developers hoped that, given the right types of property, upwardly mobile people would stay in Hoogvliet. In addition, Hoogvliet offered private developers an opportunity to create something new and innovative with a municipality willing to help them with that.

Social facilities and non-market project components
It was mentioned earlier that the regeneration scheme involves the replacement of the existing social housing stock with a mix of tenures. The new non-market housing is provided by housing associations that aim to cross-subsidise it from the sale of market housing.

As this is an intervention in a social housing estate, the main non-market component has to do with amenities, infrastructure and social facilities. Infrastructure provision and maintenance in Hoogvliet is the responsibility of the local council, which is funded by the municipality. The municipality is also partly funded by central government for the infrastructure connecting Hoogvliet to the surrounding areas. New infrastructure has been funded by income related to new development: as the municipality takes charge of the land development through the OBR, it receives income from selling serviced building plots. Private developers and housing associations also pay a percentage of the income that they receive through rents or sales. All parties involved in the development pay into an infrastructure fund to be disbursed by the council. This money is then used for funding on-site infrastructure and amenities such as green space, which are considered beneficial for the attractiveness of the area. It is noteworthy that the environmental improvements funded through this mechanism were the trigger that convinced private developers to express their interest in the scheme. It was only after the public sector had invested in place making that the private actors saw an opportunity materialising and realised that this scheme could have interesting potential for them.

Organisation

Governance arrangements and partnership members
The regeneration of Hoogvliet was led by the public sector, with the local (district) council and the municipality of Rotterdam coordinating the development and defining its terms, schedule and types of work, whereas the housing associations (and private developers) assumed a delivery role but had strong input in formulating the plans. Central government funding was crucial in pushing forward the regeneration programme. Around €200 million invested in the area between 2005 and 2009 originated from central government funds. The local authority had to initiate development in Hoogvliet, but it was the role of housing associations to produce the main bulk of market housing, in order to change the composition of the housing stock.

In 1998 it was decided to put an informal steering group in charge of the whole operation. Central government, the municipality, the local council and the two housing associations were represented in this group and its tasks and remit were defined and agreed upon, but were not formalised in a policy document. Participation and adherence to the decision of the group are as much a matter of trust as a matter of contractual obligation. At a time when the market was buoyant this worked smoothly; however, when the market turned some friction did occur.

This steering group discusses dwelling and tenure mixes, phasing, programme, funding etc. on a regular basis. Renegotiations of the initial plans are also done in this steering group. For example, the revision of the initial programme in response to the credit crunch, towards more rental housing and fewer dwellings for sale, was discussed and agreed in the steering group. Thus the regeneration of Hoogvliet is a process of co-production between the key actors participating in the steering group and the private sector.

The local council and the municipality have also established regular relationships with private developers. If a developer was interested in building in Hoogvliet, the local council would be approached to find out if a site was available. For private developers and housing associations alike, each project in Hoogvliet began with discussions with the OBR to acquire land for construction. Regardless of being part of the municipality, the OBR has to make a profit in order to fund its activities. The credit crunch forced developers to negotiate with the OBR to slow their rates of production so as to adjust to falling demand. In cases where the local government was unsatisfied with the change in production rates, developers faced the possibility of the steering group's overturning OBR decisions that allowed slower production rates.

The sale of land to a developer by the OBR is always subject to negotiations in which the steering group also has a say before the final decision is taken by the municipal council. More precisely, the steering group issues a programme (number of units and tenure) for each particular project. Guidelines on the physical form of each development are set in the local land-use plan and in more detailed planning guidance that is issued by the municipality. Within these conditions, the delivery vehicle – either housing associations of private house-builders – draws up a proposal, in negotiation with the OBR for issues concerning the residual land price calculation, and with the steering group on programmatic and design aspects. Once a suitable solution on all issues and for all parties has been reached, an agreement is signed between the parties and the developer initiates the project.

The regeneration of Hoogvliet involves four central actors, which are the two housing associations Woonbron and Vestia, the local community council of Hoogvliet and the municipality of Rotterdam. At the development level, housing associations and private developers often work in partnership. The municipal council of Rotterdam has to provide planning permission and supervise the project, and it therefore has the final say. Within the municipality, the OBR is a key player in that it is directly and proactively involved in the wholesale process as a land developer. The overall strategy for the regeneration of the area results from negotiations between these four actors (the two housing associations, community council, municipality). At a later stage, private housebuilders become involved for the building of houses. As such, they have some influence on the building programmes, but they generally operate within the boundaries set by the OBR and the local plan of the municipality, and are concerned only with building development. Housing associations have an advantage over private developers in terms of financing, as they can get cheap credit from the BNG, often backed up by central government guarantees.

Although the OBR was a part of the municipality and therefore a public body, it was still obliged to engage in profitable activities. As such, the OBR had an interest in land development and it preferred to boost housing production in order to generate as much income as possible, although as a public body it could always count on the state to underwrite its activities.

Between 2005 and 2009, the OBR invested €20–30 million in Hoogvliet. Throughout the 2000s the OBR was making an annual profit of €10–20 million through its land-buying activities in Rotterdam. So, the municipality was very keen to lend to the OBR because of its profitability and its generally risk-averse behaviour. As the OBR had access to secure, cheap and long-term funding, there was no need for it to divest until conditions called for it. Some of the money generated by the OBR through buying and selling land throughout Rotterdam was deposited into a central municipal revolving fund that the municipality used to finance other projects and actions.

Thus, the OBR does not make the development or regeneration plans, but it does play a key role in their realisation. Notwithstanding its direct activity in the land market, the OBR is a public and not a private actor. It is subject to political control and is obliged to work together with representatives of other departments of the municipality of Rotterdam.

Organisation aims and their evolution

Regeneration of a housing area on such a large scale as in Hoogvliet is quite unique in the Netherlands. It is a reaction to a situation of deprivation and economic decline that Dutch society perceived to be unacceptable and that lasted for several years, in spite of the many smaller projects that have tried to improve the situation. The main thrust of the programme is to change the housing stock structurally, thus effecting change in an area that faces a challenge from both a social and a housing association asset-management point of view. Measures to reduce social problems, in particular those that were crime and drugs related, had been deployed in the 1990s, but had not been sufficient to make a lasting change in the residential quality of the area. They did, however, set the scene for the radical physical transformation effort that was to be realised in the decade afterwards.

At the beginning of the programme a change of the area's image was required in order to make it an attractive residential area. Even though this physical renewal has not been realised at the pace that was planned, it has succeeded to an extent in putting the Hoogvliet area back on the map of property investors and homebuyers in the Rotterdam area. In due course, this is expected to contribute to a qualitative improvement in all domains (social, economic, urban) of the area.

Municipalities in the Netherlands can engage in land development along a spectrum from very active engagement to mere facilitation of market actors. In Hoogvliet the municipality assumed a role somewhere in the middle of that spectrum. It facilitated spatial planning procedures, engaged in land servicing, but left property development itself to market participants (including the housing associations). The municipality, via the OBR, sold land to developers and the developers sold public space, e.g. roads, parks etc., in their developments back to the municipality. Most of the sites were owned by housing associations and the rationale for the project was to introduce alternative tenures without adversely affecting the material and social conditions of the housing association tenants. The decisions taken to rehouse any affected social tenants either locally or elsewhere also contributed in attenuating the negative effects of a project with elements of both social engineering and endogenous development.

The choice to regenerate the area of Hoogvliet through the production of market dwellings was deliberate. A little over ten years from the start of the operation, this strategy is still supported by the key actors. The housing associations, whose central aim is to provide housing for the less well-off, have mostly been producing market housing, very often in cooperation with private housebuilders. This was thought to be necessary and reflects the new role of the housing associations, a role that would have been unthinkable before 1995. As housing prices rose throughout the 2000s, it became more and more difficult for people at the low end of the housing market to purchase suitable dwellings in the area. As a result, housing associations started to think again about how also to provide a sufficient amount of non-market dwellings.

Risks and uncertainties
In a similar fashion to IJoevers, the Hoogvliet site covers a very big area, which in itself amplifies certain risks. A second crucial factor that has to be taken into account when thinking about the uncertainties affecting the project is the

difficult market conditions. From a commercial point of view the downturn in the property markets has exacerbated an already difficult situation for a stigmatised area of low demand. These two factors led to a development strategy based firstly on the OBR's assuming responsibility for the wholesale development function, and secondly on the division of the area into separate projects, with not just one or a few large investors but several partners (public and private) jointly or separately tackling smaller development lots. The two factors also explain to a large extent the much more prominent role of the housing associations.

The option in the past would have been for the housing associations to use their own resources, with the aid of the municipality, to assume most of the market, finance and construction risks, while having a large degree of control over development outputs. This approach was actually tried in previous attempts at refurbishing flats; and indeed, in the early days of the current scheme housing associations did try to develop and sell housing for the open market. However, they quickly realised that the private sector housebuilders were much better at assessing market need and formulating products suitable for that need.

The present approach separates the risks and uncertainties associated with the municipality's pursuit of the main aims and objectives of the redevelopment of the whole area from the risks and uncertainties linked to the development of individual land parcels, which are borne by the various development consortia. For the municipality, having bought the land and invested in public facilities, the main uncertainty was whether development would take place, and if it would, then that it would lead to the expected outcomes. These risks have been addressed through variations in the structure of the project to cope with property market volatility and changes in demand (e.g. the different mix of uses of various development plots and the phasing of those developments over a relatively long period of time), in the context of a clear master plan and supported by the long-term ownership of land.

Although Woonbron and Vestia are housing associations they are considered by the local council to be market actors, and indeed they have partially operated as such since 1995. Woonbron and Vestia must still make a profit from renting and selling market housing in order to finance their social housing activities. However, their not-for-profit scope and their concern for social issues allow them to engage in operations with less-favourable risk/reward profiles than private developers would accept.

Housing associations retain the ownership of the dwellings that they build and rent them out. It is for this reason that the quality of the finishings in housing association dwellings is quite high, in order to withstand the wear and tear of several occupants over a long period and thus reduce maintenance costs in the long run. This strategy makes business sense for social rental dwellings, but costly for housebuilders who build owner-occupied dwellings that are sold in the open market. This is where the expertise of private developers comes in, and housing associations sometimes hire private developers to develop projects for sale in the open market. They pay them a certain percentage of the costs of operation and give them a share in the possible profits.

After having established the price at which the starter homes were to be sold, the municipality worked backwards to calculate the price at which it would sell its land. If the sale prices rose during the development, the council would be able to share in this by raising the land price. Private developers do not immediately become the owners of the land; the transfer of ownership often takes place several months after obtaining planning permission.

The shift of housing association production to more non-market housing, in spite of the original intentions, was partly related to the credit crunch and the subsequent economic downturn in 2008–9 as a result of which the sale of dwellings became problematic and the situation of lower-income households deteriorated. One of the reactions to this situation has been the introduction of a tenure type in which renters get the right to buy after several years of renting a property. The rent they have paid is considered as a contribution towards the buying price. Another reaction has been that the municipal council has asked housing associations to buy houses from private developers, in order to rent them out. This poses some problems in terms of the quality standards to which houses are being built. Generally, the housing associations require higher standards than private developers tend to realise. As a result, notwithstanding indirect subsidies from the municipality in the form of lower land prices, the sale of private developer dwellings to housing associations does not take place on a large scale. Central government has also introduced subsidies for new housebuilding, which supports production to an extent. The brief case study in Box 4.1 shows how the municipality and a private developer had to adjust their agreements and their approach in the face of the market downturn.

4.1 Credit crunch and private housing development: a case study

Developer A is a private housebuilding company based in Rotterdam, with an annual production of 200–300 dwellings. In 2005 the Hoogvliet steering group agreed on a development brief on a plot that was of interest to this housebuilder. The brief specified a block of apartments including a minimum of 140 residential units. The municipality originally provided the land at a price based on 140 units being built. Developer A proposed an alternative plan, which it considered to better reflect demand. It specified single-family, starter homes with gardens instead of apartments, as there was oversupply of apartments in the area. The steering group agreed with the developer and the municipality commissioned the project.

Confident that Hoogvliet would be a success, based on a mini project that sold off very quickly, Developer A began a 45-unit residential development in 2006. The developer and the municipality had agreed to set prices for each unit at between €180,000 and €190,000. As the housing market boomed, expected prices went up to €200,000. But in mid-2008 the market turned and the developer was able to sell only seven dwellings off-plan after one year. Poor presales prompted the developer to enter negotiations with the municipality to amend the project's conditions. The developer had agreed to proceed with construction regardless of the number of presales. It now asked for the project to be separated into two phases of 25 and 20 units. Even then, 7 of 25 properties sold were still too few to start the second phase. Developer A had agreed to begin construction when 60 per cent of the units were presold, but asked the municipality permission to start at 50 per cent. In order to balance the budget of the project, the developer asked for funding from the municipal crisis fund for building projects facing difficulties, as well as from central government for new-build subsidies. The developer also tried to negotiate a lower land price from the municipality that could be paid after each future sale. On the demand side, the developer and the municipalities offered incentives to prospective buyers, including mortgage loans such as mortgage guarantees for first-time buyers.

Still, sales did not pick up and the developer was forced to consider offering unsold units in the private rental market. This required a shift in its strategy, as the developer ordinarily financed its projects from its own equity. Renting the units forced the developer to seek external financing. The finance available to the developer was more expensive and came with less-favourable conditions than the finance available to competing housing associations, which were able to borrow from the BNG on good terms and often with government guarantees. Eventually the developer reached a financing agreement that meant that it would not earn anything whilst renting the properties and would profit only when the property was sold.

Eager to profit from a buoyant housing market that was expected to continue growing, the developer had agreed to purchase land from the municipality once planning permission had been granted, and more land once again before 31 December 2008. It now had to negotiate with the municipality in order to avoid the second purchase, which had been priced at the time of the housing boom. In the current conditions, that price would make the project financially unviable. The argument that convinced the local council to accept these modifications was that it was in nobody's interest to have empty buildings and a bankrupt developer, as this would damage Hoogvliet's image and its reputation with the private housebuilders.

Conclusions

A most striking feature of both case studies is their scale and level of complexity, which caused previous regeneration efforts either to collapse or to prove ineffective. In both cases the central government has exerted its influence through general urban policy and local authority funding regimes. It was the local government that pursued an ambitious agenda, sometimes in opposition to central government policies, albeit it inevitably had to be realistic and reach a compromise. Local authorities played a key role as coordinators of development not only by creating a cohesive context for the project via masterplans/development plans but also by actively assembling and leasing or trading land, by frontloading the provision of infrastructure, by attracting investors and by creating and sustaining a climate of certainty through their commitment to the project. Their involvement spanned both the strategic and the operational levels, essentially using private developers for a specific function: to deliver suitable products by developing specific sites.

In both cases, public sector landownership and the capacity to service and lease or even trade the land proved crucial in achieving the social goals of the project, in providing merit and public goods and in enforcing a rather tight but still flexible planning regime. It is also worth noting that after 2007–8 the development on publicly owned land continued, albeit with difficulty, whereas plans for privately owned sites were frozen. This is a clear indication of the capacity of the Dutch state to assume market risks that the private sector is unable or unwilling to deal with. This practice is under criticism at the moment due to the losses incurred during the prolonged property downturn. By the same token, however, public actors recognised that, as a rule of thumb, private developers are more in tune with market demand and have the ability to assess the capacity of any given site to offer developments suitable for specific market segments.

Thus, a crucial aspect in both cases is that the local state decided to join forces with the private sector because of the push from central government, and also in order to pool financial and organisational resources. In both case studies the relations between actors had to be negotiated as all parties slowly began to recognise that the public sector's long-term view brought in more stability and certainty, whereas the private sector's market astuteness brought in potentially higher returns (for all parties) and more desirable final product configurations. The negotiations between local authority, housing associations and developers were occasionally quite difficult, but public sector landownership, combined with a central government policy imperative to leave plot development to the market, created a balance of power between public and private actors that eventually led to a workable compromise. In a fashion similar to that in France, the profits from the land leasing or trading activities are channelled into funding infrastructure, public realm and public facilities, albeit in both cases this happens both directly and indirectly, through a revolving fund operating at the level of the municipality.

The regeneration programme for Hoogvliet was a major departure from previous practices of state intervention in social housing estates in the Netherlands and was closely aligned to the new trends in Dutch urban policy that emphasised mix of uses, functions, tenures, demographics and income in urban areas. It was an initiative with an explicit social engineering agenda about which the municipality, council and housing associations were upfront. Combined with this agenda came the attempt of two housing associations to restructure and valorise their asset portfolio. The decision made in the post-war years to build a single-tenancy dormitory satellite town with eventually unsuitable housing stock increased the spatial concentration of poor, unemployed individuals and households when the local economic base declined and planning as well as political priorities changed.

There was some potential for conflict in the aim to keep everyone in the area who wanted to stay there, whilst replacing social housing stock with market dwellings. Yet it is argued that both aims were achieved to a large extent. In spite of the market-oriented agenda and the need to introduce market dynamics, both the local authority and the housing associations consistently pursued an agenda that reflected a wider metropolitan-level strategy to redistribute tenures in Rotterdam without detrimentally affecting housing association tenants and the overall stock. That having been said, the approach of urban restructuring has been subject to criticism, due to its effects on social capital and the revanchist attitudes that it could reinforce (Kleinhans, 2009; Uitermark *et al.* 2007).

IJoevers, on the other hand, was also a departure from past practices in the sense that the municipality gave more freedom to housing associations and private housebuilders to influence the details of each development parcel. However, it was the dedication of the local authority to promoting regeneration that sparked private interest and made the project possible, indicating that partnership between public and private actors is a constantly evolving learning process. A previous PPP initiative was plagued by issues of risk management and risk/return allocation and was abandoned by the private partners (ING). That was a crucial lesson for the local authority as to the limitations of the private sector in undertaking large, complex, long-term regeneration projects. Thus a new form of partnership was promoted, one where each actor had rather distinct roles and assumed the related risks and returns. The different tiers of government in general operate within clearly defined remits, with centralised institutions (like the BNG or central government funding mechanisms) operating as a stabilising factor in spite of periodic changes in policy (which, broadly speaking, are more evolutionary than revolutionary).

In both cases housing associations, usually the preferred development partners of the local authority, tested their capacity to operate and deliver in their new role following the grossing of 1995. Very quickly, the housing associations realised that private housebuilders were better at sensing market trends and at responding with suitable products. After the investment in merit and public goods (infrastructure, amenities, public spaces etc.) had increased the attractiveness of the area and reinstated some private developer interest, the public sector actors and the housing associations brought in private housebuilders to deliver suitable products where necessary. This, however, did not undermine the goal of achieving certain proportions of non-market housing as well as social infrastructure; rather the opposite applied, as the housing associations were able to benefit from private development in order to cross-subsidise the non-market housing element of their tenure-blind schemes.

The mix of uses, tenures, functions and phases as well as off-plan sales and multi-developer partnerships were used effectively in both cases in order to manage market and construction risks. An enhanced degree of coordination between actors was necessary in order to employ these techniques and to embed flexibility in policies, plans and regulations. The development agreements between the municipality and the private sector had to be renegotiated when the market turned down after the onset of the financial crisis. The role of institutions like the Hoogvliet steering group, the OBR, the IJoevers 'Project Offices' and the municipal services of Amsterdam was paramount in allowing actors to reach compromises based on the trust that had been built between actors up to that point.

The effect that these changes and renegotiations had on the types of built environments produced varies according to local conditions, but is not negligible. The more stable parameters of both schemes have to do with the hard infrastructure provision (like transport), whereas aspects such as the mix of uses, tenures, timetabling etc. are more variable. It is noteworthy, however, that in both cases local authorities tried to facilitate housebuilders (housing associations and private developers) by giving them flexibility to alter their product and/or their cash flow, but were reluctant to effect major changes to amenity provision or to the production of public goods more generally. On the contrary, investment in merit and public goods provision (especially non-market housing) was seen as a way to alleviate uncertainty and dampen market volatility. One could plausibly argue that if the downturn in demand lasts much longer, then this variability could effectively alter the trajectory of these schemes by altering their strategic aim to introduce market dynamics into the areas concerned. Unsurprisingly, this potentiality sounds more probable for Hoogvliet than for IJoevers.

Last but not least, one should not underestimate the capacity of the state to provide cheap finance. Apart from crucially important direct funding in the form of emergency government subsidies or loans to housing associations, the local authority funded or guaranteed the funding of land preparation, public good provision (frontloading infrastructure investment) and stop-gap funding when the crisis struck. The housing associations played a similar role by changing their development mix towards more non-market housing when market demand decreased. This uncertainty reduction and risk attenuation at project level was possible only through mechanisms counterbalancing market cyclicality and volatility at the municipal and national levels, namely the BNG, the municipal and national (revolving) funds and the central government subsidy scheme for new-build dwellings.

Chapter 5
French case studies

Introduction

As discussed in Chapter 2, urban regeneration projects in France can be broadly divided into two categories. Therefore, studying both types will give a more comprehensive picture of how merit and public goods are provided through MUURSs. The project in Carré-de-Soie, in the Lyon agglomeration, is a locally initiated regeneration initiative in an area that has become derelict following the loss of much of its industrial activities. There was no central government subsidy available and the Greater Lyon Authority needed to convince private investors to come to the area if it wanted the project to succeed. The case of La Duchère, also in the Lyon agglomeration, is an example of the type of regeneration in which central state funding is used in order to turn around a declining suburban social housing estate.

Both projects can be considered as 'avant garde' in their respective domains. In Carré de Soie the local planning authority decided not to engage in temporary landownership and thus not to get involved directly in the development process. Development in both cases has relied to some extent on market mechanisms, although in Carré de Soie the state intervened to correct a market failure and in La Duchère the state intervened to correct a government failure. Means of coordination and of negotiation between the public and private sector actors had to be found in this context, and in both cases establishing an organisation ('*Mission*') responsible for leading the project was the preferred option.

Carré de Soie allows the study of the potential and the limits of the recent market-based approaches that are deployed in French regeneration projects for the provision of non-market housing and public goods. The local state has assumed a key coordinating role in development, mitigated risks and provided infrastructure in order to attract private sector investors into an area abandoned by industrial activities. The private sector has brought with it substantial investment potential that, combined with the local authority's efforts, has created a positive dynamic for the area. La Duchère, on the other hand, is an effort to fix what today are perceived to be the side-effects of past urban policy, namely the concentration of low-income social strata under a single tenure in areas dominated by a small variety of dwelling types of poor quality. It was the first project to obtain central state funding under the ANRU regime, and, although a major part of its funding is public and the state acts as intermediary landowner, it has managed to attract private investors and hence to generate income through the sale of building plots. La Duchère therefore allows the study of the consequences of the changing approach to urban regeneration in an area where market dynamics has been replaced and has remained absent for several decades.

La Duchère, Lyon

Context

Site conditions
The area of La Duchère is situated in the municipality of Lyon, which is part of the Greater Lyon Authority – an inter-municipal cooperation structure. It covers 120 hectares, which were developed between 1956 and 1958 as a large, high-rise housing estate of 20,000 inhabitants, with 5,200 dwellings, of which 80 per cent (4,060) was social housing. The area also contains a relatively small shopping centre and some public facilities (post office, town hall etc.). The construction quality of the dwellings is not particularly high, as they were built during a period in which there was severe shortage of housing and therefore speed of construction was the primary concern. Because of the poor quality of the materials, the buildings have aged prematurely. The structure of the land use in the area is typical of the large, high-rise housing estates that were built at the time. Only 15 per cent of the site is occupied by buildings and the rest has remained unbuilt, to be used as public space. There is no privately owned vacant space.

Similarly to many other large, high-rise social housing estates, various attempts in the 1980s and 1990s did not succeed in reversing the social and economic decline of the area. However, La Duchère is close to the centre of Lyon (Figure 5.1), is well connected to infrastructure networks, has an attractive physical environment and is surrounded by some of the most attractive municipalities of the Lyon agglomeration in terms of residential environment and job opportunities. A consequence of this favourable geographical position is that La Duchère is probably more likely than other high-rise social housing areas to attract new residents who will pursue homeownership through the market and will not turn to the public sector to satisfy their housing needs. This combination of persisting social problems with good development potential has prompted an approach to regeneration that promotes the demolition of existing buildings and construction of new types of dwellings for a variety of tenures.

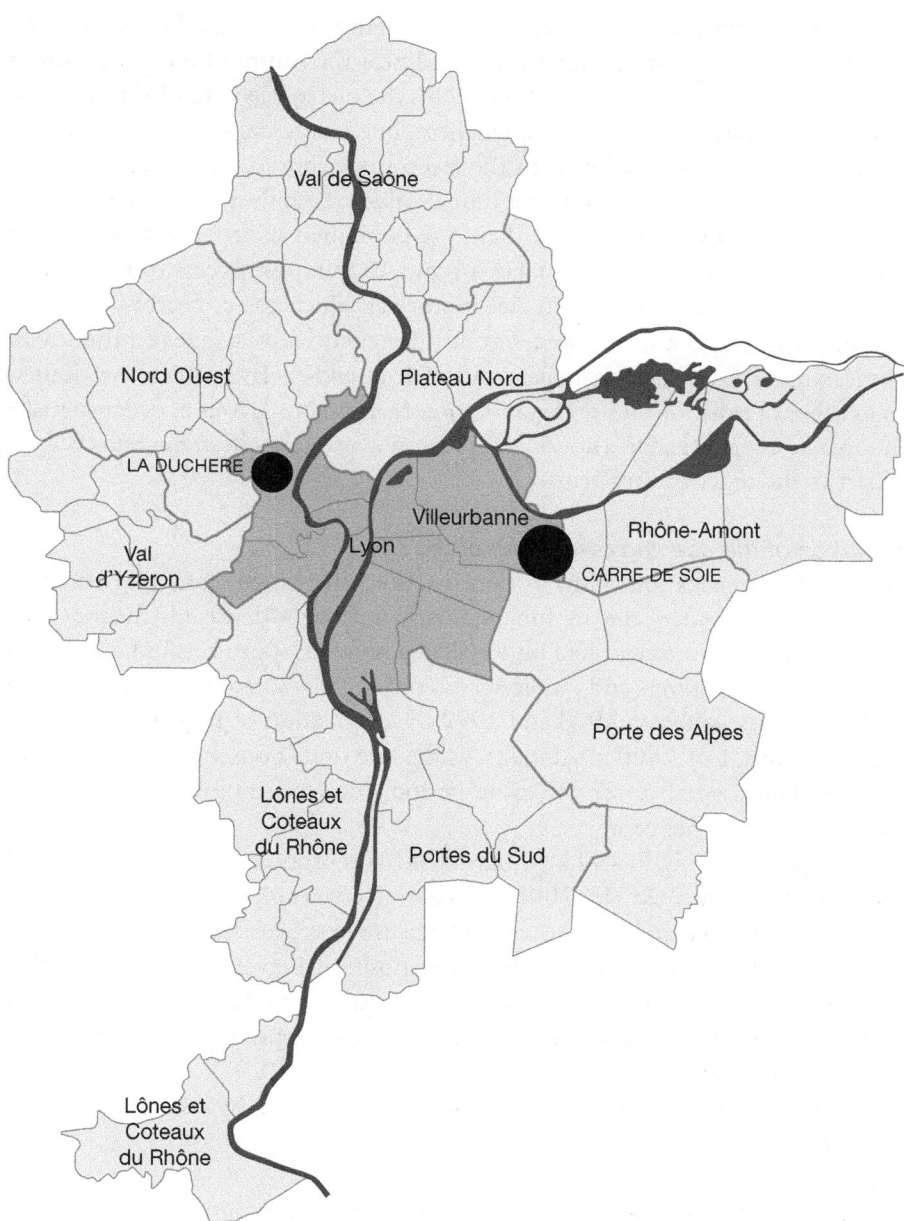

Figure 5.1 The location of La Duchère and Carré de Soie

The accessibility of La Duchère by public transport remained poor until the end of the 1990s, even though it is situated near the centre of the city (about 5 kilometres away). In the course of the 1990s the metro was extended to Gare de Vaise, at the edge of the area of La Duchère, but a large rail yard adjacent to the train station, in combination with the steep slope, posed a physical barrier. It was not until the construction of a tunnel under the railway yard in 2000 that this barrier was overcome. Since then, the combined metro–bus trip from La Duchère to the centre of Lyon takes around 15 minutes. Access to the area by car has always been good, via the A6, motorway which passes nearby.

The road network in the area was not designed with linkages to the urban fabric in mind. La Duchère felt like a sort of dead-end enclave, which contributed to its sense of isolation and segregation. Reorganising its layout in order to make the area more 'permeable' (not only for cars, but also for pedestrians and cyclists) is part of the regeneration plans.

Evolution of the use and ownership of the site
During the decades following its construction, the estate's buildings became increasingly degraded and its inhabitants increasingly deprived. By the mid-1980s, central government had undertaken a number of projects in La Duchère to improve its buildings and public spaces and halt the estate's decline, but with limited success. Between 1990 and 1999 the population of La Duchère fell, by almost a tenth, to 12,800 inhabitants, as the size of its households declined and the population aged. Over the same period, local unemployment rose from 14 per cent to 21 per cent.

In response to this, in 1998 the mayor of Lyon proposed a plan for the social renewal of La Duchère. In 2001 the central government together with the municipality funded and administered a large urban project that aimed to change its physical form and socio-economic composition between 2003 and 2012, beginning with the demolition of one of its high-rise buildings. The focus was more on physically improving La Duchère, and thus achieving social change via physical transformation.

At the start of the project, land in the area was owned by a small number of landowners:

- the city of Lyon (sports facilities, schools and social facilities, *parc du vallon* (public space);
- the Greater Lyon Authority (roads and public spaces, fire station, secondary school – college);
- social landlords (OPAC du Rhône, OPAC de Lyon, SACVEL, AXIADE), owning 80 per cent of the housing stock;

- central government (the secondary school – *lycée*);
- private homeowners, owning 20 per cent of the housing stock.

Land assembly was facilitated by the Société d'Equipement du Rhône et de Lyon (SERL), a uniquely French institution whose operation, as discussed previously, is based on the principles of a mixed market economy. The SERL temporarily owns the land during the development process: it acquires all of the land from the public landowners at the start of the regeneration process, takes care of its transformation and then sells it as building plots to private developers or social landlords, or transfers it as public space to the planning authority. In the case of La Duchère, the planning authority delegated its pre-emption and expropriation rights to the SERL but the majority of the land transactions were dealt with amicably. This was possible because of the predominantly public character of the landowners.

Property and financial market conditions

Ever since it was built in the 1960s, the area of La Duchère has never been part of the property market of Lyon; the area consisted almost exclusively of social housing and there were few transactions. The negative image that the area acquired over the years as a degraded, high-rise social housing area did not attract many investors either. In an interview in *Le Monde* (2002), Gérard Collomb, the mayor of Lyon, admitted that the regeneration plans "encounter difficulties in attracting investors to La Duchère" and said that he hoped "to convince them within three years by presenting them a renewed environment".

The regeneration project aimed to reintroduce property market dynamics, an objective that has been partially achieved today. Generally speaking, prior to 2007 the Lyon property market was booming and in 2005 an agreement was reached to build 600 new market residences in La Duchère. All projects that started before 2007 were completed but some of them required the relaxing of municipal building standards so as to lower construction costs for private developers. After the downturn in the property market, the start of new construction projects by private developers became more difficult. The regeneration project continued almost exclusively through projects developed by social landlords, whose investment capacity is less dependent on market conditions.

Policy environment

The intention at the local level to tackle social problematics through the physical transformation of the site and by reinstalling market dynamics was in line with national policy initiated at that time. As previously mentioned, important investment in the refurbishment of large, high-rise social housing estates in the mid-1980s did not have lasting effects on the socio-economic characteristics of these areas. The policy discourse therefore began to shift in favour of a more radical approach to the regeneration of such areas. The demolition of some of the existing buildings in order to construct different types of dwellings and insert new forms of tenure was expected to result in a greater social mix, with physical and socio-economic characteristics closer to the rest of the city.

La Duchère was the first project to benefit from ANRU funding but was not meant to be carried out with public funds alone. Indeed, as discussed already, another principle of the SRU and the Borloo laws is the regeneration of deprived areas through private sector investment. Under the ANRU regime public funds must be complemented by revenues generated from private property sales; thus, raising property values through projects with market appeal has become both an objective and a means of urban regeneration in France, and in La Duchère more specifically.

The SRU law of 2000 advocated a more project-led approach to urban regeneration, aiming at 'reinserting' deprived areas into the property market in order to stimulate market-driven renewal. The Borloo law of 2003 transferred this idea to the large, high-rise social housing areas by advocating an approach centred on their physical renewal, often through demolition and reconstruction. Because of these requirements, the demolition of high-rise buildings is a frequently used approach in projects receiving ANRU support, as it releases land and contributes to a change in the image of the area. This land is then used by private developers for the construction of new dwellings to be sold on the open market, thus creating an additional funding stream that can be channelled back into the project.

Content

Project structure, form and design

The regeneration plan for La Duchère envisages the transformation of the area from a high-rise housing estate into a more traditional urban form of building blocks. In a way, it highlights the ineffectiveness of the post-war spatial determinist utopia that advocated that radical changes in physical form would immediately tackle social problematics. The plan therefore involves large-scale demolition and reconstruction of the area, a choice that is illustrative of the change in policy approach that started to occur throughout France at the end of the 1990s.

In La Duchère the transformation effort is framed by the procedure of a ZAC, which provides legal possibilities for the local planning authority to initiate and

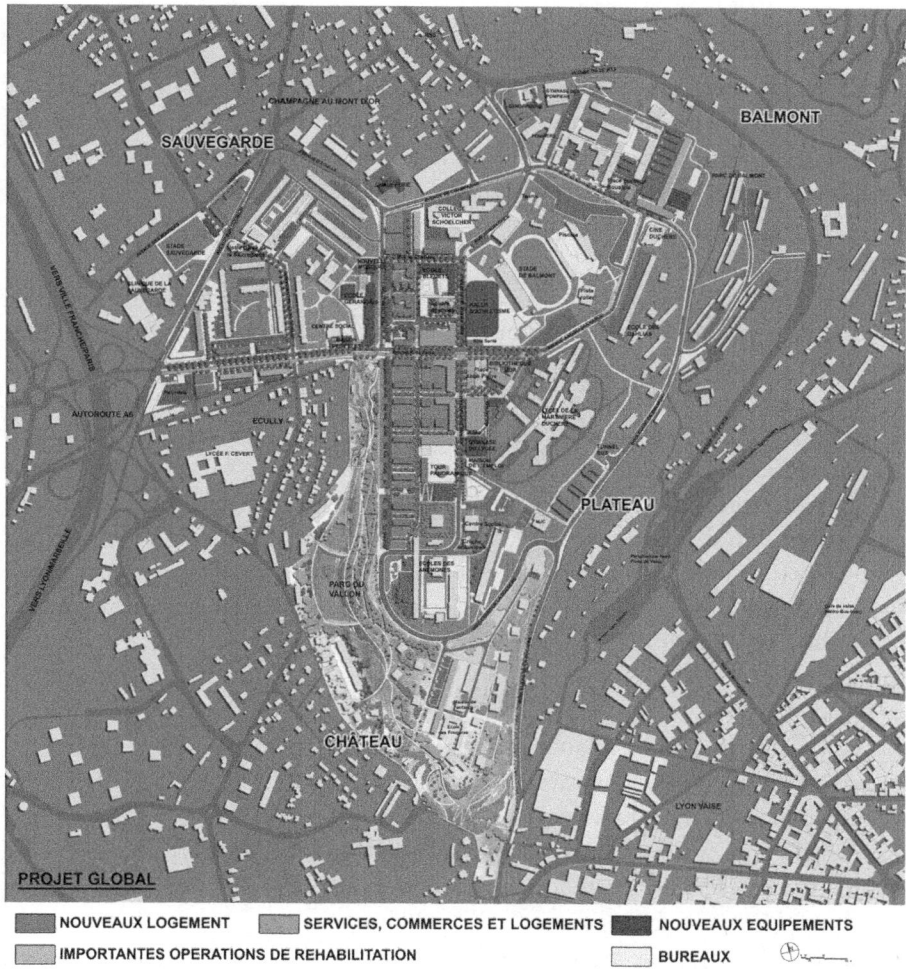

Figure 5.2 Plan of La Duchère regeneration scheme (SERL. Used with permission)

manage urban development and regeneration projects. The ZAC, created in 2004, foresees the construction of 422,000 m² of new development, comprising 333,000 m² for housing, 19,000 m² of commercial space and 70,000 m² of public facilities.

The project is organised in two phases. The objective of the first phase (2003–10) was to start the transformation of the area and change its image and attractiveness. The activities in the first phase that affected the form and design of the site were the demolition of 1,286 dwellings and construction of a new road lay-out and new public spaces. The main objective of the second phase of the project, from 2010 to 2016, is to open up the area to its surroundings. This involves improving the accessibility of the area, providing facilities to attract people from other parts of the city and 'normalisation' of the area's urban fabric. The main activity relating to the form of the project in this phase is the creation of new east–west through roads and the improvement of public transport facilities.

Use and tenure mix

One of the main objectives of the programme, as mentioned in the previous paragraph, is the introduction of a mix of uses and tenures into the area. In 2004, when the ZAC was approved, almost 80 per cent of the housing stock was owned by social landlords and the retail provision was limited. The aim was to bring the proportion of social housing down to 55 per cent through demolition and reconstruction. The demolished social dwellings were to be replaced by new social rental housing and by market housing both for rent and for owner occupation. However, the market housing should be sold at prices not more than €2,500 per m², which is below current market levels. In order to achieve this, local authorities would need to sell the land to housebuilders at reduced prices.

In the first phase of the project the following activities affected the use and tenure mix:

- refurbishment of the remaining high-rise buildings;
- restructuring of the commercial facilities (7,000 m² of shopping facilities, provided in the new building blocks);
- construction of three 'activity zones' (18,000 m² of floorspace);
- creation of a service centre for new economic activities ('*maison de la creation d'entreprise*') and for assistance in job seeking;
- 18 new housing projects, totalling 1,025 new dwellings with different tenures: owner-occupancy (albeit at lower prices), private rental, social rental.

The following activities relating to the change of the use and tenure mix are planned for the second phase:

- complete renewal of commercial infrastructure (demolition of old shopping centre, new shops at street level);
- demolition of 442 dwellings;
- construction of 675 new dwellings;
- development of 20,000 m² for economic activity.

Social facilities and non-market project components
Due to the nature of the project, some important non-market elements (namely the change in tenure composition) have been covered in the preceding paragraphs. The ZAC procedure provides a legal framework that allows the public sector to delimit an area for future development and to negotiate the programme to be developed in the area with the potential developers (either public or private). During these negotiations the potential revenue from the development of the real estate in the area is balanced against the required or desired investment in public facilities and non-market housing. The real estate developers obtain their building rights only in exchange for a contribution towards public facilities or, in the case of La Duchère, towards affordable housing.

In addition to what has been already mentioned, it is worth noting that by the end of the first phase the percentage of social rental housing was reduced to 63 per cent of all housing in La Duchère (compared to 80 per cent at the start of the project), and it is planned to go down to 55 per cent by the end of the project. This transformation requires the demolition of 1,700 social sector dwellings and the rebuilding of 1,500 dwellings predominantly for private rental or purchase.

Under French law, each demolished public dwelling has to be replaced by a new one, but not necessarily in the same area. This means that eventually 1,700 households will have to be rehoused, either to another dwelling in La Duchère or elsewhere in Lyon, posing a great challenge for the project. Given the tenure-mix targets of the scheme, rehousing in a different area of the conurbation seems to be the likely option. Thus, 1,700 replacement social dwellings will have to be built in the agglomeration of Lyon by 2016. By that date, 1,150 social dwellings in the remaining high-rise buildings will have been refurbished.

Apart from non-market housing, the construction or refurbishment of public facilities and the provision of public space is a key element of the project. Public funding of these aspects is considered necessary in order to transform the area into an attractive residential neighbourhood. The funding that the project receives from the ANRU is crucial in making the project financially feasible but the financial involvement of the local authorities is also important.

The main investment in public good provision (other than social housing) in the first phase was the construction of new and the renovation of existing public facilities, mainly for young people and families (children's nursery, sports facilities, schools). There is a clear link here to making the project more attractive to households with children that would wish to buy a property. In the second phase more emphasis is being placed on the construction of public facilities (mosque, athletics hall, library, community centre) and public spaces (Place Abbé Pierre, Place Bachaga Boualem, Parc du Vallon). These facilities and public places benefit larger areas than just La Duchère, serving the purpose of functionally linking it with its immediate neighbourhood.

Organisation

Governance arrangements and partnership members

In effect, decisions to undertake the regeneration of an area are influenced by the central government through the ANRU. The ANRU will only fund schemes that meet its criteria, which include estimates of the prospects for private sector investment. The competencies required for the regeneration of the area of La Duchère are divided between two levels of local government, with the Greater Lyon Authority having responsibility for urban planning and the municipality of Lyon being in charge of social issues. In order to manage the project of La Duchère, a *Mission* was created that linked the municipality of Lyon, the Greater Lyon Authority and the departmental and regional levels of government. This 'made to measure' coordination structure allows a comprehensive, transversal approach to the management of the project. It is the central actor in the network of actors involved in the regeneration of the area, and plays a key role in the ZAC procedure. The 'Mission La Duchère' was created and physically situated in La Duchère at the start of the regeneration project in 2003

The 'Mission La Duchère' commissioned the SERL to prepare the area for new construction (demolition, land preparation, infrastructure provision). The SERL operates with private sector logic, acts as an intermediate landowner and is responsible for the financial balance of the operation. It has to prepare a budget for the operation and make an appraisal that takes into account the price at which it has acquired the land, the price at which it is supposed to sell serviced plots and the funding it receives from the ANRU and from the local planning authority. Responsibility for the regeneration scheme ultimately lies with the municipality, but all public actors were strongly committed to the project, reassuring the private sector actors who might want to become involved in La Duchère. As a senior SERL officer put it:

> We expect from them that they propose prices which are acceptable for first-time buyers and low-income households (. . .). In exchange, they can count on the engagement of the public sector for the realisation of new facilities and meeting the announced time schedule.

The land was sold to the SERL by the municipality at a discount and the SERL received public funds from the ANRU as well as from the municipality to finance its activities. As a result, the SERL was able to sell its land to developers below the prevailing market prices in Lyon. This discount was necessary not only in order to attract private developers but also in order to allow the SERL to choose the buyers and to have leverage that allowed it to attach conditions that ensured that private development complied with the municipality's plans. In addition, the municipality expected that, with the offer of cheap land, developers would keep the price of new market housing below €2,500 per m².

Under the ZAC procedure the private developers who buy land from an intermediary (in this case the SERL, which temporarily owned the land during the development process) are exempt from the *Taxe Locale d'Equipement*, a tax usually paid by developers in order to contribute to the required public facilities in a development project. Instead, a programme of public investment is drawn up jointly by the planning authority and the intermediary. The latter has to finance a negotiated part of the investments by incorporating the extra costs into the price charged when the land is sold to the private developer. For the building of specific plots, the SERL enrols private developers through tendering procedures.

Organisation aims and their evolution

The idea to promote a regeneration initiative that aimed to attract private investment into La Duchère was influenced by experience in the adjacent area of Vaise. Following the departure of the industrial activities in the late 1970s, unemployment rates in Vaise rose and the area became both socially and physically deprived. During the 1990s the Greater Lyon Authority decided to regenerate the area based on a strategy to make it attractive to private investors. In order to achieve this aim, the public sector invested in public space, public transport and public facilities and offered financial incentives to property owners to refurbish their property. This strategy was successful in the sense that Vaise has managed to attract private investment. It is no longer a run-down area, old industrial sites were converted into modern premises that are attractive for tertiary activities and property prices have risen accordingly.

For the local authorities in Lyon the challenge at the beginning of 2000 was to replicate these dynamics in the adjacent area of La Duchère. However, the physical structure of a high-rise housing estate is very different from the structure of Vaise, a more traditional, mixed urban area with more possibilities for small-scale improvements. The demolition of existing buildings and construction of new buildings were deemed necessary as part of the local government's regeneration strategy for La Duchère (Figure 5.3).

When the regeneration project – including large-scale demolition – was approved by the council of the Greater Lyon Authority (Conseil Communautaire du Grand Lyon, 2004), the aim was to:

Figure 5.3 Housing blocks in La Duchère in the early 2000s

Recapture this strategic area by means of an urban project, the objectives of which aim at eradicating the urban and social dysfunctions by which the neighbourhood is confronted.

Increasing the 'social mix' in the area via the provision of mixed tenure housing at affordable prices, attracting private investment and reinserting the area into the property markets are key objectives of the project. Attracting private housebuilders and investors into La Duchère in order to provide owner-occupied and private rental housing was reasonably successful in the initial years of the project (2004–7).

In 2008 the average price per m² of floorspace for dwellings was €2,400 in La Duchère, as against €3,600 in the municipality of Lyon. Thus, low land prices were crucial to the financial viability of the housing schemes completed in La Duchère and are probably also a reason why the real estate market in La Duchère, although in bad shape, is rather less affected by the financial and economic crisis than most of the rest of Lyon.

Risks and uncertainties

La Duchère is a case where a lot of the uncertainties and risks related to property development have been tackled by the public sector. The main reason for this is

Figure 5.4 New buildings in La Duchère in 2010 (Laurence Danière. Used with permission)

the operation of the public sector as an interim landowner, via the SERL. This is a potentially costly option, as it requires substantial up-front costs for land purchase and preparation, and the low sell-on price is an additional cost for the public purse, or at least an opportunity cost. There is, however, a strong rationale for this 'deflationary' intervention by the state. Public landownership offers the local planning authority the opportunity to use the land price as an adjustment mechanism: by offering the land at reduced prices it can compensate private developers for the reduced income resulting from the development of non-market housing without foregoing control of the outputs.

In La Duchère the price for a square metre of serviced building land was fixed at €150/m² in the first instance, a low price compared to prices in other areas of Lyon. The price was deliberately fixed at a comparatively low level in order to attract investors to an area where there had been virtually no transactions since the construction of the housing estate, so there was no reference price. Later, the price was lifted to €180/m² for social landlords and €240/m² for private housebuilders. The idea behind this was that the first developers took on a bigger market risk, which had to be compensated by a potentially higher return. Even though the land sale price remained modest throughout the regeneration process, it did provide income to the SERL, which it could use to invest in public facilities.

The initial financial balance of the operation in the early days of the ZAC shows that, of the €146 million required for the land preparation and basic infrastructure and amenity provision, around €30 million were expected to be covered through land sales: a little less than €15 million came for transactions of building land and the other €15 million resulted from the transfer of public space between the land developer and the Greater Lyon Authority. Of the remaining €116 million, a little less than €34 million were covered by ANRU, and the Greater Lyon Authority covered the remaining €82 million. One has to remember here that this is a site that is 100 per cent owned by public sector organisations that have a social mission to fulfil. The fact that 20 per cent of the cost of land preparation, infrastructure and amenity provision was covered by capturing some of the land value uplift, whilst 80 per cent was paid from state coffers, must be weighed against the goals that were achieved, namely, increased certainty for private developers regarding the quality of the land, control of the form and quality of the public realm, provision of basic infrastructure (road access, utilities etc.) and provision of low-cost housing by private developers without necessarily affecting their margins. An important thing to note here is that the purpose of this approach is to ensure that the state assumes certain risks (e.g. that the land will remain unsold, that the costs of servicing will exceed the budget etc.) and in return it extracts value from the land development process to provide certain merit and public goods. Although some of that value is monetised during the sale of land to private developers, another part is not immediately translated to a 'bottom line'. The benefits of the externalities achieved (from an enhanced public realm to cheaper housing to an increased tax base to better quality of life or even to social peace, health improvements etc.) are substantial. This use of public spending fits the 'republican' tradition we mentioned earlier.

Because it owns the land, the SERL has some discretion in choosing the actors with whom it wants to have a contractual relationship. It uses that discretion in order to specify the degrees of freedom of those actors. The development programme is specified in the project plan and the actual influence of the developers on the project is limited to the design of the buildings they develop. Thus, private developers assume the risks associated with the design, finance and construction of their developments, while the uncertainties surrounding the estimation of demand are to a large extent shared between the public and private sectors through the tendering process, which provides strong signals to the SERL about the way market actors perceive its development programme.

The relationship between the ANRU and the Greater Lyon Authority has been explained in preceding sections. In this section the focus is on the relationship between public and private partners, especially in view of the important role that private developers were called upon to play. In the early days of the scheme it was uncertain whether anyone would be willing to acquire housing or shops in La Duchère, as it had not been tried before and the reputation of the area was not attractive to potential homeowners. Due to the significant market uncertainty the regeneration partners of La Duchère were faced with in the early days, the SERL preferred to sell land to larger companies operating at regional and national level, under the assumption that these larger companies had a better capacity to assume risks.

These developers had an opportunity to discuss the public sector plans and to express their wishes and concerns. The actual choice of developers was made through a tendering procedure, with the aim of selecting a developer/ housebuilder for each building block. The first tender process was launched in 2004, on eight building blocks in three different parts of the area with a capacity of 600 dwellings. The scale of the tender was large in order to create a 'critical mass' of operations in the area, which would transmit a message of radical change in the area's character from the very beginning, thus reducing uncertainty about its future. Even though this move might be seen as increasing the commercial risks taken on by the SERL, it reassured the developers and the market at large that the state was determined to go ahead with the required improvements in the development potential of the area, and thus it actually reduced commercial risks both for the SERL and for the private sector (admittedly, market conditions were favourable). It has to be noted that at this point market conditions were buoyant and developers were searching for developable land throughout the Lyon metropolitan area. The modestly priced land in La Duchère appeared as an interesting opportunity, notwithstanding the uncertainties that the first investors undeniably faced with regard to future demand for property in the area.

However, the financial crisis and the subsequent downturn in the property market in 2008 seem to have slowed down the activity of the private sector, especially in housing. Of the 18 housing projects planned in the first phase, 7 were finished at the start of 2010. Seven other projects were under construction, two were in the preparatory stages of building work, one was still in planning and one had to be relaunched because of the withdrawal of the private housebuilder. In total only 417 dwellings were completed on schedule, considerably fewer than the 1,025 dwellings that had been planned.

Whereas at the very start of the scheme the time horizon for its completion was 2012, this has now become 2016, yet it is not easy to pinpoint to what extent this is related to changes in the property market or to changes in other circumstances. A delay of several years in a large-scale urban project such as La Duchère is not unusual, and in any case it is undeniable that the area of La Duchère was reinserted into Lyon's property market at affordable prices.

Even so, La Duchère remains a 'risky' area for private housing development, due to its characteristics as a predominantly social housing area. At the same time, the project benefits from a high political priority. Stopping the operation is not a politically attractive option, so at the time when these words were written (mid-2010) it seemed that there might be a decision to build more non-market housing or to provide more public funding than was originally planned. Given the recent involvement of the CDC in funding additional housebuilding in regeneration areas throughout the country, it is likely that both scenarios could materialise.

Carré de Soie, Lyon

Context

Site conditions

Carré de Soie is an urban regeneration scheme within the Lyon conurbation, located east of the city centre in the communes of Vaulx-en-Velin and Villeurbanne. The entire area of the project covers 500 hectares, on land once used primarily for industry. However, the entire area of 500 hectares will not be brought into development in one go and its regeneration is an objective that extends over the next 30 years. This section focuses on the first projects in the Carré-de-Soie area, which are the central shopping and leisure centre, some office development and a 700- to 800-dwelling housing development.

In order to understand the evolution of the project it is necessary to take a closer look at the site and its characteristics. The area of Carré de Soie is situated to the east of the city centre of Lyon, just outside of the city's main ring road, which forms a physical and psychological barrier between the area and the city of Lyon. At the beginning of the project, the area had a mixed urban fabric (former and still partly active industrial sites, different types of housing, small-scale manufacturing and maintenance workshops) that was becoming derelict in many places.

The area is situated in the part of the Lyon conurbation referred to as the *premier couronne est*, which faces multiple issues of deprivation (poor housing conditions, concentration of low-income groups, high unemployment rates etc.). At the same time, the area has certain physical advantages, in particular its good accessibility and also the presence of large areas of green space and water. There is thus potential there, which the Greater Lyon Authority wants to seize in order to develop a commercially attractive urban area. The rationale underpinning the project is that the regeneration of the area should contribute to the improvement of conditions in the *premier couronne est*.

At the end of the 1990s the mayors of the municipalities of Vaulx-en-Velin and Villeurbanne and the Greater Lyon Authority identified the development potential of the area. The local authority envisaged acquiring the race-course in order to redevelop it as a leisure centre. Further interest in the regeneration project came from the cinema group Pathé Cinéma, which wanted to develop a large cinema complex (*multiplex*) in the eastern part of the Lyon agglomeration. Pathé considered the area to be a good location for its *multiplex*, and by deciding to locate the project there it created an opportunity for the local authority to use this investment in order to instigate a larger regeneration scheme structured around a commercial and leisure centre in the area, including the redevelopment of the race-course. In this case, swift action by the local authority, combined with Pathé's commitment to invest, reduced the uncertainty surrounding the future of that area and increased its development potential.

In the following years, new public transport links reinforced the attractiveness of the area and the leisure centre became the core of a project that was to be developed gradually. However, the sites in which actual development takes place at any one time represent only a small proportion of the whole area. The overall objective of the project is to create a high-quality urban area with housing, offices, workplaces, leisure space and transport infrastructure by 2030. The 500 hectare area should eventually house 25,000 to 30,000 people (compared to a population of 14,000 at the start of the project) and offer employment for 35,000 (compared to 10,000 at the start of the project). The first part of the project, on which this case study focuses, combines a shopping and leisure centre, office development and housing development with considerable investment in public transport and public space.

Because of its location just beyond Lyon's eastern ring road and close to motorway connections to the east of the Lyon agglomeration, the area of Carré de Soie is easily accessible by car, both from the city of Lyon and from the eastern suburban areas. Good car accessibility was probably one of the reasons why Pathé planned its *multiplex* in the area, but in addition to this, important decisions were made concerning public transport that dramatically increased the accessibility of the area and thus changed its situation within the Lyon conurbation. Initially, these decisions were independent of the proposed development on the site, but shortly after their announcement they became part of the regeneration plan.

At the end of the nineteenth century a railway line extended east through Carré de Soie from the centre of Lyon. Passenger services to Carré de Soie stopped in 1947, but freight traffic continued, peaked in the 1960s and dwindled thereafter. However, this railway legacy allowed the Greater Lyon Authority to commit to developing a multimodal transportation hub adjacent to the leisure and shopping development. The *département* of the Rhône also engaged in this development, because it decided in 2001 to use the abandoned railway line as part of a light railway link between the airport Lyon-Saint Exupéry – to the east of Lyon – and the railway station of Part-Dieu, at the centre of Lyon. This decision situated Carré de Soie right in the middle, between the city of Lyon and the airport, roughly 15 minutes from each destination. At the same time, the Greater Lyon Authority decided to extend the metro line B to Carré de Soie in order to create a multimodal hub connecting the metro network to the light railway/tramline and eight bus lines, with 450 car-parking spaces available for park-and-ride purposes.

The first section of the tramline was opened in 2006 and the extension of the metro line has been operational since 2007. Even though the completion of the tramline to the airport underwent some delays, it has been fully operational since the summer of 2010, thus completing the new public transport connections of Carré de Soie to the city of Lyon and its surroundings. The greater accessibility of the area of Carré de Soie that resulted from these investments, as well as the long-term commitment of the local planning authority to the development of the site, dramatically increased the development potential of the area.

Evolution of the use and ownership of the site

Currently, Carré de Soie is a mixed land-use area with partly abandoned industrial activities on large plots as well as smaller workshops and housing of different types (a 1960s high-rise area, a 1930s garden suburb and a lot of dispersed, small-scale housing developments mainly built in the second half of the twentieth century). Due to this history, there are several quite small landowners in the area and a few bigger ones. The area where the leisure and commercial centre is located, to the south of the rue Bohlèn, had previously been used by Peugeot and Renault for industrial purposes but fell into disuse. In 2000 Pathé bought 30,000 m² of land on the site to build its *multiplex*.

The Greater Lyon Authority had already been considering whether acquiring the race-course opposite the planned *multiplex* would help to change the area's dynamic by reinforcing its sports infrastructure. At the same time Pathé promoted the idea of transforming Carré de Soie into an entertainment destination. In 2002 the public sector partners agreed to create a leisure attraction that would offer entertainment as well as commercial activities.

In order to give shape to this idea, in 2002 the Greater Lyon Authority and the municipality of Vaulx-en-Velin commissioned an architect to propose a masterplan for the site. However, the planning authority decided to stick to a role of facilitation and regulation and not to become directly involved in the development of the area through temporary landownership. In the words of a high-ranking Greater Lyon official:

> In the operation of the leisure centre, it has been decided to elaborate a schedule of conditions in order to deal with potential investors (. . .) Taking into account the interest that several investors had in the project of a leisure centre, it was decided that the Greater Lyon Authority will not pursue an active land policy in the area. Moreover, it is clear that currently the Greater Lyon Authority is incapable of establishing the acceptable land price because this depends of the final project, the number of square metres of floorspace, the type of buildings (. . .) The Greater Lyon Authority therefore has to play a role of 'facilitator' in this operation. An innovative role, but one that is difficult to assume when the private owners do not accept the proposed approach.

Prior to elaborating its strategy in 2001, the Greater Lyon Authority had acquired 7,800 m² of land south of rue Bohlèn adjacent to the land purchased by Pathé. In 2003 it launched a tender for the development of a leisure and commercial centre on this land, which had to take the Pathé *multiplex* into account. The commercial developer Altarea won the tender and started developing the project at the end of 2006 (see 'Governance arrangements' below).

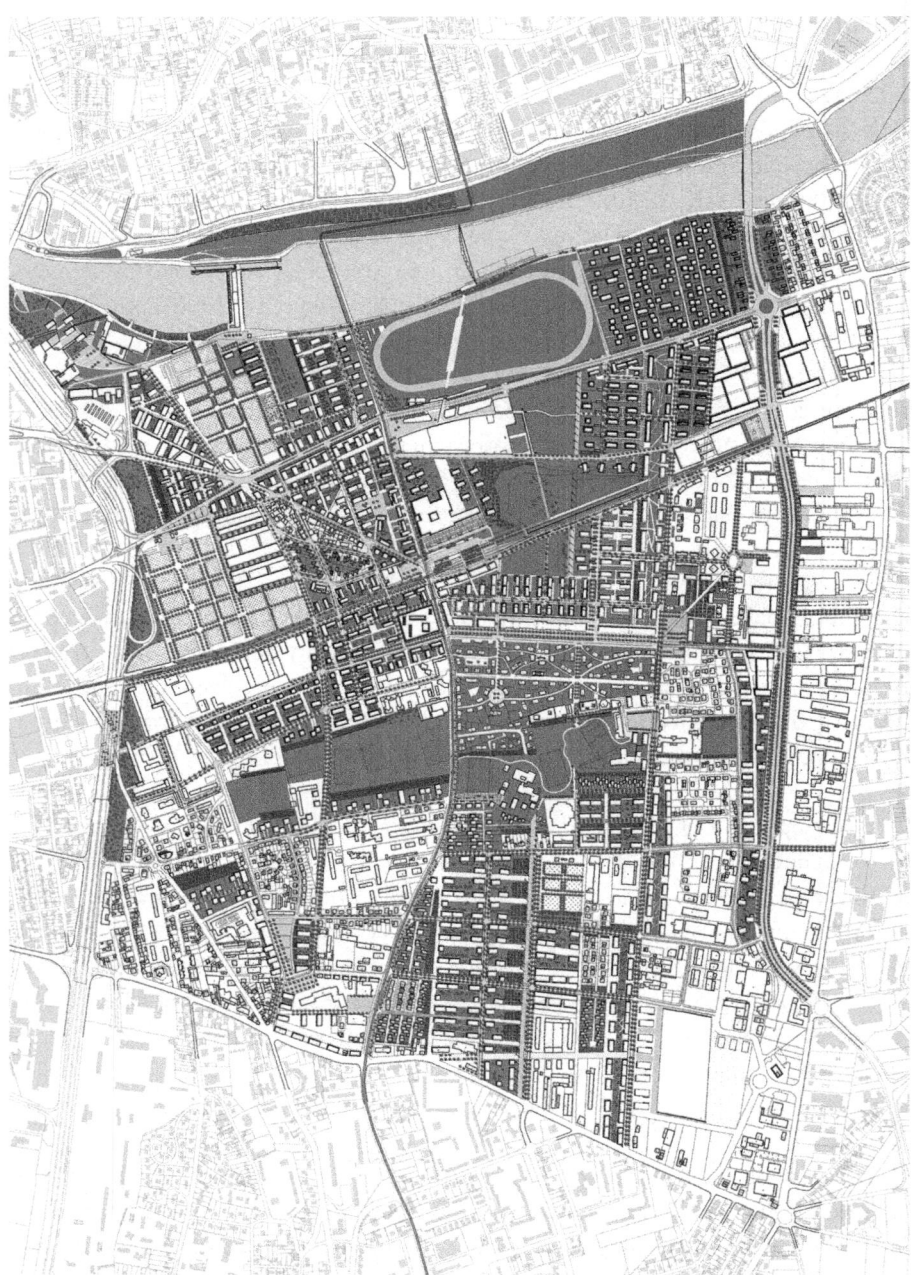

Figure 5.5 Plan of the Carré de Soie regeneration scheme (Bruno Demetier. Used with permission)

In parallel with the development of the shopping and leisure centre by Altarea, investor interest for the area increased. The projects that were realised and planned as part of the regeneration scheme (see 'Market conditions' below) incentivised private investors to buy land speculatively in the area, in anticipation of future changes in zoning that would allow the land to be developed as housing or offices. The first development project, apart from the shopping and leisure centre and a small office development on publicly owned land, was a 3.5 hectare site adjacent to the leisure centre. This site had been an artificial silk (viscose) factory owned by the Tase company. The factory buildings still stood on the site, but they had been abandoned and were gradually becoming derelict. Developer Bouwfonds-Marignan acquired the land in 2006, with a view to developing it. It proposed the development of housing on the site, which would require a change of the zoning in the local land-use plan from industrial use to housing.

In 2006 the Greater Lyon Authority also decided to acquire land in the area in order to improve its negotiating position with private investors. It exercised a pre-emption right that allowed it to acquire roughly 25 per cent of three different sites measuring 43 hectares in the immediate surroundings of the commercial and leisure hub and the tram and metro stops (Tase, Ferraileurs, Yoplait). Notwithstanding these land acquisitions, the strategy for the redevelopment of

Figure 5.6 Carre de Soié in the early 2000s before redevelopment (Agence d'Urbanisme de Lyon. Used with permission)

the area remained unchanged through time: the investment should be carried out predominantly by the private sector, and the role of the planning authority is to frame and to facilitate these transformations, using the mechanisms at its disposal as leverage.

The reason for this approach was neatly summarised by an officer at the land and real estate directorate of the Greater Lyon Authority:

> We do not have the means. Today, financially speaking, on this project I would need, I don't know, ten times the amount I have in my hands today. You have to try to be realistic. If a developer can realise an operation in which we do not have any financial engagement, and which fits into the urban project, we win in financial terms in this case, and the money we save here we can invest somewhere else.

Property and financial market conditions

In the period between 1930 and 1970 the area of Carré de Soie attracted investment from industrial firms searching for a location near the city of Lyon but outside its boundaries. Thereafter it did not attract considerable investment in new development until the beginning of 2000, when Pathé decided to develop its *multiplex*. Combined with the decision of the Greater Lyon Authority to develop the area as part of a regeneration scheme, this renewed interest changed the market situation for the whole area. It has to be noted that these decisions were taken in a period during which property prices in France were undergoing high inflation. Prices had started to increase in the second half of the 1990s and this growth continued apace through the early and mid-2000s.

As a result of the increasing property prices in Lyon, access to housing in the Lyon conurbation became problematic, in particular but not exclusively for first-time buyers. In order to be able to offer housing to meet this demand, developers became interested in areas in which land prices still enabled the redevelopment of housing that could be sold at moderate prices. They found this land in areas that until then had been considered less attractive because of their physical state and their location at the edge of the city centre, like Carré de Soie.

In addition, the inclusion of the area in a long-term regeneration scheme reassured investors of its medium-term investment potential, thus reducing market uncertainty. The potential difference in land and property prices in the area before and after regeneration incentivised private actors to speculate on land, even when the zoning allocation was still industrial. Land purchases multiplied in the early 2000s after the uncertainty surrounding the future commitment of the state and of Pathé was lifted. As the uncertainty was gradually reduced, the combination of the general property market context and the specific plans for Carré de Soie made the area attractive for further private sector investment.

Clearly, actors were aware of the importance of market conditions for the development of the area. As a senior officer of the Mission Carré de Soie stated at the peak of the property boom: "At the moment, we have a frenzy, well, a frenzy, a surge of development. If ever we have a reversal of the situation in the real estate markets, and I speak not of the leisure centre, but of the other operations, will they then be delayed?"

That situation occurred with the credit crunch and the subsequent economic crisis in 2007–8. The conditions in the property market became much less favourable, and as a result private investors became reluctant to invest. Even though this was a general phenomenon, not restricted to Carré de Soie, the effects on the regeneration scheme were important. In order to promote development and to ensure delivery of the required public facilities, the Greater Lyon Authority had negotiated a PAE (Box 5.1) at the peak of the boom, in 2006. This PAE facilitated market housing development in exchange for financial contributions by the developer to specified public facilities. Following the financial crisis and the property market decline the project was mothballed, which meant that the development of the public realm and the delivery of other public goods could not progress. This posed a significant risk to the dynamics of the whole regeneration scheme. Similarly, at the Tase site the developer who bought the land in 2007 had not started operations in 2010.

Box 5.1 The Programme d'Aménagement d'Ensemble (PAE)

The objective of the PAE is to obtain contributions from private developers to finance public facilities in urban development projects, which are directly related to the project. If it wants to use this procedure, the planning authority determines the boundaries of the area to which it applies, and draws up a list of facilities to be completed in the area. It then decides, on the basis of the principles of causality and proportionality, which part of the costs of these facilities will be paid by the developers, and the way in which these costs will be distributed amongst the different types of development. The developers can pay their share either in money, or in kind by building the required facilities by themselves.

This procedure allows the planning authority to obtain 'made to measure' funding for facilities, rather than applying a general, lump-sum payment. It therefore applies particularly well to areas that are under-equipped in terms of social infrastructure and public goods provision. However, it has its limitations, as it imposes costs on private developers. In a depressed real estate market, this may discourage investors and stifle development. The PAE also transfers a risk onto the local authority. If the contributions are financial and not in kind, then the local authority has to build the facilities itself after the passage of a set time period (usually around ten years; nine

---

years in the case of the Tase site). If real estate development is delayed and does not take place within this period, the costs of the facilities are borne entirely by the planning authority. Partly for this reason, even though the mechanism of the PAE seems to be rather attractive, it is not used frequently in urban development.

Notwithstanding the important efforts made by the public sector to increase the development potential of the area and the significant private investment that has been attracted there, Carré de Soie still has to prove its attractiveness as a residential location. In the current economic climate developers are not necessarily eager to engage in the process. This delays the realisation of the regeneration project. As a senior officer of the Misson Carré de Soie puts it:

> What happens is that they want higher densities and a reduced design quality. But this request deteriorates the situation: it is a vicious cycle. You have difficulty in selling, so you say: "I will reduce my costs and increase densities in order to proceed." But if you increase densities, you have fewer arguments to sell because it is dense and the design quality is reduced.

Policy environment

Even though the municipality of Vaulx-en-Velin played an important role in the initial phases of the project, the planning authority responsible for the regeneration of the area is the Greater Lyon Authority (Communauté Urbaine du Grand Lyon). This is an inter-municipal cooperation structure that includes 57 municipalities with around 1.3 million inhabitants. It is one of the oldest *Communautés Urbaines* in France, dating back to 1969, and is generally considered as one of the most active in the field of urban development. The municipalities that compose the Greater Lyon Authority have transferred responsibility for urban planning (which in principle is at the municipal level) to the Greater Lyon Authority.

In order to supervise and coordinate the regeneration project, the Greater Lyon Authority has created a dedicated agency – the Mission Carré de Soie, a central actor in the process. Unlike in many other large French urban development projects, at the start of the project the planning authority decided not to be directly involved in the development of the area as a land developer, although it got involved in the land market in order to gain some influence. It was an explicit goal of the Council of the Greater Lyon Authority (Conseil Communautaire du Grand Lyon, 2006) that the regeneration should be carried out by private actors. The planning authority is directly involved only in the launch of the project (the tender for the shopping and leisure centre), in the realisation of public facilities (public space, main infrastructure, public transport) and in safeguarding the realisation of a certain amount of social and affordable housing. The local planning authority influences the flow of land available for development by changing the zoning allocations of its local land-use plan and by playing an informal but crucial brokerage role between landowners and potential developers in order to promote development projects that suit both the private developers and the planning authority.

As mentioned already, in order to ensure some influence in such informal dealings, the Greater Lyon Authority acquired 'strategic' plots of land in the area in 2006. The objective of these land acquisitions was not so much to proceed with direct public land development but to engage in negotiations concerning future development projects as a landowner and not just as a regulatory body. So far as public investment is concerned, in addition to the Greater Lyon Authority, it was the municipalities of Vaulx-en-Velin and of Villeurbanne that contributed to public realm interventions, and the Rhône *département* that played a key role in developing the tramway link to the airport.

Content

Project structure, form and design

The Greater Lyon Authority chose to intervene in Carré de Soie as part of an effort to integrate the area with the rest of the city. The development of Carré de Soie was expected to drive the regeneration of the surrounding areas as well. Following the departure of key industries, what remained was the stigma of dereliction as well as a local population with high unemployment rates and low incomes. The area became isolated from the property and labour markets of the rest of Lyon and little investment was attracted to it. Public and private investment in the commercial and leisure hub aimed to create conditions that would reinvigorate the area's economy and allow it to enter a virtuous cycle of growth. In order to achieve this aim, the Greater Lyon Authority launched an ambitious regeneration project, starting with central sites and extending over a much larger area in subsequent phases. In terms of structure, the evolution of the regeneration scheme can be divided into two stages.

Improving the quality of public space and increasing the accessibility of the site were key elements of the first stage (before 2010), which aimed at increasing the attractiveness of the area to investment. The plan for this phase of the regeneration of Carré de Soie consisted of four main components: construction of the shopping and leisure centre; revitalisation of the public realm; construction

Figure 5.7 Office building under construction in Carré de Soie in 2010 (Cristophe Durand. Used with permission)

of new public transport infrastructure; and provision of housing on the Tase and Touly sites. The following activities were part of this stage:

- improvement of the main roads of the area (avenue Böhlen, rue de la Poudrette, rue Jara, rue Jacquard);
- construction of the T3 tramway line, linking Carré de Soie to the centre of Lyon, and of the tramway line between the city of Lyon and the Airport;
- extension of metro line A to Carré de Soie;
- construction of a park-and-ride facility of 400 spaces and a bus station;
- extension of the *Boulevard Urbain Est* to improve accessibility by car;
- development of the commercial and leisure hub;
- first development project (30,000 m² of floorspace) of office and housing directly adjacent to the tram and metro stops (Îlot Touly).

The development of housing on the Tase site, where a PAE was used, has been delayed and had not yet started when this research was undertaken.

The second stage (after 2010) consists mainly of the development of housing, offices and commercial projects with a total floorspace of around 150,000 m². Further regeneration activity in the area depends on the initiative of the private sector. It is therefore unclear which projects will go ahead and the planning of the area is rather tentative.

Use and tenure mix

The commercial hub in Carré de Soie comprises a three-storey commercial centre with 40,000 m² of retail space on two levels comprising eight major stores and 40 other shops and restaurants, as well as 1,600 parking places, all managed by Altarea. In terms of the leisure hub, Carré de Soie includes a 15-screen multiplex, a renovated race-course run by UCPA, a pony club and go-karting as well as restaurants, promenades and an aquatic centre along the Jonage canal. Some dwellings have been built in a development project immediately south of the tram and metro stop, on the Touly site. The Greater Lyon Authority acquired the land on this site from the public transport company, in order to contribute directly to the regeneration of the area. The total development programme for the site comprises 30,000 m² of floorspace, of which 10,000 m² is for housing and 20,000 m² for offices, as well as a target of 20 per cent social housing set by the Greater Lyon Authority. This project, completed in 2007–9, was the first private investment development in the area, together with the commercial and leisure centre.

The future housing development in the area, the pending project on the Tase site, will be part of a mixed development with a total of 105,000 m² of floorspace, 68,600 m² of which will be allocated to housing (again including 20 per cent social housing), 22,800 m² to commercial development and 13,500 m² to a hotel. As the Carré de Soie project proceeds and Tase is developed, housing development will become a more dominant land use in the area. However, even though the plans for this project are at an advanced stage and the PAE specifying the contributions of the investor to public facilities has been agreed, the time-frame for its completion has become uncertain following the downturn in the property markets in 2008.

Private initiatives for development in the area are framed by the (indicative) masterplan of the planning authority. In the masterplan, Carré de Soie is conceived as a '*parc urbain*': residences and economic activity should be accommodated in detached buildings of diverse architectural styles and of maximum height of six storeys, in a green setting. In order to be binding, the masterplan has to be written into the local land-use plan. A balance has to be found between the precision of the regulations and the flexibility necessary to induce private housebuilders to invest in the area. The conditions of the property market affect this balance: given the state of the market in 2010, there are concerns that too detailed regulations might act as an additional brake on private sector investment.

Social facilities and non-market project components

Private investment in the development of the commercial hub was accompanied by investment by the Greater Lyon Authority and the municipalities of Vaulx-en-Velin and Villeurbanne in the public space surrounding the hub. This investment aimed at an improvement of the road and footpath network in the immediate surroundings of the hub. As mentioned already, in 2010 public investment in Carré de Soie was mainly directed towards the provision of infrastructure, with some private sector contributions towards non-market components. The requirement to specify developers' contributions to non-market components in the commercial and leisure hub was part of the terms of reference of the tender won by Altarea. These terms of reference were drawn up by the local planning authority, which owned part of the site. The other significant landowner, Pathé Cinema, agreed to the terms of reference of the tender and allowed the planning authority to ask for bids, on condition that a large cinema complex would be part of the commercial and leisure centre and that Pathé would be designated to run the cinema complex. The planning authority also expressed an intention to buy or, if necessary, expropriate smaller plots covered by the bid area if it should turn out to be impossible for the winning bidder to buy the land from the initial landowners.

Total developer contributions towards non-market components for the first phase of the project amounted to almost €6 million. Altarea's proposal, which eventually won the tender, envisaged a pedestrian link between the multimodal transport hub and the leisure centre. This included a footbridge over the tramline and amounted to a total cost of €2.2 million. The developer also committed to providing a park area at the centre of the race-course at a cost of €2.9 million and to building a public promenade on the banks of the canal to the north of the race-course, at a total cost of €0.85 million.

In the second phase of the project, private sector contributions to public facilities and non-market components will be dealt with through the PAE for the Tase site. As mentioned already, this mechanism allows the planning authority to make the award of a planning permit dependent on specified financial contributions by the developer. The PAE allows the planning authority to use this power in order to obtain funding for public facilities. In exchange for a planning permit for the construction of 105,000 m² of floorspace the developer will pay 68 per cent of the cost of the following:

- on-site infrastructure;
- improvement of infrastructure to access the site;

- street lighting;
- a childcare facility for 20 children;
- a primary school with eight classrooms.

Organisation

Governance arrangements and partnership members

The regeneration of Carré de Soie involves both public and private actors but there is no partnership vehicle through which overall risks and revenues are negotiated; these discussions take place between the local authority and potential developers, often within the context of legal frameworks like the PAE. Rather than speaking of partnership members, it would be better to speak of different actors involved in a lengthy process of co-production as part of a regeneration scheme.

Apart from the Greater Lyon Authority, an important actor is the municipality of Vaulx-en-Velin. When Pathé expressed its interest in investment, it was the mayor of Vaulx-en-Velin – quickly followed by the Greater Lyon Authority – who used this as leverage for the larger regeneration project. In order to integrate the *multiplex* into the regeneration project, the Greater Lyon Authority asked Pathé to delay its investment. The latter accepted because it was also in its interest to integrate its investment into a larger, coherent leisure and commercial centre.

In July 2002 the Greater Lyon Authority, together with the municipalities of Vaux-en-Velin and Villeurbanne, formed the Mission Carré de Soie, a small governance structure that coordinates the different services of the Greater Lyon Authority and the municipalities involved in the development. The Mission therefore became a key actor in the development process.

The planning authority used its key competency of effecting the allocation of property rights through the local land-use plan as a bargaining tool in order to extract contributions to public facilities and infrastructure from the developer. Initially, the site was designated as industrial land, thus it was impossible to develop a potentially profitable mixed housing and office project. A revision of the local land-use plan was required in order to maximise the development potential of the area. As an officer of the Mission Carré de Soie says:

> Because our power is in the land rights, as long as the developers do not have development rights, they cannot do anything. It is the local land-use plan that is in charge. It is really the central element, and the developer, the one who owns the four hectares of land, he is very aware of that.

Choosing the PAE to frame the development of the area was in line with the decision of the planning authority to rely on private actors for the regeneration of the area. Other procedures, in particular that of the ZAC, allow the planning authority to acquire land and assume a developer role, but take longer, are more complicated from a legal point of view and, more importantly, require a stronger financial involvement of the public sector. The PAE appeared to be a more suitable vehicle because there was a developer who expressed an interest in developing the site and because the planning authority wanted to start the development quickly.

Altarea entered into an informal partnership via the tendering procedure for the commercial and leisure hub. The procedure was launched by the Greater Lyon Authority at the end of 2002, but although the developer had been chosen by September 2003 it was not until three years later, in 2006, that construction began. Other actors entered and left the regeneration process as it proceeded. The original landowner of the Tase site was an important actor until it sold the land in 2006 to the developer, Bouwfonds-Marignan, who then renegotiated the previously agreed PAE. On other parts of Carré de Soie other landowners and/or developers can enter this informal partnership in a similar way, from the moment that they express an interest in developing their site.

Organisation aims and their evolution
In comparison to many other large-scale French regeneration projects, the aim of the Greater Lyon Authority and of the local municipalities was to act as initiators and facilitators of a market-driven regeneration process. They wanted to seize development opportunities as they occurred, in order to redevelop the area without taking too many risks on their own, within a fiscally restrained context. The choice of the public sector not to become an intermediate land-owner was made largely for this reason, and thus direct public investment was channelled to infrastructure and the public realm in order to trigger development by increasing the attractiveness of the area. The single most important decision to that effect was the decision to bring the tramway and the metro to the area. This involved substantial public investment and boosted the accessibility of the site. With increased accessibility came increased development potential and this led to a repositioning of the Greater Lyon Authority. Whereas at the beginning of the project the development was supposed to be mainly residential now office development seemed to be a viable option as well. The flexibility of the planning framework allowed for such modifications.

The idea behind this front-loaded approach was that private investors attracted by the development potential of the site would step in and carry the development further. However, the credit crunch and the subsequent downturn in the real estate market have derailed this scenario. That having been said, the commitment to develop the area as a leisure, commercial and residential hub of metropolitan significance has remained largely unchanged throughout the first stage of the development. The aims of stage two have not changed much either, but it is possible that the way these aims are pursued will differ.

Risks and uncertainties

The Carré de Soie regeneration is a complex scheme comprising a number of smaller operations, each with its own stakeholders. As discussed, the Greater Lyon Authority made a deliberate choice not to use intermediary public land-ownership to organise the development of the area. One has to bear in mind that temporary landownership by a public actor is common practice in urban projects of this type in France, since there are several landowners and in many cases the land has to be assembled. By choosing not to act as a temporary intermediate landowner the public sector knew from the beginning that it was entering into a process that would require innovative solutions in order to be managed effectively.

The approach chosen by the Greater Lyon Authority has been to leave a lot of leeway for the project to evolve during its planning and development. A framework plan for the entire area of Carré de Soie has been drawn up but development is taking place in smaller plots. These projects have to respect the framework plan but there is a great deal of flexibility in terms of programme, design and functions in order to adapt the projects to the conditions and the investment opportunities prevailing at the time when they are developed. Such flexibility is required because of the size of the area (500 hectares) and the time-scale of its development, which spans 25 years. In French regeneration practice, however, this is a rather innovative approach; in many other cases public inter-vention involves acquisition of the land, land servicing and the sale of serviced building plots to developers by the state.

This approach has attracted a wider range of investors than usually is the case, but at the same time it has changed the nature and time-frame of the risks assumed by the public sector. A relatively robust start, with Pathé's *multiplex*, was followed by a freeze in private investment and the scheme came to a virtual standstill. This illustrates the pro-cyclical character of this type of approach: as long as the property market context makes investment in regeneration projects a relatively low-risk proposition, private developers and investors are attracted and the project advances. When market uncertainty (or any other form of uncer-tainty) makes investment in regeneration unattractive for the private sector, the public sector has little leverage by which to push or attract investment.

The reliance of public sector goals on the investment decisions of private actors is something with which the Greater Lyon Authority has little experience. The only important negotiating tool that the planning authority has in this situation is the development rights. The use of the PAE procedure shows how these rights can be used in order to frame the co-production of merit and public goods in a large-scale development project. The fact that the development of the Îlot Tase has still not taken off illustrates the sensitivity of this approach to market conditions.

In this approach the direct financial outlays, and thus the risks that the local authority assumes, are rather limited in comparison to other large-scale regeneration projects in France (see also the case of La Duchère). This risk-averse attitude came about in response to cuts in public funding that meant that, in terms of political priorities, the Carré de Soie project came behind several other large-scale regeneration projects in the Lyon conurbation, such as the Confluence project and the La Duchère project.

Interestingly, in the absence of any public land acquisitions prior to the project, the local authority paid a high price for the land that it acquired, but did so in order to build public facilities or in order to improve its negotiating position. In the absence of a detailed plan and with only partial public landownership, the public sector relied on the rapid completion of the first developments (in particular the commercial and leisure centre) in order to persuade new investors to come to the area. In return for granting development rights, the public sector will eventually benefit directly via the facilities provided through the PAE, and indirectly via the increased level of economic activity, increased population etc., which all translate into a wider tax base.

Under this arrangement, market uncertainty, and construction and design risks, have to be dealt with by the private sector, which, in a buoyant market, should indeed be better equipped to deal with those risks. Although it has invested significantly in the area, the public sector has only a partial influence on the outcomes of development but is need of results in order to justify the investment outlay. In effect, the state is not dealing with market risks, which have been taken on by the private sector. In exchange it has lost some control over the development and thus assumed greater political risks, both short and long term. In this instance, private sector actors responded to the market downturn by freezing development. This reaction can indirectly devalue the public investment and makes the regeneration scheme less palatable politically, which may put the scheme's long-term future in danger.

Under the terms of the PAE it will be the public sector that will have to provide all the necessary facilities if private development does not take place within nine years from the day of agreement. Thus, so far as the public sector is concerned, a distinction is made between political risks and short- to medium-term market and financial risks. From a private sector's point of view, however, more short- and medium-term market and financial risks have been taken on without losing the potential for long-term state support, due to the political risk that will still be dealt with by the state.

In view of the response of the private sector, and in order to keep the momentum going, the planning authority has decided to play a more proactive role. It is likely to initiate the development of new parts of the area – especially those where private investors are reluctant to take the initiative – using the public-led procedure of the ZAC. This will allow it to take charge of land preparation, but will also mean that it will assume a larger part of the associated risks.

Conclusions

The case studies discussed in this chapter are projects that between them demonstrate much of the variety of French policy initiatives and implementation mechanisms that structure regeneration schemes. Both case studies are long-term, mixed-use schemes involving private developers as well as different tiers of government. Both regeneration initiatives involve radical physical transformation and have taken shape under the direct influence of a political and legal framework that has structured the ways in which stakeholders could become involved in the process and the roles that they have been allowed to play. Different levels of government have engaged in a variety of roles, often complementary to each other, and the key theme of their involvement has been to cooperate so as to ensure the long-term commitment of the state in both schemes.

Thus, in Carré de Soie the policy imperatives for market-driven regeneration, combined with the lack of adequate public funding, were translated locally into a rather loosely defined regeneration scheme with clear strategic aims but a flexible planning framework and a reduced role for the state as landowner. In La Duchère the local and central governments were prepared to channel substantial resources in order to tackle what was broadly perceived to be an enclave of persistent social deprivation. The project was a much higher political priority, which meant that public institutions were mobilised to a larger extent and took on a very proactive role, both as intermediate landowners and also in terms of coordination, planning and funding of merit and public goods provision. In both cases, physical transformation was combined with the provision of merit and public goods both locally and at the metropolitan scale in order to ensure a positive net balance of public goods provision for the city.

In the case of Carré de Soie the local state played a crucial role in attracting investors, providing the planning framework, putting infrastructure into place and ensuring the provision of merit and public goods through a PAE. The local government also engaged in land purchases and thus was actively engaged in shaping the local land market and in benefiting from the uplifts in value caused by the regeneration initiative, albeit arguably at a higher price than would otherwise have been the case. The developer role, and thus the estimation of future demand and the resulting development programme was left to the private sector, which could operate within a relatively flexible planning framework. The state engaged with this process as a facilitator by ensuring that adequate public facilities, social housing and public spaces would be provided in return for allowing developers to go ahead with the development of the area. In La Duchère, because the ZAC was the preferred institutional tool and the land was mostly owned by public bodies, a hybrid entity (the SERL) assumed the responsibility of assembling and preparing the land for development before selling it on to the private sector. Developers could express their interest via a tendering process and dealt with the construction and sales within a rather tight planning and development framework.

In both cases, the public sector invested in local and metropolitan infrastructure early on, and used public good provision (public realm etc.) as a means to enhance the sites' development potential and to give a strong message of long-term commitment. Landownership was seen by the state as a way to increase its leverage in the negotiations with the developers in order to achieve its aims. In both cases the public bodies involved set up a coordinating institution, a 'Mission', whose remit was to promote the regeneration scheme by streamlining public and private resources. The role of the 'Mission' was crucial in creating trust between stakeholders and thus in allowing them to respond flexibly to changes in the market. However, the role of both central and local public institutions as ultimate guarantors of the stability of the system should not be underestimated. It was only through the sustained commitment and investment of central and local government that these areas became attractive to private investors and continued to be an option for investment following the post-2007 downturn in the property markets. In both cases the immediate response of the private sector to the property market downturn was to reduce its level of engagement and either to stop development completely (in Carré de Soie) or to lengthen the delivery time-scale (in La Duchère). In both cases the public sector's response was to increase its involvement in project development, mainly by shifting resources to the delivery of merit and public goods.

In France both the institutional framework and the institutional capacity that allow the state to play the role of a 'backstop' predate the credit crunch and provide the flexibility for the public sector to increase or decrease its level of involvement, depending on the circumstances, and to receive some financial return. It is noteworthy, however, that in Carré de Soie, other than investing in the development potential of the site, the state had very little leverage to reinvigorate the development process once it stopped. As a matter of fact the combination of public investment and partial engagement of the local authority in landownership without control of the development value chain meant that market uncertainty was transformed into political risk, which inevitably prompted a post-hoc public sector intervention. In La Duchère public landownership and the management of the development under the SERL/ZAC combination allowed the state to have much more control over the development value chain: it deflated land prices, allowed some of the accrual in land value through development to be captured and recycled into merit and public goods provision and offered developers the opportunity to buy land at cheaper prices whilst also benefiting the end consumer (who was offered cheaper housing). In short, control over the value chain was translated into an enhanced capacity to promote a welfarist agenda. This role of the state had a counter-cyclical effect and reduced volatility and developer exposure to the scheme (at a short-term financial cost to the public sector), which meant that developers could adjust to the market downturn without disengaging from the development altogether. Increased state commitment and engagement (both in financial and in planning terms) in the case of La Duchère actually lowered both the commercial and the political risks of the development for all the actors involved, but required a greater commitment of public sector resources.

In both schemes a variety of mechanisms were used to manage uncertainties and risks at both the scheme and project levels. The choice of mechanisms often depended on the needs of each case and, for example, included coordination by a state agency, public landownership (be it intermediate or not), early demonstration projects, flexibility of the planning framework, manipulation of the time-scale, changes in mixity (tenure, uses etc.), changes in density and the degree of land exploitation more generally, increased state funding and a mix of developers who were allocated sites for development.

Similarly to the Netherlands, if continued for a significant period of time, the variability in factors such as the mix of uses and tenures and the increased investment in merit and public goods during the downturn may pose a threat to the strategic aim of reintroducing market dynamics into the areas concerned. In the short to medium term, however, these interventions alleviate uncertainty about the future of the scheme and act counter-cyclically, thus reducing volatility. The actual physical form of the scheme varies according to how and when these techniques are employed and indicates the path-dependent character of such schemes.

Chapter 6
English case studies

Introduction

Regeneration policy in England and the UK as a whole was also influenced by the shift towards 'mixity', which in this case came to complement the turn towards market-based regeneration that occurred during the 1980s. In a way, the rise of the Labour Party to power meant that the state, at the level of rhetoric at least, launched an effort to transform urban spaces along the lines of an agenda similar to those pursued in France and the Netherlands. The two case studies included in this chapter, both located in England, are also similar to those explored in the other countries, in the sense that one is a failed estate and the other is a site on previously developed land. In both cases the reliance of policy delivery on the market cycle is evident. Each case, however, represents a different configuration of public and private interests in urban regeneration, as well as a different set of mechanisms that have been used in order to deliver the outputs and outcomes expected by the various actors.

The Paddington Waterside regeneration project is one of the biggest such projects in Europe. A key aspect of the Paddington case study is that it sheds light on the approach to regeneration that prevailed in many areas in the UK, especially those with buoyant property markets. It demonstrates how a local authority, with little direct financial assistance from central government, engaged with a major scheme that aimed at attracting private investment to an underused and sporadically derelict area. Indeed, given its rather privileged and well-connected location, it may come as a surprise that it took several decades before a scheme to regenerate the area actually materialised.

There were several plans covering larger or smaller parts of the present-day Paddington Special Policy Area (PSPA), but they never took off. This attests to the complexity, size and the significance of the site, and also to the reduced capacity of the private, and to some extent also the public actors, to engage effectively with the uncertainties and externalities surrounding the project. Eventually the project materialised when the lead developers and the local authority got the market timing right and had everything in place at the start of a growth cycle in 1998, when the development potential of the site was boosted by the operation of Heathrow Express (see below).

New Islington, on the other hand, is a case where central government and local authorities played a more prominent role in organising development in a failed social housing development (Cardroom Estate) at the fringe of the city centre and within the context of a more challenging property market situation. The attempt was to put a very difficult site back into the market and, given that the public sector owned the land and had an expressed goal to use the scheme for demonstration purposes, it is illuminating to look into how its leverage was used. Canniffe (2010, p. 3) describes the scheme as "a situation where there is the attempt to accommodate both divergent ends of Manchester's socially divided spectrum". One can also approach New Islington as an interesting, largely experimental, public sector-driven effort to develop and apply a relatively novel set of arrangements between public and private sector actors: in Paddington publicly owned land was sold outright or leased for the long term prior to development, in New Islington it was used as an asset from which more than just a market price could be gained.

New Islington, Manchester[1]

Context

Site conditions
New Islington is a mixed-use regeneration scheme located immediately north of Manchester city centre, within the New East Manchester regeneration area. It was conceived in the early 2000s, riding a wave of optimism created by the Commonwealth Games. A first masterplan by Will Alsop was prepared in 2002. Work began in 2003 and was initially expected to be completed by 2012, but the progress of work since 2007–8 has been severely limited, due to the downturn in the residential property markets.

The New Islington site was historically a part of Ancoats, an area that was a major centre of the textile industry in the nineteenth century. Ancoats was particularly well served by a network of canals, as it was crossed by both the Rochdale and the Ashton canals. Aside from the large number of cotton and textile mills, other industries such as engineering and foundries were set up locally. This industrial cluster required a substantial work-force and Ancoats became one of the most densely populated areas in Manchester as workers moved to the area, into terrace homes built amongst the factories. With such large numbers of poor residents living in a small space with few amenities, the deprivation of Ancoats became so pronounced that Friedrich Engels researched the area in his study of English industrialisation and the conditions of the working class.

In the early twentieth century the cotton industry declined and the industrial sites of Ancoats were left derelict. Between the 1920s and the 1970s many canals were filled in, many of the 'slum' terraces were cleared and much of the local population was rehoused, mostly to large council housing estates. The Miles Platting Estate was built in stages in the 1960s and 1970s just to the north-east. In 1976 the Cardroom Estate was built on the site where New Islington is today (Figure 6.1). In reaction to the failure of high-rise and high-density tower blocks built in previous years, it comprised low-rise housing with low population densities and was intended to have a village-like feel. However, as with many council housing estates in Manchester, it gradually became riddled with social problems and physical deterioration. The development of a retail park at its southern border in the 1980s cut it off from the city centre and accelerated the decline. By the early 2000s the majority of the 204 houses in the Cardroom Estate had been abandoned.

The site is located in the immediate periphery of the city centre (Figure 6.2) and it borders other large regeneration sites: Ancoats Millennium Village to the

Figure 6.1 The housing stock on the old Cardroom Estate (Denna Jones. Used with permission)

Figure 6.2 The location of New Islington

north-west, Miles Platting to the north, the city centre and its Northern Quarter, with Piccadilly Gateway just further to the south. As with Ancoats and Miles Platting, it is part of the large East Manchester regeneration area.

The site itself was occupied by the largely abandoned Cardroom housing estate and a number of old industrial buildings, most of which had to be demolished. Because of the area's industrial past, the site also required soil and water remediation and the remediation of its canals. It is within a ten-minute walk of Manchester city centre and Manchester Piccadilly, the city's main train station. There was a proposal for a new Manchester Metrolink tram stop to be built in New Islington as part of the East Manchester Line extension. However, the proposal was hampered by funding issues, as cost estimates for the extension had grown substantially above the original estimates made in 2000. In 2004 the central government withdrew its funding, but several years later, in 2008, it restored funding and at the time of writing the line was expected to be fully completed by the winter of 2013–14, with interim steps like New Islington to be opened sooner than that.

Evolution of the use and ownership of the site

Because of its previous use, most of the land of New Islington was owned freehold by Manchester City Council (MCC), with some pockets of private land. At the time when the scheme started, many plots that remained in private ownership were acquired by the MCC under compulsory purchase orders. As part of the structure of the New Islington project, the council land was leased to EP (which later was merged with the HCA), the central government urban regeneration and economic development quango, in a 250-year lease. To this pool of land were added a few neighbouring plots belonging to developers Urban Splash.

As the site develops, this landownership set-up will evolve. Developers of the different parcels that make up the project will get subsidiary leases from EP/HCA. Leasehold ownership of buildings will pass to the final property owners (households, housing associations, investors, health and education bodies), whereas the public realm will be passed on to a community trust.

Property and financial market conditions

The redevelopment of the Cardroom Estate and its transformation into New Islington first started in the early 2000s. At the time, the UK has just emerged from a languid property market that saw average house prices peak in 1989, then fall and then rise again seven years later, from 1996 onward. In 2003, house prices finally reached their 1989 levels. Afterwards, house prices began to rise further at rapid rate, with both housebuilding and housing demand fuelled by cheap and easy credit.

As with other regeneration-related projects in and around central Manchester, the New Islington project concept relied on the growing strength and dynamism of the housing market, and especially of the urban apartments section of that market, as well as on an abundant supply of mortgage and development finance. In the case of New Islington, the site was slightly marginal to the active Manchester city centre apartment market and therefore part of the project strategy was to bring it to the core of that market through better transport connections, and also by changing perceptions.

During the rest of the decade, preparatory work on some sites in New Islington advanced and detailed proposals for sites were made, including the commissioning of developers. However, in 2007–8 the property market crashed and within a short period aspiring homeowners became unable to buy dwellings and housebuilders either stopped building or lost interest. The collapse of the market led to a glut of new residential units all over Manchester facing very low demand in general, and on the New Islington site in particular. By then only a couple of developments in New Islington had been completed, and most had not even been started. Bank finance for projects became increasingly difficult to obtain, not only because of the general restriction on credit but also because of the scheme's characteristics, which made it appear to banks to be excessively risky (a complex profit matrix, overall costs, project dependence on uncertain transport infrastructure investment). From that time, private development came to a halt and only publicly funded housing association work continued for a while, together with some investment in infrastructure. As put by a consultant involved in the project:

> It's very difficult to get construction on site at the moment. The only work that's really been taking place has been the investment in the public realm, investment in setting the scene, the village neighbourhood structure for a community. The private investment that has followed in on the back of that has been limited. However, what's not in question is that the value of that investment, while not being immediately realised, clearly sets up onward development and hopefully as the market begins to return, you will see the different plots plug into that wider framework.

This strategy, however, creates a landscape where a few buildings are dotted around swathes of public open space, sometimes finished and open to the public and sometimes under construction and closed off. Canniffe (2010, p. 4) conveys the image that he saw and the feelings that the site in its current form generated in him, calling it "a key example of contemporary urban *anomie*". What makes sense from a planner's or long-term investor's point of view does not always sit nicely with the expectations and needs of the present user of a site.

Policy environment

New Islington is one of seven Millennium Communities projects in England, a national initiative designed to create sustainable communities in 'difficult' locations through a series of demonstration projects. The chosen projects were supposed to showcase partnership work between local authorities, regeneration agencies, housebuilders and communities and to emphasise sustainability and place making.

New Islington was conceived in the context of a strong policy push to transform the housing stock in the north of England in terms of tenure and quality through demolition and reconstruction. The Northern Way, an influential

partnership between key stakeholders from the north of England, with a com-
petitiveness and territorial cohesion agenda, was a major promoter of that
discourse. Regeneration strategies along similar lines (mixed-use, high-density,
home-ownership based projects) sprung up all over the north of England and as
part of regeneration efforts in Manchester city centre and East Manchester. These
projects have relied on the strength of private property development to deliver
policy aims (articulated around ideas of mixed tenures and mix of uses) and thus
to replace decaying, mono-functional and single-use council housing estates and
revive derelict industrial districts.

Architectural and urban design quality and the policies addressing them have
been important determinants of these projects, both to create demand for a city-
living life-style and to attract buyers and wealthier residents into areas previously
dominated by social renting. More recently, New Islington has not managed to
benefit fully from policy mechanisms designed to protect key development
projects from the consequences of the economic downturn. Before the 2010
public spending cuts, the scheme had secured North West Development Agency
(NWDA) pledges for investment worth £4.4 million in basic infrastructure and
public realm improvements.

Content

Project structure, form and design

New Islington was an urban regeneration scheme for a derelict and deprived part
of Manchester's city centre, on 12.5 hectares in what was originally a Victorian-
era industrial site and later the site of a failed social housing estate of the 1970s.
The partnership between MCC, EP and Urban Splash originally planned to
build a mixed-use scheme of around 1,400 new homes, including 66 houses,
500 large two- and three-storey apartments and 600 one- and two-bedroom
apartments, around 20 shops and restaurants and some office space and workshops. Additional public services and amenities that were to be provided within
the development included a health centre and a primary school as well as
100,000 m² of parks and gardens, a marina, a new canal and two miles of canalside promenades. A masterplan by Will Alsop, elaborated in 2002, articulated
those uses based on the concept of 'fingers' (Figure 6.3).

In addition to New Islington's being within convenient walking distance of
Manchester city centre and the main train station, the site was also to be served
by its own tram stop – part of the Metrolink network – several new bus stops and
1,400 on-street and underground car-parking spaces.

The structure of the project as described above was shaped by urban regeneration strategies that were based on public investment triggering private-led

Figure 6.3 Plan of the New Islington regeneration scheme (Alsop Architects/Urban Splash. Used with permission)

development within a masterplan. The overall content of the project was decided on the basis of calculations of the profitability of developments in a buoyant residential market, as well as an acceptable return on public investment (including land) through a share in developers' profits. The showcase nature of the project (as a practical exemplar of how to incorporate ideas of sustainability, communities, place making, desirable densities) was another factor explaining the mix of uses and tenures, the overall layout and building design and specifications. It was also responsible for the nature, extent and location of public facilities, including public realm elements. As mentioned already, the spatial outcomes of this approach have already drawn some criticism (Canniffe, 2010), albeit the scheme is not yet finished and will in all likelihood look and feel very different when completed.

At the time when the fieldwork was done, the HCA and Urban Splash were considering whether they should modify the tenure mix and overall densities towards more low-density housing with more conventional architecture, as well as more publicly funded social/affordable housing, which does not depend on banking finance, in an effort to attract more market interest.

Use and tenure mix

The use mix in the original project tried to create a viable, vibrant urban environment by complementing the dominant residential use with social facilities (school, health centre), shops, some other commercial uses and leisure spaces/public realm. Given the size and complexity of the project, the specific mix of use and tenure, in its many components, has evolved with varying dynamics to cope with changes in housing demand and financial constraints. At the beginning of the development of New Islington in 2003, 1,400 new homes were proposed; several years later, as the housing market boomed, 1,700 new homes were planned; and, as the market slowed down severely in the late 2000s, the number of new homes to be delivered was scaled back again to 1,400.

The only social housing included in the original project was destined for the 100 families who had remained in the Cardroom Estate. As social housing tenants, these families were granted the right to return to equivalent accommodation in the area. The Manchester Methodist Housing Group (MMHG) was selected as the social landlord member for the New Islington partnership. The original assumption was that the residents would agree to be rehoused in the new apartments planned for New Islington, but this turned out not to be the case and family houses had to be developed to accommodate them. As the main developer partner and manager of the masterplan, Urban Splash had to allocate a site within New Islington for the MMHG's social housing, so as to satisfy the residents' concerns that they would not be rehoused at the development's periphery. With funding from the Housing Corporation, the MMHG planned to provide between 80 and 100 social houses for rent.

The first MMHG social housing development was Islington Square, comprising 23 houses. Prospective residents chose the design in 2003 and construction began in early 2005 and was completed in March 2006, at a cost of £2.3 million. Around the same time, in January 2006, work started on the second MMHG development, Guest Street, comprising 14 homes. It was completed in March 2007 and cost £1.4 million. In summer 2007 the MMHG was selected as the new landlord for the tenants of 12 existing social houses on Weybridge Road, on the border of New Islington. As these houses were in relatively good condition the tenants did not want to be relocated. Respecting their wishes, Urban Splash incorporated the Weybridge Road houses into the development plan for New Islington and the MMHG spent £34,000 on improvements in each of the homes.

The vast majority of planned new housing in New Islington was intended for sale to the private market. The most prominent project within New Islington was 'Chips', a residential apartment building designed by Will Alsop to resemble a stack of chips on a plate and developed by Urban Splash on its own land adjacent to the main site. Off-plan sales for the apartments began in May 2005, and 109 of the 134 planned apartments had been reserved by September 2005. Construction started in January 2006, the building was topped out in December 2007 and completion was planned for 2008. However, there were a number of delays as well as a change in the development and tenure mix. The plans for 'Chips' were altered to mixed use and to include 142 one-, two- and three-bedroom apartments as well as 12,000 sq ft of ground-floor commercial space. Roughly £3 million in funding was made available by the HCA to make 50 of the apartments available for shared ownership and around 20 apartments available for the HCA's 'Rent to HomeBuy' programme, an intermediate form of tenure. As a form of non-market housing, both sets of apartments are under the management of the MMHG. In July 2008 every apartment had been sold off-plan, and in summer 2009 'Chips' was finally completed at a cost of £20 million. Since then, sales for a number of both market and shared-ownership apartments have fallen through, due to the inability of the buyers to obtain mortgages.

By early 2009 the financial crisis and the non-existent demand for housing had taken their toll on New Islington; changes in the composition of the project

Figure 6.4 View of the New Islington site in 2009 (EG focus. Used with permission)

and a prolonged time-frame for construction were used as ways to tackle the effects of the property-market downturn. Only 4 out of 11 residential schemes (Islington Square, Guest Street, Weybridge Road and Chips) have been completed, delivering 191 of the planned 1,400 dwellings, since the New Islington development began in 2003. In 2010 work continued only on the refurbishment project at the Dispensary and Urban Splash began talks with the HCA and the NWDA to dispose of a number of development sites.

Infrastructure and provision of amenities fared better, due to public funding; so, of seven such projects, only two were not started (Redhill Street Bridge and the primary school), whilst the remaining five projects (Bascule Bridge, Cotton Field, Health Centre, Old Mill Street and the Canal) ranged from being under construction to being fully completed. It has to be noted here, however, that the prolonged uncertainty about the future of Metrolink and the withdrawal of the funding by the government affected the development potential of the scheme adversely and undermined the confidence of market actors in the scheme's potential.

The severity of the downturn put original plans under pressure in the short term, with implications for the long term. The decline in the local development and mortgage market, together with pressure from government to show results and returns on public investment, created pressure for changes in the use and tenure mix towards use and tenure types that could be perceived by banks/ investors as less risky and for which there might still be a demand. Conversion of housing into hotel uses was being discussed, as well as an increase in housing association-rented housing that could benefit from public money for development and acquisition. There was also some discussion about decoupling tenure from income, introducing private renting and finding ways of creating a mixed-income community without relying solely on owner-occupation. As stated by a senior local manager at the HCA:

> We are also discussing how we can involve the private renting sector. Government policy has focused on owner occupation or social housing for rent. Private renting has not featured highly. We think that with restrictions on the supply of mortgages and aspirations for high-quality dwellings there are real opportunities for private sector renting, and New Islington is one of the areas for that.

Social facilities and non-market project components

The project aspires to provide local services and amenities on a level that befits the demonstration character of New Islington as a prototype of a sustainable, high-density mixed community. Much of the public sector funding (which up to 2010 had amounted to £22 million) has gone to amenity and public realm investment, with the creation of parks, water features and boulevards. On the one hand, this investment was justified as part of a 'place making' strategy, in tune with New Islington's sustainability aims. On the other, it is also part of the commercial strategy to make the area an attractive proposition to private developers, investors and homeowners. The new public realm, with its streets, canals, lakes and parks (and also the already-excavated basement areas of the proposed buildings) forms the platform upon which private developers should work. This strategy is described by a senior project consultant as follows:

> This is a demonstration project showing what a sustainable area should be like, not only from an environmental point of view but by creating a place where people (families as well as singles) would like to live in the long run. Public space is key in making this place desirable.

The finance for developing non-market components involved, as a rule, up-front investment by the EP/HCA or Urban Splash on their behalf, either in land preparation or in building work, and the recovery of those costs through sale of land leases to developers and planning obligations (section 106 etc.). Thus, developers' contributions are a key source of funds for the non-market housing component of the project. This meant that, beyond an initial up-front investment by EP/HCA deemed necessary to trigger development, further investment and completion of facilities and amenities were linked to the sale and development of sites.

Construction began on a new health centre in April 2006 and was completed in January 2008 at a cost of £6.5 million. The 2,250 m² health centre was one of the largest in Manchester and was designed to serve residents in the surrounding area, as well as to have the capacity to serve a much larger population in the future. Work started on New Islington's urban water park, Cotton Fields, in March 2006 and was to be completed by summer 2007. This 1.6 hectare park includes a lake, several islands and an urban beach. Although the work was mostly completed, funding issues left the park closed to the public and, at the time of field work, discussions were on-going as to how to cover the costs necessary to open it, even if no new developments materialise around it in the short term.

With the economic downturn, investment in public goods provision came to depend more strongly on public funding with uncertain return. The result has been a focus on the more sensitive elements of the local services and amenities, those with the greater potential to influence private investment decisions, such as the social facilities mentioned above, bridges and parts of the public realm around the more attractive development sites. However, no funding was obtained for a new primary school in New Islington, despite Urban Splash's having set aside land for its buildings and playing fields.

Organisation

Governance arrangements and partnership members

The key players in the development have been the MCC (the planning authority and freeholder of much of the land), EP/HCA (long-leaseholder and funder of much of the land preparation and infrastructure work as well as of non-market housing) and developers Urban Splash (landowners and principal developers). Additionally, an important role has been played by NWDA through the New East Manchester (NEM) regeneration company (as public sector funders), the MMHG (later renamed Great Places – the developers and managers of all the non-market housing in the project) and a number of subsidiary developers who took responsibility for individual sites and were expected to work under the guidance of Urban Splash but providing development skills and capital for their own sites.

Partnership membership and the involvement of the members have changed with time. It started with the NWDA, MCC, EP and Urban Splash. In July 2003 an agreement was signed between Urban Splash, MCC and EP to develop New Islington. These three parties formed the client body with which other parties signed agreements to provide their services. The partnership decided that EP, the government's then regeneration quango responsible for supporting English local authorities' regeneration efforts in terms of investment, skills and human resources, would take the leading role in this development, as MCC was the leading partner in the regeneration of the city centre and the NWDA was involved in the regeneration of East Manchester and Ancoats Millennium Village through NEM. The NWDA provided the policy framework and regeneration-funding umbrella for the whole site but was not directly active on site until the introduction of the Metrolink extension.

The MCC administered the regeneration of the Cardroom Estate through NEM, yet all contracts and commitments were made to MCC, not to NEM. MCC transferred its land holdings to EP/HCA early on (EP took a 250-year lease) and changed their role to that of planning authority and guarantor of the contracts related to the project. EP/HCA therefore became the lead partner, leading on contracts and employing most of the consultants/contractors. EP/HCA are also the developers for all the public realm interventions (Old Mill Street, Cotton Fields Park and the water features). The creation of HCA from the merger of EP and the Housing Corporation (HC) gave HCA control over housing-related budgets that have become increasingly important in the delivery of the project and also gave it the role of lender for non-market housing projects. For the development phase, overall management was delegated to the partner-ship, which – apart from the general benefits of such partnerships – also meant that the short- and long-term costs of significant infrastructure investments did not show up as liability for public sector partners (EP and MCC).

One point worth mentioning here is the way that the public sector approached funding issues. When asked about the role of EP in funding regeneration, and more specifically about Kickstart, EP interviewees revealed that this involved the provision of loans, grants and equity, in effect converting EP into a form of banking institution. Says an EP official:

> In terms of the 'Kickstart' approach . . . you can ask for a loan, for equity and for grants. And for many years, as you know, EP had that funding – it went to Europe and got funding for this scheme. Equity is something new in this area, but if in effect the banks aren't prepared to lend on a scheme, when we see, with our understanding, that this scheme could make money then, we could put an equity share into it. Alternatively we could offer a loan which has a rate of return, so we may be acting like a bank, effectively, because we know that this project will pay off.

Yet, when that same official was asked whether somehow formalising that role by setting up a (potentially local) banking institution to perform this function in the long run might be considered, the response was rather more cautious, yet demonstrative of how the role of government is understood:

> The fact that we operate that element of 'Kickstart' means we are becoming a bank, a lender in that way. I don't think that was the intention. The intention was to create pressure upwards from the ground where schemes aren't being funded by the lending institutions. As a public sector body we shouldn't be displacing the market, so where schemes can secure funding from the private sector they should do so . . . If the private sector can deliver it, we should do it in the private sector. Where the private sector won't step in we can argue that the government should provide alternative options and one of those options is that. [EP should not] displace the market, that's not the role of government I believe. And I don't think HCA does either. I'm not saying that when it has a portfolio across a number of projects the government won't take a view on how it recovers that money. It could then if it wanted to sell that loan book on the market. There's no reason not to do that, it could sell on competitive terms, and the government can recoup its money, but the banks can restructure it.

Urban Splash was already a landowner in and around the site and had started the flagship 'Chips' development. On the back of its reputation and its land-holdings it assumed the role of lead developer, delivering projects on its own sites and overseeing subsidiary developers on HCA sites. As the lead developer, but not the developer of every scheme, Urban Splash was not only to develop some of the site but to procure other developers to build. Urban Splash believed that at least two other developers would have to be involved, although Urban Splash would be responsible for the quality of their design and construction. Some of the sites involved multiple developers (e.g. TuttiFrutti, with its 26 individual projects), and the developer partner Urban Splash acted as an overall contractor with the independent developers.

In 2003 the MMHG was chosen by Cardroom Estate residents to be their new landlord, following a competition between four housing associations. The MMHG was a large housing association in the North-West with over 4,000 properties and extensive experience in developing affordable housing on inner-city brownfield sites as part of mixed-use community regeneration projects. The role of the MMHG was to deliver social housing so that the residents of the Cardroom Estate would be able to exercise their right to return. Acting as a developer, the MMHG bought its building sites from Urban Splash, assumed responsibility for planning and development and remained as the landowner. In New Islington, the MMHG employed architects selected by its future tenants and used its own building contractors.

After completion, general management responsibilities (and running costs) of the public and private realms, including the large infrastructure of parks and canals, is to be transferred to a Community Trust (CT). HCA's 250-year lease will also be transferred to the trust. Subsidiary management organisations in each block will contribute to the overarching CT, with tenants paying a service charge that covers both levels. Although this is not yet clear, presumably MCC will pay the CT to manage adopted roads and public spaces within the project area, employing the same routines that the CT will use for the non-adopted spaces. There is some controversy about how this double-layered management arrangement will be funded, especially in the case of a housing association and other social housing tenants, as this might considerably impact on the monthly rent.

Organisation aims and their evolution
The aims of the partnership members reflect national and regional policy objectives (the increasing emphasis on sustainability, place-making and mixed uses and incomes) as well as national views on how to achieve these, i.e. with the public sector in a mainly facilitating role and aiming to attract private investment. The strong policy objective of diversifying tenure in Manchester was meant to counteract the dominance of social renting in large areas of Greater Manchester, seen in itself as an important contributor to social, economic and physical decline, to stimulate more 'aspirational' housing and to generate higher council tax receipts. According to some interviewees, Manchester may have an excess of council housing stock but is actually facing an acute shortage of good-quality,

non-market housing, suitable for the types of households that would be its tenants. This view was unable to influence the aims of the project and, as a result, developers working in Manchester were not required to provide affordable housing as a condition of planning permission on the same terms that applied throughout most of the UK. Only 10 per cent of the 1,400 new homes planned for New Islington were to be non-market housing, as opposed to the require-ment for between 30 and 50 per cent social housing in new developments that is usually applied in other cities in the UK.

New Islington was conceived as a ten-year project, with development starting in 2003. The model chosen was one where public sector involvement in land servicing and investment in infrastructure and the public realm would reduce the actual and perceived risks of private investment and development. This was quite different from the neighbouring, private finance initiative- (PFI) based Miles Platting housing estate, where the private sector would regenerate the estate and manage it against an annual fee for services specified in a Local Services Agreement for the duration of the 30-year contract. It was also different from East Manchester, where council land was often sold to private developers, coupled with gap funding. According to the partnership, the choice of model for New Islington and the decision on greater public sector involvement resulted from the demon-stration character of the project. The chosen model required significant up-front investment from the public sector in order to demonstrate commitment to the area and to improve the development potential of a difficult location.

The New Islington project was conceived from the start as the insertion of a much broader tenure mix into an area previously dominated by council-owned housing, so as to create a functioning local housing market catering for a variety of needs and aspirations and to improve the local urban environment. Indeed, the whole of the NEM regeneration strategy, of which it is a part, has targeted primarily owner-occupation, with some private renting as preferred tenures, whilst limiting social renting to the relocation of resident population with rights to return (about 100 households). This is how developer Urban Splash describes the mixed-tenure objectives:

> The idea was to address that by replacing the social housing that is not working, putting in more private housing and more intermediate housing, getting more mixed tenures . . . What we would like particularly would be for that area to cover all market niches from your first home, your starter house or flat, right up to where you're planning to retire. And within that there are a range of different housing prices, a range of different affordability levels.

As the main landowner, MCC first considered the regeneration of Cardroom Estate in 2001 as part of its broader effort to regenerate East Manchester. In

March 2001, Urban Splash was selected by the MCC as the lead developer of the estate. Urban Splash was a private developer that specialised in the regeneration of urban, previously used land sites for mixed use through innovative planning, design and architecture. Aside from property development, Urban Splash was also a landlord and managed a portfolio of commercial and residential rental properties. Will Alsop was commissioned to draw up a masterplan for the Cardroom Estate, and in May 2003 Urban Splash's 'New Islington' scheme was granted planning permission.

NEM was established in 1999 as a partnership between MCC, EP and the NWDA in order to lead the physical regeneration of East Manchester, integrate social and economic initiatives and promote the area to new businesses. Following extensive consultation with residents of East Manchester in 1999, NEM developed a regeneration framework. The planned construction of over 1,400 new homes in New Islington was to contribute to NEM's goal of delivering 12,500 new homes in East Manchester. Infrastructure planned for New Islington, such as the Metrolink, was to serve as a physical link between the city centre and other areas of East Manchester, and planned amenities such as the health centre and the urban park were to be designed to accommodate New Islington's residents, as well as residents of surrounding areas.

EP selected the New Islington development as the third of seven Millennium Communities in England, as part of its Millennium Communities Programme. The £170 million programme was launched in 2000 to support the development of sustainable and 'environmentally innovative' communities in challenging locations throughout England and deliver 6,000 new homes by 2010. As a Millennium Community, the community's development plan and the design and construction of its buildings were to adhere to a number of sustainability and environmental standards in order to be eligible for the programme's funds. The New Islington development was meant to showcase the role of high-quality urban design and public realm in sustainable living. In December 2008, EP was merged with the HC, another quango that funded the construction of new affordable housing, to form a new housing and regeneration agency, the HCA.

Through the Millennium Communities Programme the HCA contributed roughly £27 million towards the development of New Islington, including previous contributions by EP and the HC. At the beginning of the development in 2003, EP spent £22 million on demolishing the Cardroom Estate and other buildings, remediating the soil and water and constructing infrastructure, including roads and canals. It also funded the compulsory purchase of land in New Islington for site assembly. By undertaking these works through a significant outlay of public capital, EP hoped to create a more stable development environment that would introduce certainty into the planning process so that developers would consider working in New Islington a managed risk.

The market downturn and the slow pace of development have forced HCA to consider enlarging its role in the project and consequently to change some of the private-delivery philosophy that informed it from the start: There is some discussion about HCA equity involvement in some of the sites, and extending its role as lenders. As the main conduit for public money into housing in general and social housing in particular, it has become the main lender for the project, de facto replacing market lending. Thus, in response to the credit crunch and the reduced demand for housing, the HCA provided £2 million in funding through its National Affordable Homes Programme to convert 50 existing market apartments in the 'Chips' development to shared-ownership apartments under the management of the MMHG. The HCA also contributed an additional £1.3 million to convert about 20 existing market apartments in 'Chips' to 'Rent to HomeBuy' apartments.

The HCA responded to the market downturn by launching a housing stimulus programme to support housebuilding activities that had been severely curtailed as a result of the credit crunch. The 'Kickstart' housing delivery programme was launched in April 2009 and was one of six programmes making up the stimulus plan. 'Kickstart' focused on mixed-tenure residential projects that had stalled at the construction stage and that could restart immediately. When markets improved, the HCA would seek to recover its investment and share in any uplift in values. The New Islington scheme sounds like an ideal candidate, but unfortunately it did not receive any funding. This went to other schemes, including projects in the aforementioned Miles Platting and NEM schemes. We do not know the rationale for those decisions, but we consider it noteworthy that central government preferred to fund projects in schemes in which it had much less control over the land and thus over the value chain. CABE later criticised the HCA for funding schemes with low design and public realm standards (Hurst, 2010).

After having been selected as a beneficiary of the first round of funding under the 'Kickstart' programme, Urban Splash received nearly £40 million from the HCA in May 2010 to continue building at three residential sites where construction had stalled. Although none of these sites was in New Islington, the injection of money into Urban Splash's £130 million residential programme could help to balance the company's finances and retain its presence in New Islington. In yet another twist to the story, in the summer of 2010 the HCA decided to freeze uncommitted 'Kickstart' funds in an effort to save money, whereas the new Coalition government considered closing it down altogether.

Risks and uncertainties

It has been mentioned already that at the beginning of the project demand for dwellings in the area did not exist, either for market or for non-market housing. In essence, this demand had to be created, and it was decided that the way to do this would be to recreate a local market for housing. Thus, the whole project was predicated on the idea that public funding of infrastructure would attract private development and this, in turn, would generate profits from uplifts in land value that would pay back public investment. A main risk in this model was that infrastructure investment might not generate interest from developers and investors, especially if the long-term commitment of the state was not a given (which turned out to be the case so far as central government is concerned). The success of the project was therefore linked to property-market cycles, because what is an attractive investment proposal in a booming market may no longer be attractive in a downturn. The demonstration character of the project, and its relatively peripheral location in relation to established Manchester housing sub-markets, added to the perception of riskiness and these factors were expected to play a part in risk/returns estimations by developers and funders.

The sensitivity of the scheme to market volatility was understood by key public sector actors from the beginning as a risk, especially given the long-term scope of the project. Political and financial capital was invested in the project, and for the public sector these investments could have been wasted if the project did not deliver significant results within an acceptable time-frame. The key issues facing the promoters of the scheme were: firstly, the ability to attract developers to individual sites (a function of developers' expectations of housing demand, of variations in the cost and availability of finance and of their perception of the public sector commitment to the project), and secondly, the possibility that developers would not honour their commitments or could go bankrupt. Both issues were factored into the project design (flexibility in the masterplan, break-up of the project into much smaller development sites) and informed contractual arrangements.

Overall, the management of the risks as identified from the start of the project seems to have relied on the flexibility of the masterplan, on control of ownership of the land (EP/HCA with a long lease from MCC and Urban Splash), on public infrastructure investment and on partnership arrangements. The whole project was conceived as a collection of separate individual developments unified by a platform of infrastructure, public realm and a strategic masterplan. Although the overall project should deliver a mixed-use, mixed-tenure, high-density development, there is enough flexibility in the masterplan for sites to be brought forward or held back and for the mix and specifications of each component to be modified to suit fluctuations in the property market.

As in the wider NEM scheme, the regeneration strategy for New Islington is predicated on creating a mixed income/use/tenure environment as a condition for sustainable regeneration and sustainable private investment returns. However, pressure from financiers for more guarantees in the form of pre-sales may lead to increases in the proportion of units being acquired by wholesale investors looking for outlets for investment capital rather than for homes to live in. Moreover, in a context of decreasing property prices, social renting has become an attractive alternative for investors left with vacant residential properties. There are fears that these factors could compromise the long-term objectives for tenure mix and the capacity to maintain the long-term value of public and private investment in the area. These risks became more apparent and important as the scheme progressed and market conditions changed. However, the level of contributions required from private developers to build and maintain those non-market elements in a weak market has increased the perception of risk associated with New Islington on the part of developers and financial institutions. Strategies by the project partnership to attenuate the uncertainties surrounding the project were aimed at different levels. At one level, the large amount of public sector investment enhanced development potential (better public realm and infrastructure) and made the scheme more attractive for private sector investors and developers. As it was put by an EP official:

> To change the area, the public sector has to invest a massive amount of capital to create the public realm, the infrastructure and the development platform which would remove uncertainty for the private sector. Nothing below the ground needs doing.

Also, when it came to investment above ground, the EP used the public realm to enhance the development potential of the site and further attenuate uncertainty. As a senior local EP manager said:

> The public realm then becomes a risk-minimisation strategy against competition. Competition started off well by offering high-quality flats, but as land prices increased developers started squeezing more and more flats out of sites and the whole thing went down the drain. In New Islington, the good quality of public space, amenities and standards makes it more competitive in the market and better prepared for the market turnaround.

In this set-up, the public sector took over most of the risks associated with land-remediation costs and infrastructure investment, whereas most operational risks (construction costs, development finance, commercialisation of units) were transferred to private sector developers. This is one of the key reasons why the Metrolink was crucial for the success of the scheme: it would obviously improve the scheme's accessibility but at the same time it would signal the commitment to the scheme of all the tiers of government. Unfortunately, even though the Metrolink is now going forward, the ambivalent approach of central government towards it severely undermined the credibility of the public sector commitment to the New Islington regeneration scheme. The reluctance of the HCA to back the scheme via 'Kickstart' had a similar effect, although one can imagine that things could have been worse if a project had been selected, only for the money to be withdrawn later on (as turned out to be the case with several other projects).

Within these parameters, each actor deployed its own specific risk-management strategies. Lenders, for their part, increased the proportion of forward sales that they required in order to provide development finance as the market situation deteriorated. For public sector organisations, and especially the HCA, the risk is for a demonstration project in which government has invested so much to stall or to fail altogether, thus compounding legal and financial responsibilities for managing the land, its uses and the people living on it. From the start, the money spent by the EP/HCA was regarded as investment that would equate to a percentage of the value to be created by the development. Future returns from the project were to be allocated according to those percentages. Therefore, if the development does not progress, there is the risk that the investment in infrastructure and remediation will not be paid back. It is therefore crucial for the HCA to ensure that some form of development keeps happening on the site. On the other hand, the creation of the CT to manage the development platform is an attempt to transfer responsibility for long-term management to someone other than the HCA.

For Urban Splash, the risks are those associated with involvement in any development during an economic downturn, albeit reduced in this case because the costs of remediation and land acquisition were borne by the public sector. For Urban Splash, as well as for other private developers, freezing development activities has been a way to manage risks for sites on which development had not started. More sites were diverted to publicly funded housing association developments in order to secure some momentum for the project; specifications for residential units were altered to match variations in demand; and attracting buy-to-let investors was seriously considered. The varied use and type mix was also part of a strategy designed to tackle competition from other development sites around Manchester, mostly offering a narrower range of unit types, uses, public facilities and amenities.

To share some of the risk of developing New Islington, Urban Splash invited private developers to enter competitions to win the right to develop schemes on specified building sites. In early 2006 Bryant Homes won the first of these developer competitions with its proposal to build 'The Tree House' and 'The

Botanic' and entered into a joint venture with Urban Splash as the first 'outside' private developer involved in New Islington. However, the poor property market in the UK brought Bryant Homes' parent company, Taylor Wimpey, close to bankruptcy, so Bryant Homes was forced to withdraw from 'The Botanic' and construction stopped in March 2009.

After Bryant Homes won the right to develop 'The Botanic' no further competitions were held by Urban Splash to involve other outside developers. Several other sites were also granted planning permission in 2007, but construction never started on those either. As a result, the development brief for the site gradually changed and the expected number of dwellings to be constructed fell (see section on use and tenure mix).

Finally, for the communities living in and around the project site, the very real risk is that the project will never be fully completed and they will be condemned to live in and around a partly completed building site with high management costs and precarious infrastructure. For them, the only course of action – apart from moving out – may be to hope that the next upturn in the property cycle creates the conditions for the project to continue in a form that meets at least the most important of their expectations. As a design consultant involved in the project put it:

> There's certainly an air of frustration by a whole variety of stakeholders, not least of which the local community, because that community have made sacrifices or have been affected by the construction work or left with vacant open sites on their doorstep with no construction activity on them. So they're understandably asking themselves the question when are these shops going to appear, and when is this park going to open etc. . . . And the question needs to be properly asked and debated whether or not that's a price worth paying.

Paddington Waterside, London[2]

Context

Site conditions
The PSPA, which delineates the project's boundaries, covers an area of around 32 hectares, currently comprising 13 different developments with office, retail and leisure uses. Around 900 dwellings of both market and non-market housing had already been built at the time of writing this book and another 1,400 are planned.

The land-use evolution of the sites currently forming the PSPA was closely associated with the evolution of its transport infrastructure and was directly affected by the changes in the economic geography of the UK. Paddington Basin was first developed in 1801 as a terminus of the Grand Union Canal, resulting in the construction of warehouses and in small-scale industrial activity in the area. The role of Paddington as a major transportation hub was greatly enhanced by the construction of Paddington Station in 1854 as the London terminus of the Great Western Railway (GWR). To service freight and passenger traffic, GWR also built the Paddington Goods Yard north-west of the station and the Great Western Hotel at the station entrance facing Praed Street. The connectedness of Paddington increased further with the opening of Paddington underground station as the western terminus of Metropolitan Railways in 1863, followed by four more underground lines by the early twentieth century.

The arrival of motorised freight traffic had a disruptive influence on the area's economy. The local warehousing infrastructure became redundant and the construction of the A40 Westway in the 1970s contributed significantly to fracturing the urban fabric, dispersing the local community and reinforcing the present-day PSPA area's isolation. The A40 formed an urban barrier to the north-north-west, complementing the railway lines and the train station, which made the area

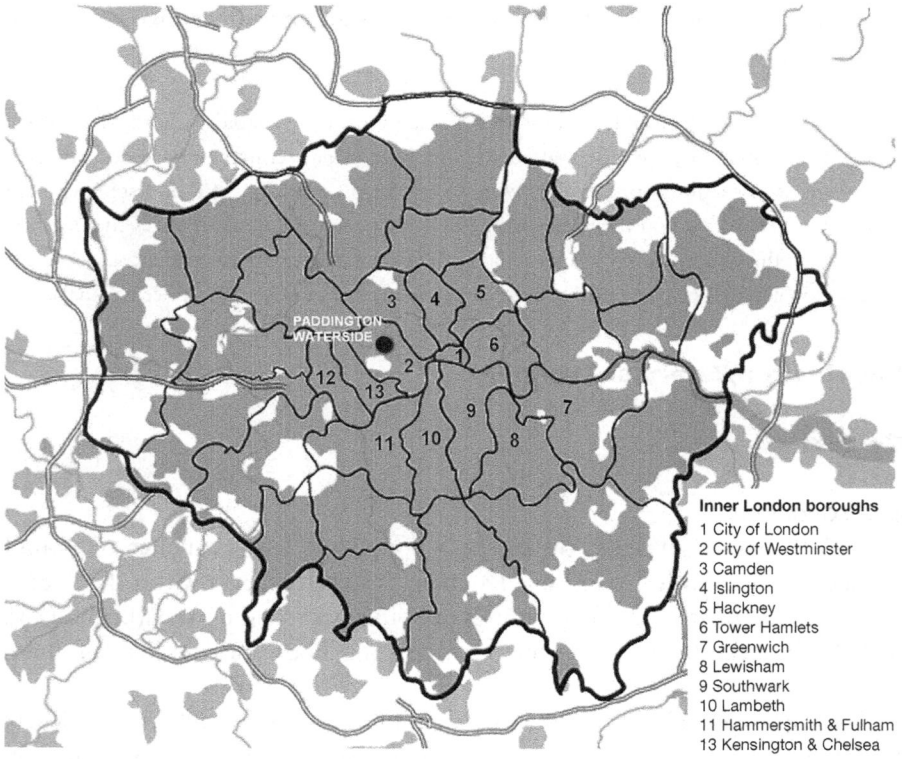

Inner London boroughs
1 City of London
2 City of Westminster
3 Camden
4 Islington
5 Hackney
6 Tower Hamlets
7 Greenwich
8 Lewisham
9 Southwark
10 Lambeth
11 Hammersmith & Fulham
13 Kensington & Chelsea

Figure 6.5 The location of Paddington Waterside

impermeable from the south-south-west. The situation deteriorated further with the addition of St Mary's Hospital in the 1980s, which blocked access to the site from the east.

The slow decline of the local economy, which had gained momentum after the 1970s and 1980s, combined with the lack of access routes to and from the canal, created a mosaic of derelict buildings, buildings in sub-optimal use and limited-access areas (mainly next to the canal itself), which were used as dumping grounds. Several sites in the PSPA area required land servicing, including remediation and decontamination, especially in and around the canal and the goods yards, although the conditions were not so serious as to derail the project. The most important factor in enhancing the site's development potential was the improvement of accessibility, which in the case of the Paddington Goods Yard site entailed extensive decking so as to raise it to the same level as the neighbouring sites and thus make it more easily accessible from the new road and bridge.

Perhaps unsurprisingly, two transport projects have radically shaped the area's future: Heathrow Express and Crossrail. The opening of the Heathrow Express in 1998, which made it possible to travel non-stop from Paddington to Heathrow in 15 minutes, was a catalyst for the regeneration of Paddington. As well as being nearer to Heathrow and offering a shorter journey time compared to the alternatives, Paddington had the added advantage of being nearer to hotels in Westminster and therefore more convenient for passengers travelling to and from Heathrow Express.

In October 2007, following years of deliberations, the then Labour government approved Crossrail, a £16 billion railway project extending from Maidenhead and Heathrow in the west to Shenfield and Abbey Wood in the east. The train service will run underground from Paddington to Canary Wharf and is planned to be completed in 2017.

Evolution of the use and ownership of the site

The evolution of use and ownership of the major sites comprising the PSPA is listed below. An interesting aspect in terms of landownership is the fact that Westminster City Council (WCC) owns two plots immediately adjacent to the PSPA (between Westway and the Basin) but has not included them in the PSPA, nor has it sought to actively develop them or use them as leverage. It has, however, used them as strategic assets in a proposed land swap that would make the development of St Mary's Hospital Campus possible.

PADDINGTON BASIN

British Waterways was the original owner of a 3.6 hectare site surrounding the canal. The site accommodated a variety of uses, predominantly warehousing and light industry, which began to decline after the 1960s. From then and until the mid-1990s there were two major changes in landownership, the first in 1978, when the land between the canal and South Wharf Road was compulsorily purchased to allow St Mary's Hospital to expand its facilities, and the second in 1988, when British Waterways entered into a joint venture with Trafalgar House and sold a 999-year leasehold to it in exchange for an obligation to develop the property, share the proceeds of the development and pay a fixed rent for several years. The recession in the property market at that time stalled most developments in the area.

In 1996, Trafalgar House was bought by a Swedish company, Kvaener, and later that year Chelsfield formed a joint venture with European Land to acquire the basin site and exploit the potential that the Heathrow Express project would generate. The joint venture, called Paddington Development Corporation Limited, bought out Trafalgar House's 999-year lease. The land surrounding the basin still had several occupiers, so Chelsfield and European Land had to buy out these leases as well and thus completely empty the site prior to redevelopment.

Immediately after buying the site in 1996, Chelsfield and European Land sold two acres of land along the south-eastern side of the basin to Rialto Homes and Frogmore Estates, and eventually European Land's 50 per cent stake in the remaining part was bought some time later in 2000 by Pearcroft. Pearcroft allowed Chelsfield to manage its investment in the Paddington development on its behalf.

In 1998 WCC passed a resolution to grant outline planning permission for a 140,000 m² development scheme valued at £1 billion. The development would be carried out in three phases, together with an associated development at nearby site: a residential scheme on the land purchased by Rialto and Frogmore; a 7,000 m² commercial scheme including around 4,600 m² of office space; and a mixed-use building at Hermitage Street. Chelsfield and European Land were prepared to speculatively build up to 3,000 m² of office space once a pre-let was secured.

In November 1999, a detailed planning application was submitted to WCC for the second phase of the Paddington Basin development. However, the development of Paddington Basin was delayed when European Land, encouraged by the sale of the neighbouring Paddington Goods Yard in autumn 1999, decided to put its 50 per cent share in Paddington Basin on the market for £50 million in May 2000.

In May 2001, whilst blocks B and C were being built, Marks & Spencer agreed to a 20-year lease for £9.1 million in annualised rent to occupy 22,800 m² in both blocks combined for its new headquarters. In addition to the lease, Marks & Spencer would pay an additional £20 million to fit out and move into the new building, called 'The Waterside'.

In 2002, Orange was told by its new owners, France Telecom, that it was not to move from its existing headquarters to 'The Point' (an office building in the second phase of the Paddington Basin development), as the cost of fitting out and relocating to the new building was too high; instead Orange was to sublet the building. Waterside was completed in May 2003 for £56 million and Marks & Spencer relocated its headquarters to the building in spring 2004.

In February 2004 Elliott Bernerd, the chairman of Chelsfield, executed a management buyout of Chelsfield and privatised the development company. Once private, Chelsfield adopted a strategy of selling its income-producing assets so to reduce its debt, and it put 'The Point' and 'The Waterside' up for sale. In October 2004 Chelsfield sold 'The Point' to WELPUT (West End of London Property Unit Trust) of Schroders. In autumn 2004, two Australian companies, Westfield and Multiplex, entered into a bidding war to take over Chelsfield. Eventually Westfield and Multiplex joined with the Reuben brothers to acquire Chelsfield for £2.1 billion including £585 million in equity and £1.5 billion in debt. Multiplex and Aldersgate entered into a joint venture and took over 50 per cent of Chelsfield, and Westfield took over the other 50 per cent. After dividing Chelsfield's assets with Westfield, Multiplex and Aldersgate were left with a combined 50 per cent interest in the Paddington Basin development (25 per cent each). Pearcroft, involved in Paddington Basin since 2000, had retained its 50 per cent share. The new partnership later decided to operate under the name of European Land and Property.

In May 2006 Multiplex sold its 25 per cent share in the Paddington Basin development to Aldersgate as part of a property portfolio worth £68 million, leaving the Reuben brothers and the Jarvis family each with a 50 per cent share.

PADDINGTON GOODS YARD

The Paddington Goods Yard was a 5 hectare site north of the railway tracks leading to Paddington Station. In 1968 the Paddington Goods Yard was closed and ownership was transferred to the National Freight Corporation (NFC). In 1999, after several failed attempts to develop the site, Regalian and NFC put the Paddington Goods Yard on the market, when it was bought by Development Securities, who eventually developed it into Kingdom Street and Sheldon Square with the backing of two institutional investors (Equitable Life and Norwich Union).

In November 2004 Aviva (formerly known as Norwich Union) was left as the sole institutional investor for Kingdom Street after buying out Equitable Life's share of the remainder of the Paddington Central development. Equitable Life had been experiencing financial difficulties since 2002 and was unable to fund any more projects. Equitable Life withdrew from Kingdom Street but remained a partner in Sheldon Square as the development was complete and producing rental income. It eventually sold its share in Sheldon Square to an American investment fund and is no longer involved in Paddington Central.

10–50 EASTBOURNE TERRACE

Land Securities became interested in the Paddington development in the late 1990s, with the completion of the Heathrow Express and the prospect of a new rail station as part of the planned Crossrail line. After failing to purchase Paddington Goods Yard, Land Securities remained interested in Paddington and instead acquired the first of five office buildings on Eastbourne Terrace, facing Paddington Station, at the south-west edge of the PSPA. Eventually, Land Securities purchased 10, 20, 30, 40 and 50 Eastbourne Terrace. Although these offices were built in the 1960s, the buildings' tenants offered Land Securities attractive rental yields and the buildings themselves presented refurbishment opportunities.

TELSTAR HOUSE AND 53–73 NORTH WHARF ROAD

Derwent acquired Telstar House, a 1960s office building, at Two Eastbourne Terrace. Although physically outside the PSPA, it was considered as part of the Paddington development. Telstar House had been fully let to Transport for London (TfL) and Derwent simply collected rent until summer 2003, when Telstar House burned down. On the completion of its rebuilding, Derwent sold Telstar House to Prudential, retaining no further interest in the building.

Within the Paddington development, Derwent acquired 55–73 North Wharf Road, a 8,500 m², 1960s office building in poor condition the immediate appeal of which was its good location and its redevelopment potential. The building was already fully let to a number of different occupiers until 2008–9 and generating a rental income stream. The onset of the credit crunch forced Derwent to abandon its plans when all the original leases expired in 2009. Instead, the occupiers' leases were extended to 2014 and the new development scheme will be reconsidered at that point.

THE TRIANGLE SITE

Railtrack owned the 'Triangle' site located between the railway tracks leading to Paddington Station and the Paddington Arm canal works. The land was surplus to the station's operational requirements, so Railtrack sold the 20,000 m² site to Hammerson in 2002 as part of a portfolio of 24 properties. However, the site is key to the redevelopment of Paddington Station and crucial in connecting it to both the Basin and the Goods Yard. Hammerson had plans to develop it but eventually the site was compulsorily purchased in 2008 for the needs of the Crossrail project. Hammerson will still be offered the right to first refusal for development of the airspace above the site once the Crossrail-related infra-structure has been completed.

Property and financial market conditions

Various plans have been put forward for the redevelopment of different sites in Paddington Waterside since the 1970s at least. All of these plans have eventually been shelved, due to a variety of factors, more often than not bad market timing or an unfavourable local planning authority. Even when development proposals were accepted and planning permission was granted, the difficulties and costs of tackling site complexities meant that the upswing in the market cycle was difficult to take advantage of.

The right ingredients came together in the mid-1990s. The market was just about to enter a growth phase, the arrival of the Heathrow Express boosted the development potential of the area and WCC had introduced a strategic frame-work. Indeed, in 1998 developers were confident that the market was in a boom phase, interest rates were falling steadily and demand for commercial and residen-tial space was growing rapidly. This market environment allowed developers to attempt to 'rebase the local property market' without losing the confidence of their financiers.

In the years that followed this bet paid off handsomely, as developers were able to let the new schemes for rents two to three times higher per m^2 compared to the norm in the local market prior to 1998. This was aptly described by a senior manager in a development company involved in one of the schemes:

> because you're starting from a very low base and there's the catching up to do, once people realise that this is as good as being in the West End the discount that they apply for being in Paddington rather than the West End will narrow, so you will see exceptional rate of growth (. . .) we were basing our appraisal on a very heavily discounted rent at a time when the prime rent in the core of the West End would have been £70 or more, we were basing our appraisal on £35 a foot here, which is 50 per cent discount. It doesn't deserve a 50 per cent discount but that reflected the fact that you had to persuade people to come here in the first place. In the end we were achieving rents of up to £45 because in the very short period of time between the time we started building and the time that they were there, somewhere to move into, literally a two-year period, people's perceptions of Paddington changed so much that they were actually prepared to pay a significantly higher price than we thought they would. They were competing with each other for space, they were seeing the quality of the occupiers that were coming along.

In 2007 the market turned once more, and in the years that followed demand for office space collapsed, whereas the devaluation of the pound inflated construction costs. Despite the physical undersupply of office space in the West End, the drastic reduction in demand for such space still makes developers and financiers very hesitant to initiate new projects. In 2010 the uncertainty of economic recovery was compounded by the political uncertainty of Coalition government and the spectre of massive public sector cuts. Although the cost of moving office was small compared to general operating costs for most companies, prospective tenants remained unwilling not only to commit to a lease but even to discuss specific office-space needs.

Although debt finance in general was severely curtailed by the credit crunch, Aviva and Development Securities were unaffected in Paddington Central, as Aviva had set aside funding for the development many years ago, in the late 1990s and early 2000s. However, having earlier decided to complete each Kingdom Street building in a partnership, Aviva faced the prospect of finding a partner amongst a smaller pool of investors asking for more stringent terms, thus making the investment more difficult to justify. Still, in 2009 and 2010 there was some investor demand for commercial property in prime locations. However, as a senior manager for a major developer involved in Paddington pointed out:

> although there is a reasonable appetite for commercial properties as an investment, because the stock market is so terrible, everyone is suffering in the same way in terms of raising bank finance.

During the financial crisis, Aviva and Development Securities faced more problems in finding tenants for their buildings in Paddington than in finding investors to finance their properties. In the words of a senior manager who had been involved in the project for several years:

> I think the bigger concern for us is on the demand side, which has affected every business that there is, not just in terms of finance . . . Particularly where they have leases coming to an end. They have to say "what do we do?" That is the thing we are probably feeling the most . . . Demand isn't strong . . . plenty of people have been coming to look at the building and say "we have a requirement this year, next year, whenever", but nobody has said "we want seriously to take x thousand square feet of your building, we want to talk terms with you" . . . that is the greater worry we have, rather than the financing side. Maybe that's because we're not out there looking for financing at this time and if we were we might be equally worried. Going away from Paddington, we have a number of other schemes that we can't finance.

The residential market took less of a hit and recovered relatively better. This means that during 2010 residential properties had a better risk/return profile, as compared to office and retail, and thus residential development could be financed more easily. European Land & Property decided to press on with more residential developments because they needed to sell only 20 to 30 per cent of the value of the residential development before a bank loan could be taken out. The hotel market was also relatively less affected by the downturn, mainly due to the devaluation of the pound and the expectations that the coming 2012 Olympic Games were creating in the tourism sector.

Policy environment

In the early 1980s WCC was reconsidering its policy for the Paddington area. Its rejection of a proposal for a mixed-use commercial and residential development at the nearby Paddington Goods Yard had been overturned by the Secretary of State, so WCC decided to allow other commercial developments in the Paddington area. This prompted British Waterways to study other uses for its land, including filling in the basin. In 1988 WCC introduced Special Policy Area status for an area in Paddington defined by the Westway to the north, Praed Street to the south-east and the railway tracks into Paddington Station to the south-west. In the centre of the PSPA lay the Paddington Canal Basin. The site was considered by WCC to be a strategic development site that offered excellent transportation links, a view with which the Government Office for London (GOL) agreed. More importantly, Paddington was a brownfield site offering room for development at the edge of some of the most expensive real estate in the world, in the West End and Mayfair.

The ensuing property downturn that depressed the market well into the 1990s gave WCC the opportunity to develop its policy framework further. WCC hoped to direct developers' attention to Paddington, which was close to the edge of the West End and still within the City of Westminster. With fewer constraints, developers would be able to construct large, modern buildings there to meet demand, and be able to use design and architecture more loosely in ways that would not have been permitted in the West End. WCC saw the PSPA as a safety valve that would relieve the pressure for commercial space in the West End, where development was constrained by a number of issues.

It wanted the development of Paddington to be flexible and to happen organically. Within the PSPA, WCC decided to deal with each development on its own merits but still be consistent with the PSPA framework. WCC argued that there were many different developments that were in competition with each other, therefore it was important that the planning framework should play a coordinating role.

Finally, local community views were also important in affecting the scheme, for example much of the concern about building height was the result of close consultations with Westminster residents. WCC were very conscious that the community in and around Paddington were wealthy, influential and vocal. It is a stable and consistently Conservative borough and the planning authority is considered to have well-defined sets of planning rules, policies and guidance. The implementation of these rules, policies and guidance is also consistent as its planning team has been in place for a long time and has low staff turnover.

Content

Project structure, form and design

Significantly, WCC did not create a masterplan for the PSPA because it did not want to become involved in a large public consultation, nor did it intend to finance any compulsory purchase to assemble land. There was opposition from private developers to the idea of the public sector's composing a masterplan, as it was seen as a potential source of conflict and delay. Later on however, the failure of several high-profile public sector development projects within the PSPA, including St Mary's Hospital, Paddington Station and North Westminster Community School, was attributed to the lack of a public sector masterplan. In any case, the lead developers commissioned masterplans for both Paddington Goods Yard and the Paddington Basin, in their attempt to formalise and advertise or communicate their plans about the future of the sites. However, when it came to applying for planning permission, developers often opted for solutions that would fit with their expectations as to future demand.

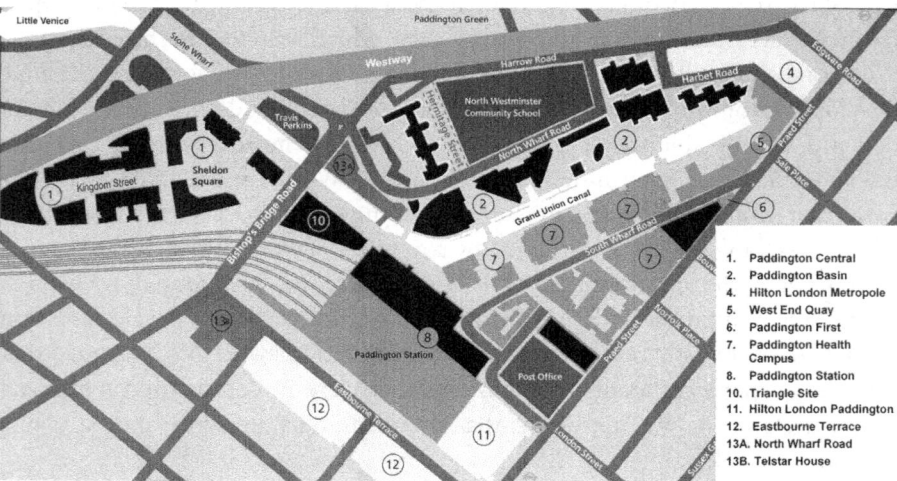

Figure 6.6 Plan of the Paddington regeneration scheme

Although Paddington was promoted as a place for modern buildings, WCC was strict regarding the quality of the public realm and adopted a PSPA Public Realm Strategy in 2003, in collaboration with Paddington Waterside Partnership (PWP). WCC was also relatively strict regarding building heights. Developers noted that Paddington was surrounded by several tall council tower blocks as well as the 91 m, 24-storey Hilton London Metropole hotel and convention centre within the PSPA itself, and submitted several schemes proposing buildings up to 42 storeys high to match Tower 42, the tallest building in the City of London. Instead, WCC preferred buildings to be 8 storeys high and a maximum of 10 to 12 storeys to match the height of the nearby 46 m, 11-storey Queen Elizabeth the Queen Mother building at St Mary's Hospital, also within the PSPA. Still, flexibility was a key parameter: after earlier tall buildings at Paddington were rejected or cancelled in 2007, WCC granted planning permission for a 132 m residential tower, the Blade, at Paddington Basin.

In 2010, 15 years after the development of Paddington had begun in earnest, the decision not to apply a masterplan to the whole estate but to rely on a policy framework was seen as a success by WCC, says a senior borough officer involved in the planning process:

> It's obviously not intent on our part other than I think we tried to construct a framework. We haven't been overly explicit about this because we don't need to be . . . I've always wanted it to be relatively robust because it takes a number of decades to do things as big as this . . . And that is going to be ensured not by how much money anyone's got but by how they value their money. Good people value their money over longer periods of time.
>
> The policies were part of it, and they were quite clear as to what we wanted. The major clients haven't had building briefs, they have had, however, a relatively consistent approach to all the planning applications and often they had relatively recent planning permissions, so there's a real benchmark there. Then it's easier to make sense of the scheme, so people have not had to invent things completely new each time . . . it works principally on the basis of one thing we have been very clear on: if you've recently argued a case in front of the planning committee and then you want to change it, you've got to go over those arguments again and prove to us that the same or better output is derived from the new design.

As a result of allowing many developers each to pursue their different schemes within the PSPA during a buoyant market, the physical transformation of the estate progressed relatively quickly towards completion. Although some social infrastructure, for example a school, was funded by central government, the key public sector project (the PPP for the new hospital) never materialised.

Use and tenure mix

The scheme is a bundle of projects that are in constant flux; in addition, a small number of projects lie outside the PSPA boundaries and will not be mentioned here. The onset of the credit crunch forced some developers to modify their plans, due to a combined lack of demand and difficulty in financing projects. By 2010, the Paddington estate was more than half developed in terms of commercial space: about 175,000 m² had been completed, with about 160,000 m² remaining in the pipeline. The evolution of the tenure and use mix of the main projects of the scheme is detailed below.

PADDINGTON BASIN

In 2000, as uncertainty surrounded the start of the second phase of Paddington Basin ('The Point', 'The Waterside' and Paddington Walk), work began on the first phase of the development owned by Rialto and Frogmore. As part of the initial planning application for all of the basin, Rialto and Frogmore had proposed to build 472 residential units. In May 2000 Frogmore sold its share in the development to Rialto (a developer focused on short-term speculative projects), which then formed a consortium called West End Quay to complete the development. In July 2000 West End Quay was granted conditional planning permission to build 468 units and 2,205 m² of retail space on the site. Construction began immediately and was completed in 2004 and was a financial success, although it took some time to find occupants for the retail part.

In July 2000 Chelsfield submitted another detailed planning application for the third phase of its Paddington Basin development, seeking approval for the Grand Union Building, a mixed-use building comprising three towers rising to a height of 164 m. Meanwhile, Chelsfield began construction of The Point (building A). In March 2001 work also began at Chelsfield's Hermitage Street site, called Paddington Walk. The approved plans were for a mostly residential development of four buildings offering 232 units, including 79 affordable units. There was also to be some retail and community space. Paddington Walk was completed in 2003 at a cost of £42 million.

As work on The Point, The Waterside and Paddington Walk progressed, Chelsfield applied for permission to build the Grand Union Building, which was approved in 2004 following several years of negotiations and modifications due to the concerns raised by the project's proposed height. The Point was completed in February 2003, but in 2004 work at the Paddington Basin came to a halt, due to the financial difficulties faced by Chelsfield. The uncertainty regarding Chelsfield's management further complicated development plans for the neighbouring St Mary's Hospital, where a land-swap deal between Chelsfield and the NHS had been reached. However, in April 2005 the UK government

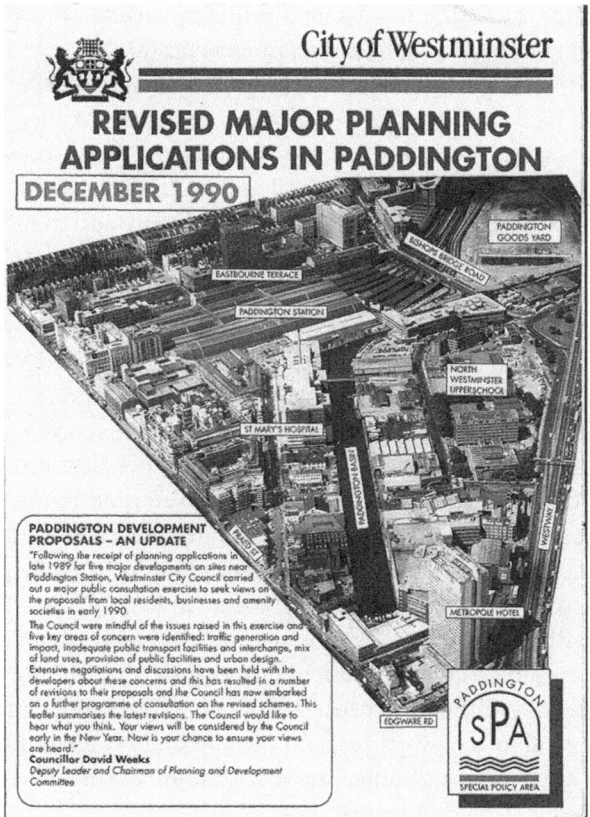

Figure 6.7 Paddington Basin in the 1990s (Westminster City Council. Used with permission)

cancelled the deal, due to its cost of £98 million, as well as opposition to the hospital closures, and so plans for the new hospital were abandoned.

In February 2006 European Land & Property officially abandoned plans for the Grand Union Building and prepared plans for a new, 168,000 m² mixed-use scheme, called Merchant Square, for the third phase of the Paddington Basin development. Merchant Square, valued at £800 million, comprised six buildings, A to F, of which three were to be office buildings offering 75,000 m² of space and three were to be primarily residential buildings (with some retail) offering 559 units, of which 30 per cent were to be affordable. Wishing to maintain the landmark height of the Grand Union Building, European Land & Property proposed a 132 m residential tower, Building A (The Blade), for Merchant Square. Also, the two buildings from the second phase of the Paddington Basin project that had not been started, the Windings, were incorporated into plans for

Merchant Square. WCC granted detailed planning permission for two buildings in Merchant Square, buildings D and E, in March 2007.

The residential property boom that preceded the credit crunch had raised house prices so high that by 2010, even when the credit crunch had depressed both office-space rents and house prices, residential property was worth more per square metre than office space. European Land & Property (the new vehicle that had replaced Chelsfield) decided to change its plan and build a residential building instead of an office building as its next scheme. This was a response both to the lack of available finance for office construction and to the fact that residential development could sell out much more quickly. An interesting side story to this was that European Land & Property had hedged its currency exposure, and thus it was not hit by the devaluation of the pound, although a lot of the construction materials that it buys are made in the eurozone.

In September 2007 European Land & Property began the speculative construction of the Carmine building, followed by Waterline House in November of the same year. After the completion of Waterline House and Carmine in 2010, detailed planning permission still was in place for four more buildings in Merchant Square – two office buildings, Topaz and Azure, and two residential buildings, The Blade and The Wave. At the time, no financing was available for an office building unless a large pre-let had been secured. However, securing a pre-let was generally difficult because the credit crunch prevented most businesses from moving into new offices, and this difficulty was compounded within Paddington by the amount of office space both immediately available and in the pipeline from competing developers.

Exercising the flexibility of being a privately held company, European Land & Property decided that it could not afford to wait for a pre-let and decided to change its plans and replace one office building with a residential building; the remaining development at Merchant Square would therefore comprise three residential buildings and one office building. In addition, plans for The Blade residential tower were altered to accommodate a boutique hotel. Had the credit crunch not struck, European Land & Property would have continued with another office building after completing Waterline House and Carmine.

European Land & Property expected to submit the new planning application in autumn 2010 and begin building its first residential building in summer 2011.

PADDINGTON GOODS YARD

In March 1999 Grainhurst submitted a scheme for the Paddington Goods Yard, called Bishopsbridge. Soon afterwards, in July 1999, WCC gave planning consent for 158,000 m² of office, retail and leisure space. Grainhurst intended to sell the site, as Regalian had been experiencing financial difficulties and its share in Paddington was its biggest asset. It was therefore eager to add value to the Paddington Goods Yard site by having planning permission in place. After securing planning permission, Grainhurst sold the site to Development Securities, the preferred bidder, in November 1999.

The Development Securities bid was funded by Norwich Union (now Aviva) (Morley Fund Management) and Equitable Life (Insight Investments), with each providing £100 million for the purchase and development of the site, of which they became the sole owners. The entire development scheme for the Paddington Goods Yard was to be called Paddington Central. The scheme comprised 177,000 m² of mixed-use space with a gross development value of £600 million and was considered to be the largest mixed-use development in Europe.

In summer and autumn 2000 Development Securities submitted a detailed planning application for the first of two development phases that were planned for the site. Phase A, to be called Sheldon Square, would offer a total of 58,500 m² of mixed-use space, including 18,000 m² and 13,500 m² office buildings, 9,000 m² of retail and leisure space and the two residential buildings with market and affordable housing (210 units of the latter).

When the office buildings were completed in early 2002 the economy was still suffering from the uncertainty that followed the 9/11 attacks in the United States. However, by spring 2002 the two buildings were mostly let; Visa occupied one building completely and the other building was let to several tenants, including Chiltern, Kingfisher, and Prudential. Rents were low because Paddington was still an untried location with few amenities, but still higher than Development Securities had expected when the site was purchased.

Development Securities completed the development at Two Kingdom St but stopped the development of the last two remaining buildings in phase two, while it continued to seek tenants for the remaining two-thirds of Two Kingdom St. However, Development Securities was able to modify its plan, and by making a small change in the locations of the as yet unbuilt buildings it was able to fit in a new hotel development, which received planning permission and was financed and built directly by the hotel franchise. This is characteristic of the flexibility mentioned previously, an outcome of the rapport that has developed between developers and the planning department and that allows the frictions that would otherwise emerge to be overcome.

The second phase of the Paddington Central development was called Kingdom Street and began in mid-2003 with the granting of planning permission for Two Kingdom Street, a mixed-use building with 45,500 m² of office space, 4,000 m² of studio and light industrial space and 550 m² of retail space. Several months later, in September 2003, planning permission was granted for One Kingdom Street, an office building with 33,000 m² of space.

Before any building works could be carried out Development Securities had to construct a 0.9 hectare, 8 m high steel and concrete deck under which Crossrail could lay temporary railway track to carry away soil and over which much of the development would be built. The deck cost more than had been taken into account by Development Securities when Aviva and Equitable Life bought the site. After London won its bid to host the Olympic Games in summer 2012 and as demand for hotel accommodation across central London surged, Development Securities was repeatedly approached to build a hotel in Paddington Central. After rebuffing initial requests, due to the lack of room at Kingdom Street, Development Securities eventually altered the development to include a hotel, whilst preserving the original amount of open space and office area to let. By combining buildings and moving buildings closer together, the architects were able to fit a new 206-room hotel to the development plans.

In April 2006 the revised plan for One Kingdom Street, with 32,500 m² of office space, was granted planning permission. In late 2006 Aviva and Development Securities decided to begin the development of One Kingdom Street without a pre-let. Market conditions were getting better and the developers were feeling less conservative; at the same time they wanted to get market timing right, so they had to be quick. Aviva would first finance and build the necessary infrastructure, and then offer investors the opportunity to buy into the project and partially fund the remaining construction. As the site would be fully serviced, Aviva hoped to sell a 50 per cent stake at a premium. Union Investment Real Estate, a German investment fund, bought into One Kingdom Street in April 2006. The nine-storey, 24,500 m² office building was completed in February 2008. Following this, Aviva completed several other substantial pre-lets and lets at rents much higher than expected.

Encouraged by the success of the Sheldon Square development, Aviva and Development Securities began Two Kingdom Street as One Kingdom Street neared completion. The revised building plan had been granted planning permission in August 2007. Two Kingdom Street was to be 13-storeys high, with 21,400 m² of office space and 2,000 m² of studio space.

In January 2008, Aviva decided to spread its risk and formed a 50 per cent joint venture with Quinlan Private (now Avestus Capital), an Irish equity group that was backed partly by private investors and by Anglo Irish Bank, to finance Two Kingdom Street. Quinlan was the first company involved in Paddington Central that was reliant on bank finance; previously, Development Securities had dealt with institutional investors. Thus, although Aviva's exposure was reduced as a result of the joint venture, the medium-term risk of financial problems for the project actually increased, due to the type of financing that Quinlan brought in. One year later, in May 2009, as the recession was intensifying, Development

Securities agreed a pre-let to Astra Zeneca for 4,650 m² of office space, later to rise to 7,000 m². After the Astra Zeneca let, no other tenant was found for the remaining two-thirds of the building, which was completed in early 2010. In 2010 there was speculation that Quinlan was suffering substantial losses from its investment in Two Kingdom Street, as the rental income could not cover payments for the loan that Quinlan had taken out to buy into the building.

In July 2010, One Sheldon Square, fully let to Visa, was put up for sale for £150 million by Aviva and its partners, Invista, Henderson Global Investors and Liquid Realty Partners, an American investment fund. Shortly afterwards, in August 2010, Union Investment Real Estate's 50 per cent share of One Kingdom Street was put up for sale for £118 million.

In Paddington Central, only Four and Five Kingdom Street have not been developed. Outline planning permission for the two buildings was granted in 2000, but the permission had to be repeatedly extended by WCC, due to the delays caused by the complexity of the site. Detailed planning permission was granted in mid-2010. The two office buildings will offer a total of 32,500 m² of space (Four Kingdom Street 13,000 m² and Five Kingdom Street 19,500 m²).

10–50 EASTBOURNE TERRACE

In March 2006 Land Securities completed the refurbishment of 40 Eastbourne Terrace to include 7,700 m² of office space. The refurbishment of 10 Eastbourne Terrace was completed in 2007 and offered 6,100 m² of office space. The refurbishment of 30 Eastbourne Terrace followed and was completed in summer 2009, offering 4,500 m² of office space. No work has started on the last phase, the refurbishment of 20 Eastbourne Terrace, due to deterioration of conditions in the office market.

In September 2009, 40 and 50 Eastbourne Terrace were sold for £50.5 million to an investor from the Far East; 40 Eastbourne Terrace had been fully let; 50 Eastbourne Terrace had been partially refurbished and contained 5,600 m² of office and retail space that was fully let to multiple occupiers for a total annual rent of £1.7 million.

TRIANGLE SITE

In partnership with Domaine Developments, a subsidiary of Ballymore, Hammerson was to develop a 15,000 m² office building on the Triangle site using a pre-existing planning permission that was part of an earlier development plan for Paddington Station. In March 2007, anticipating the proposed Crossrail development, Hammerson submitted a revised planning application for 20,000 m² of office and retail space to be built over a ramp allowing taxi access to Paddington Station from Bishop's Bridge Road. Hammerson then withdrew this planning application in June 2007. The Crossrail Act was passed in July 2008 and the Triangle site was compulsorily purchased by Crossrail from Hammerson to build a taxi ramp linking the station and Bishop's Bridge Road. Later, plans for the taxi ramp were combined with plans for a new Transport for London ticket hall on the Hammersmith & City line for the new Paddington Integrated Complex at the Triangle site. Crossrail planned to obtain planning permission for an office building above the complex and then to offer Hammerson the right of first refusal to develop the airspace when the complex was completed in 2014.

Enabling works for Crossrail started at Paddington in September 2009 and construction of the station, to be completed in 2016, is expected to cause major disruption in Eastbourne Terrace.

TELSTAR HOUSE AND 53–73 NORTH WHARF ROAD

Following a fire, Derwent decided to use the insurance payout to rebuild Telstar House speculatively. Planning permission was given to demolish the remnants of Telstar House and build a new, 10,000 m², eight-storey office building. After construction started, the new building was fully pre-let to Rio Tinto, in June 2006.

With the occupiers still in place, Derwent refurbished the North Wharf Road building and upwardly adjusted the rents. In June 2007, Derwent submitted a planning application to demolish the building and construct a mixed-use development comprising a 16-storey office building, 100 residential units measuring 9,300 m² in total and some retail space. Later, in January 2008, Derwent received planning permission to demolish North Wharf Road and develop one residential building with 102 units (16 affordable) and another 23,250 m² office building on the site. Derwent's original leases in Telstar House expired in 2009. Instead of the redevelopment plans going ahead, the occupiers' leases were extended to 2014, with the new development scheme to be reconsidered at that point.

Social facilities and non-market project components

Social facilities and non-market components were mainly provided under the section 106 agreement for each site and were linked to the award of planning permission; however, contrary to standard practice, a predetermined rate of contribution applied. Given the nature of the UK planning system (which favours discretion) this approach created much-needed certainty and was welcomed by developers. The allocation of planning obligation money had both a physical and a social aspect to it, the physical aspect mainly involving the provision of affordable housing, public access provision and public realm improvements, and the social aspect mainly involving job brokerage and contributions into a social community fund for the residents of Paddington and of neighbouring areas where the need was greater. This fund was also a rather innovative idea, for the UK at least, which worked well, and efforts were made to expand its use. According to a senior WCC officer:

> We have several different ones – there was a social and community fund which tried to agglomerate, draw together money from the developers based on needs assessments carried out some time ago which we then put in a fund which they could bid for. So that was straightforward. There were then funds for traffic and public transport issues and we applied for those . . . We have reviewed our policy and practice on section 106 across the whole of the city and based on the experience from Paddington to see where and if that applies city-wide. So in that respect Paddington has gone from being a bit of a one-off, something different from the norm, has become much more mainstream and we've so far – touch wood – not had any complaints.

Development Securities, for example, was subject to £14 million in section 106 planning obligations, mostly to do with public access to the goods yard and improvements to the public realm as well as an obligation to provide as affordable housing about one-third of the total number of dwellings produced during the first phase of Paddington Central.

Interestingly, in West End Quay (WEQ) the section 106 contribution came in the form of a monetary contribution to the community fund and public realm improvements. Affordable housing provision was not a compulsory policy requirement at the time, as it was to become a short while later, due to changes in national policy. According to one of the developers:

> The policy's the same, probably there is a slight shift of emphasis towards housing, relative to offices. They have come to the conclusion there's enough office accommodation there to satisfy the role for Paddington within the Westminster economy. If new sites are considered, e.g. the school site on North Wharf Road, they'll see that as being essentially a housing development. There is a greater emphasis on housing, whereas they were previously considered to be of equal standing. The policies towards affordable housing have got more demanding. The percentage that has to be affordable has increased. Apart from that, they still support the concept of it as an economic area. If our permission were to lapse through not being implemented for the last two buildings, we'd have to get a new permission and it would not be as favourable because of the new policies towards housing, and other things coming from the GLA [Greater London Authority].

Even so, the exception of WEQ from affordable housing provision is notable and can be explained if the role of this project in testing the market in the PSPA area and thus reducing uncertainty and valorising the rest of the programme is considered. WCC was reluctant to jeopardise the financial viability of the project, given the potentially large trade-off. Arguably, however, with the benefit of hindsight, an affordable housing requirement at WEQ would not have made the project unviable. It might have reduced the margins of the developer to a level that might not have been attractive, given the uncertainties surrounding the PSPA's market and development potential at the time.

Paddington First, established in 1999, soon after the formation of PWP, was a recruitment centre set up by PWP to help businesses at Paddington Waterside find qualified people from the Paddington area to fill their vacancies. By early 2009, almost 5,500 local residents had found jobs through Paddington Works, with most working at Marks & Spencer, St Mary's Hospital and Hilton Hotels. In April 2009 the European Social Fund allotted funding over two years for Paddington First.

The main vehicle for fulfilling PWP's commitment to become involved with the local area was 'Time for Paddington' (TfP). TfP developed strategies and policies to involve companies at Paddington in charitable activities within Paddington. Specifically, TfP arranged volunteer opportunities for individual employees working at Paddington Waterside, organised team challenges for companies to fundraise for local organisations and brokered the donation of companies' surplus equipment to local groups.

When PWP was first established, Paddington was neither desirable nor even known as a place for business. So, the first task for PWP was to promote Paddington Waterside. PWP generated media to publicise the site and regularly held guided walks and hosted study visits to physically familiarise people with the area. With the many different actors involved at the Paddington development, PWP became the first point of contact for people interested in the area.

In February 2005 PWP expanded the range of activities by forming the Paddington Business Improvement District (BID) to improve the local environment and the performance of local businesses within areas to the east, south and west of Paddington Waterside. In April 2009, in its second term, the Paddington BID covered 34 streets and 300 businesses. To fund its operations, PWP implemented a levy payable by those businesses with a rateable value of £15,000 or greater. One example of its activities included working with WCC to pave and relight Praed Street.

In addition, PWP offered programmes that allowed companies in Paddington to fulfil their corporate social responsibilities, such as using Paddington First to employ local residents. PWP received funding from the section 106 obligations that the companies had negotiated with WCC. Under contract from WCC, in January 2007 PWP established the Westminster Works for Business programme

Figure 6.8 Paddington Goods Yard: Sheldon Square in 2010

to work with companies to increase the employability of local residents. In addition to teaching job-hunting skills, Westminster Works for Business organised work placements, job trials, work tasters and employability days for participants with businesses at Paddington Waterside.

In 2010 the Paddington estate was halfway developed, but PWP had spent more than two-thirds of its section 106 funds and did not expect to receive any more. Before Crossrail, PWP had focused on creating an enjoyable canalside environment at Paddington. Building on its experience with Crossrail, from 2010 onwards, PWP hoped to begin offering public realm management services.

So far as public realm improvements in particular are concerned, the PWP and the WCC both recognised the benefits of a coherently organised and high-quality network of streets and public spaces and have worked collaboratively to establish a framework for its provision, design and management. This framework, the PSPA Public Realm Strategy, was published in 2003 as a WCC Supplementary Policy Guidance and is coordinated with the section 106 provision.

Organisation

Governance arrangements and partnership members
Several platforms, official and unofficial, at both programme and project level, were established and used in order to negotiate and mediate the wide range of

interests involved. Two state actors, the local authority (WCC) and the GOL, played an important role in shaping the wider network of actors and in coordinating the development process. This was, however, less due to some institutionalised organisational imperative and more due to the personal commitment of two key senior figures, one in each organisation, who wished to exercise their authority in that direction and steered the resources of the two state actors accordingly. Clearly, however, if the wider policy context had not been one favouring their approach, then their efforts would have stalled very quickly. That having been said, WCC owns two sites adjacent to the PSPA area that are on course to be redeveloped but it was unknown whether it would join PWP even after the developments received planning permission.

Influenced by the pressure of the state actors, the developers working at Paddington formed the Paddington Regeneration Partnership (PRP) in 1998 as a forum to facilitate communication between developers at the site, between the developers and other organisations and to help with coordinating the many different development schemes at Paddington. Although it started off at a time when partnering was still a novel idea in UK regeneration practice, its benefits soon became apparent. Later known as the PWP, the PRP comprised eight members, all landowners and developers. Its membership grew with time, and by 2010 the members of the PWP had grown to 18 and included both developers and occupiers.

The example of Land Securities is typical of the approach taken by several developers. Initially, Land Securities had no desire to be a member of PRP; one reason why it purchased the Eastbourne Terrace properties was that they were outside the PSPA and Land Securities believed that it would be easier to develop the buildings on its own. However, Land Securities joined PWP when it realised that it was better to work together with other developers in Paddington to present a common voice to WCC, and later to Crossrail.

Communication was vital within Paddington – on occasion up to 14 different development schemes were planned or were being carried out in parallel. During construction, most developers' sites had to be accessed through other developers' sites, and after construction, workers at each development would have to move through other developments in order to go to and from their jobs. So, PWP was necessary from a practical point of view in order to coordinate access.

Aside from facilitating access, PWP served as a means to keep developers informed of each other's schemes, allowing them the opportunity to see what was being planned or changed and to measure how their own developments would be affected. By providing a private forum, PWP served to protect the Paddington development from negative publicity by minimising objections and conflicts between developers and keeping them out of the public sphere.

Although the developers were competitors, the attitude was taken that they were not enemies, and that by working together within the partnership, they would have a collective voice that was greater than that of any one developer speaking for itself. This was particularly important with respect to dealings between PWP and public bodies such as WCC and Crossrail. PWP ensured that the developers would present a unified and consistent view to planning policy makers in WCC and in the GLA.

When occupants first started to move into Paddington, PWP was split into two forums: the developer forum and the occupant forum. When asked to comment on the success of that approach, a PWP officer said:

> I think some of the connections between the developers and the commercial occupants we tried to force. So we tried to bring commercial occupiers together with developers every six months for a joint meeting and they didn't share the same agenda. We tried to create a shared agenda for them and it didn't work, we tried to have an occupier forum and it didn't work. I think we have two sides to the Partnership, two halves, not opposing, but they have different demands and consume absolutely different services. We have to face both ways, we have to serve the developer needs and serve the commercial occupier needs.

As development activity decreased, the workings of the Partnership became increasingly geared towards the needs of the occupiers, but until the site was fully built out PWP still had to serve both the developers' needs and the occupiers' needs. In addition to mandatory section 106 commitments, developers and occupiers in Paddington made voluntary contributions to PWP through subscriptions. Subscription rates for developers were determined by the scale of their developments, whilst the rates for occupiers were based on the number of their employees and the amount of floor-space occupied. Asked about changes in membership, a PWP officer said:

> In terms of membership that we've lost, Land Securities left . . . they've stopped their refurbishment programme, which is what motivated them to join. When they stopped that they said "we have no further role here". Now they've come back in and I think the reason why is because of another big role of the partnership, which is the impact of Crossrail works on Paddington. Effectively, now the partnership has become a major communicator with Crossrail on behalf of developer partners. We all have our own separate communication as well, but in terms of coordination that's become very important and Land Securities are badly affected by the works in Eastbourne Terrace for Crossrail, so that's the developer side.

The new Crossrail station at Paddington was to be built beneath Eastbourne Terrace. Initially the plan was to partly close it, but when the works began in

2010 Crossrail demanded the full closure of Eastbourne Terrace. This closure was greatly opposed by local businesses and transport operators, as Eastbourne Terrace was one of the key routes in and out of Paddington for vehicles. For developers Derwent London and Land Securities, both members of PWP, such a closure would have meant cutting off road traffic to their office developments. Developers used the PWP forum to directly express their concerns to Crossrail with a common voice.

The impact of Crossrail was not limited to traffic; pedestrian movement and the pedestrian experience within the Paddington estate were also affected, so PWP put up signage to manage the flow of people. As Paddington was to become an even busier building site for the next ten years, developers wanted to ensure that their tenants would be able to navigate through Paddington Waterside.

When Crossrail first started its operations in Paddington its approach was simply to transmit information to local businesses and residents using generic publicity. PWP forced Crossrail to enter into a direct dialogue with those affected by Crossrail construction. Construction was expected to take place between 2009 and 2017 and severely affect people's ability to move through the Paddington estate.

Risks and uncertainties

The effects of a potential market downturn and the likelihood of a downturn's taking place during the lifetime of the programme were well understood by WCC and most private partners. Obviously, whether all of the actors were able to forecast the time the downturn correctly and to take the appropriate measures is a different matter.

So far as WCC was concerned, the decision not to have a masterplan allowed for more flexibility, thereby giving developers a chance to respond more quickly to changes in the market environment, and for proposals to be turned into projects much more efficiently. WCC's decision not to engage as a landowner and land developer (in spite of its ownership of two sites) but to keep strictly within its role of planning authority is also noteworthy.

Arguably, any attempt to develop Paddington through a sole developer (as was the case in previous attempts) would have added several years to the time of the development, whereas multiple ownership combined with multiple developers meant that the market uncertainties associated with developing the entire estate were more effectively tackled. It would have been very difficult for one developer to construct so many buildings in one place at the same time.

In most projects in Paddington Waterside the developers are backed by investors and financiers with whom they have long-term, well-established relationships. The significance of having those relationships in place cannot be underestimated within the context of the volatile and competitive West End property market. It allows for rapport to be built between stakeholders, which in turn minimises the uncertainties surrounding each other's behaviour. Development Securities and its investor scheme currently count more than ten years of continuous involvement on the site. It has been more than 15 years since Elliot Bernerd and the German financiers first started investing in the Basin projects (originally through Chelsfield). The role of WCC in selecting development partners with a longer-term investment horizon was also crucial, as it assisted in stabilising the system of actors engaging with the project.

A key strategic decision aimed at alleviating market uncertainty regarding the PSPA's potential was the sale of the 8,000 m^2 site to Frogmore & Rialto to build WEQ. It was important for this project to be developed in order to signal to other market participants that the location had development potential that would be realised, essentially proving the PSPA concept and testing the nature and strength of demand for the location and the wider regeneration scheme. It is worth noting here that WCC was acutely aware of the significance of WEQ and thus was willing to commute any planning obligations for the project in order to get it built as soon as possible.

Within this context and in order to tackle the risks surrounding market conditions and construction itself, the developers employed a series of techniques, some of which have already been encountered in other case studies (pre-let, phasing, partnering) and some novel ones (currency hedging). The strategy of pre-letting was employed on several occasions as a means to minimise the risk that speculatively built developments would remain vacant. In some cases, however, as in Paddington Basin, it was the nature of the joint venture itself that caused developers to opt for pre-letting developments. The joint venture between European Land and Chelsfield was relatively fragile and European Land was looking for people to whom to sell its share. Adding pre-lets to the joint venture portfolio instead of speculatively built projects made it more marketable.

For developers and investors involved in residential development, strong demand for residential property in central London was combined with a very limited supply. After WEQ proved the potential of Paddington, their perceptions changed to an assumption that whatever was built to a certain standard would sell. Debt finance was based on the assumption that for every 100 apartments sold, at least 80 would complete contractually with no problems, so the risk of being unable to service debt taken on for residential development was small.

Office buildings were not seen as having the same qualities – space was either let or not let, and rent was paid or not paid – and in the context of the credit crunch were considered riskier than residential development. A building that had been pre-let to a large organisation and then built to meet its requirements using debt finance was exposed to the risk of the organisation's going bankrupt.

Some developers used different arrangements at different phases of construction in order to manage development risks. For example, European Land & Property began Waterline House using its own funds to excavate and build the basement up to the ground floor. In that time, it achieved a sufficient number of pre-sales to be able to arrange bank loans to finance 100 per cent of the cost of completing the building. This model enabled the developer to reduce the risk for its lenders in several ways: as the basement was already completed, the banks were not exposed to the risk of encountering unexpected and costly ground conditions at the building site; as the basement was already paid for, European Land & Property had equity in Waterline House to leverage the loans; and, as a number of apartments were already sold, the banks faced both a lower exposure and a lower risk in that exposure.

In this context, where the mix of uses and tenures was of paramount importance as a technique to manage market uncertainty, the flexibility of the planning regime proved to be crucial, particularly with respect to the mix of uses. During the 2008 financial crisis residential property values did not fall as much as commercial property values and residential property sales created immediate returns on property investments, a trend that European Land exploited to a larger extent than did Development Securities.

This flexibility, however, may have helped to tackle market uncertainties, but it amplified risks relating to the management of construction itself and to the interaction between projects and actors. In terms of the latter, as developers changed the content and timing of their projects to reflect their anticipation of demand it was inevitable that neighbouring projects, if not the whole scheme, would be affected. Thus the role of the PWP as a mechanism for coordination increased in significance because it was a very effective platform through which the effects on the whole scheme caused by changes in its components could be tackled. This became apparent when the Crossrail project eventually materialised. In the words of one developer:

> Crossrail is the classic, where we can get together and say "This isn't just about what would be comfortable". What's essential for us is that potential occupiers here should not say "We're not coming to Paddington, because it's going to be chaos! How can we be sure that we can walk from the station? Are we going to have to walk around the block? Are we going to have to climb over footbridges? What's the noise going to be like?" So we can go to Crossrail, and say "We all have a problem with this. It's going to affect demand, it's going to affect our occupiers, it's going to affect rent values, so we need you to address that."

This brings us to the major issue of infrastructure provision. The development potential of the site was boosted after Heathrow Express was built. However, the

Goods Yard required road access that only the reconstruction of Bishop's Bridge could offer, and the whole area's future could change dramatically depending on whether Crossrail, as well as National Rail's plans to electrify the railway line, would materialise. The rejection and resubmission of numerous infrastructure proposals generated uncertainty for developers, who did not know what infrastructure would be in place and when. As a result, developers' plans were threatened by the possibility of being subject to compulsory purchase orders to accommodate a Crossrail station, as well as the possibility of being substantially revised to facilitate access to the station. In the words of a senior Development Securities manager:

> we had an issue with Crossrail. We didn't know whether we would have to build the deck. Because at that time there was no government commitment to Crossrail, so we had some financial provision for that, but it was a big risk factor, and it costs us more than we had predicted, but that was part of normal commercial risk. That could have been a problem for us if it had not been possible to reach agreement with Crossrail on the deck, as to what we would have done about it. Fortunately that strategy worked out OK. Apart from timing, it's pretty much what we had anticipated.

Development Securities attached a premium to its development at Paddington in order to account for this risk and had to spend an extra £30 million in infrastructure to allow for the rail works to take place in case Crossrail was approved. Clearly, notwithstanding the buoyant market conditions at the time, not every property developer would have been equally prepared to go down that route. In this instance it was the private developer who took the long-term view and reduced the uncertainty surrounding the scheme, whereas central government's lack of clarity and indecisiveness increased uncertainty. In that sense, the innovative approach that WCC took towards securing planning obligations also reduced uncertainty and assisted developers in taking on such risks.

This lack of commitment and long-term strategic support on behalf of central government is also highlighted by the case of the Paddington Health Campus. This project was and still is key to increasing the permeability of the Basin and the quality of its public and private realm, thus boosting the Paddington Waterside development potential, its liveability and its integration into the urban fabric. Even though opinions vary as to what went wrong, it seems that the WCC and private developers were keen to make some progress; WCC used its land as part of a land swap in order to facilitate the project. The National Audit Office (NAO, 2006, p. 24) reports on the concerns of the Department of Health on that deal:

the Department considered that the proposed land deal was unacceptable because it meant the land purchase would appear on its balance sheet, and so would count against its annual spending limit for capital projects, which it could not accommodate. The Department also considered the £62.5 million premium over open market value that would be paid to Paddington Development Corporation Limited excessive, although the District Valuer confirmed that, in his view, the land transaction represented fair value.

In the same report (p. 4) the NAO highlights three key reasons for the collapse of that project:

the sheer number and scale of risks and lack of a single sponsor; the way in which the Campus partners organised and carried through the scheme, including the failure to secure adequate land for the scheme; and the lack of active strategic support for the Campus vision.

It emerges from the report that, given the level of centralisation in the public health sector, so far as the project is concerned, central government needed to assume a different role and to have different priorities than those that it had, if it was to act in a stabilising manner.

Conclusions

The two cases represent two entirely different approaches to regeneration so far as the role of the actors and the risk/return allocation between them are concerned. On the one hand, in Paddington, the state (or the local authority more specifically) engaged in regeneration by setting the basic rules of the game within which private developers operated. Similarly to France and the Netherlands, the local authority played an important role in coordinating actors, using its urban planning competence in order to frame the development and incentivise and guide developers. It is noteworthy, for example, that no masterplan was implemented for the area, due to a preference for increased flexibility. Planning also plays an additional role in the case of Westminster: it restricts the locations to which the extremely strong demand for space in the West End can be channelled (another example of this is the Vinex locations in the Netherlands). Under the UK system, which emphasises discretion, this use of planning is, in practice, limited to zones such as conservation areas, of which Westminster has a great abundance.

The biggest parts of the site were once owned by the public sector (for example, British Rail) but were sold off several years ago, and those still owned by a public body (like British Waterways) were rapidly leased out on a long-term lease. The exception was two WCC sites that were used strategically in the land swap for the Health Campus, although WCC never sought to become actively engaged with the land development aspects by using its ownership as leverage (as it could have done if it had participated in PWP). This is a low-risk route to take in relation to public assets and landownership and has the advantage that it generates quick returns. Land assembly and preparation was left to the private sector, and thus the local authority relied exclusively on extracting value through mechanisms that apply at later stages of the development process, during or after the allocation of development rights (i.e. section 106). It has to be mentioned here that in the UK the allocation of development rights comes much later in the development process than in either France or the Netherlands. The amounts that were extracted were mainly in the form of affordable housing, public facilities and infrastructure locally, with some resources channelled into social projects that in many cases would benefit people located away from the area, in other parts of the local authority.

Key infrastructure was mainly funded by the private sector as well, and was key in lifting the area up as a whole (e.g. the Heathrow Express) or in unlocking specific sites (e.g. Bishop's Bridge). Similarly, the public realm was regulated by the local authority via planning instruments, but it was paid for by the private sector. This is an indication of the strength of the local market in the first instance, but also of the reluctance of the local authority to become involved in land development even at the stage of land or site preparation.

Given that the public sector did not get involved in functions related to development per se even when it owned the land, its main leverage in the negotiations with developers, when it came to merit and public goods provision was the lack of alternatives for developers, due to the scarcity of suitable land elsewhere and the statutory requirement for planning obligations that is imposed in developers. In booming markets like London, these conditions may be enough to ensure the provision of merit and public goods, albeit with an inflationary effect as the related costs are passed on to property prices. It is noteworthy that the model itself is predicated on rising property prices and is inflating them at the same time.

The policies of the local authority and its long-term commitment (as well as GOL commitment early on) were crucial in reassuring investors and developers about the future of the area. It was important in that sense that WCC's planning department could offer stable leadership throughout the duration of the project. It was the conscious choice of WCC planners to reject offers made by developers and investors aiming at short-term gains and to focus on attracting private actors who were happy to take the long-term view, such as pension funds etc. Thus, although several private actors joined and left the PWP, there was always a core of key players taking the project forward. This long-term perspective, together with the relations of trust between actors, which in some cases predated the scheme and in other cases were fostered by it, was an informal but effective mechanism that acted counter-cyclically and ensured that momentum was not lost, regardless of the situation in the property markets.

In that sense, the role of PWP was crucial in creating a flexible platform that served a variety of purposes, from conflict resolution between developers to effective lobbying on their behalf. The single most detrimental influence on the project was that of central government, whose inability to organise the Paddington Health Campus project and whose protracted dealings regarding Crossrail (which was very nearly cancelled) posed a major threat to the marketability of the project. This role of central government as a destabilising factor that creates uncertainty by focusing on taking items off its balance sheet is in stark contrast to both France and the Netherlands, where central or regional government involvement (mainly through the funding regime, major infrastructure provision and strategic guidance and support) is meant to enhance both short-term and long-term certainty.

New Islington, on the other hand, is a demonstration project aiming, amongst other things, to build up the development capacity of the public sector, thus offering a development approach where public, private and third sector roles are rebalanced. The public sector actors had a rather drastic ambition to physically erase the past and start with a clean slate. The main governance mechanism of the project was a partnership between public and private actors but the state also played an important role in the project via central government agencies such as EP and its successor, the HCA. EP prepared the land and provided the necessary infrastructure and public realm investment in order to boost the attractiveness of the site, whereas the HCA provided much of the funding in support of the scheme and of the housing associations that were to play an important role in rehousing social tenants and in initiating the whole scheme. The cost of that investment was to be recovered through land sales to developers. The NWDA also pledged to provide stop-gap funding after the downturn began.

Regional and local authorities assumed a coordinating role in setting the policy and planning framework through NEM, as well as through the provision of infrastructure. However, the responsibility of dealing with a lot of the uncertainties surrounding the organisation of the development process was passed on to the private sector when Urban Splash was chosen to coordinate the delivery of the development. This decision was based on the assumption that the private sector is more capable than the public sector in dealing with the risks and uncertainties of delivering a development project.

By retreating from this key role, the public sector tied the delivery of merit and public goods (and of the development itself) to the future of an otherwise very reputable private company with big exposure to the property market and thus quite vulnerable to downturns. In both cases the institutional framework that was created to support the development allowed key players to develop strong relationships that could endure the passage of time. This 'institutional thickness' ensured that the projects continued even when important partners left or when the market conditions deteriorated. In the case of Paddington, it was the long-term focus of the local authority (especially of few key people working there) and the personal commitment of a senior GOL civil servant that infused some stability into the constellation of actors involved. In Manchester it was a combination of the local and the regional authorities and government agencies who played that role.

In spite of the funding commitments of central government organisations, funding remained problematic. Although investment in infrastructure and the public realm was a key element of the strategy adopted by the two central government agencies involved, it was not possible to secure funding for a new primary school. Central government hesitated in funding the Metrolink and therefore missed an opportunity to reinforce the positive dynamic created by the launch of the regeneration initiative at a time when the property market was doing relatively well. Providing site infrastructure and public realm investment emerged as a key strategy for maintaining the momentum of the project following the credit crunch, but the scheme did not receive any funding under the two rounds of 'Kickstart' emergency grants. This may well prove detrimental to its future, although the indirect benefit of 'Kickstart' is that it gives some breathing space to Urban Splash, since 'Kickstart' is funding a couple of other projects that Urban Splash is also developing.

The uncertainty over central government funding in Manchester was compounded by the uncertainty over private funding either in the form of bank loans to developers or in the form of mortgages to the end consumer. Even so, short-term wholesale institutional investors were viewed as a mixed blessing, posing a threat to the success of the project. Their attitude is perceived as the cause of poor estate management, under-occupation of the properties or quick turnovers, and eventually may shift the tenure mix towards social security claimants. An institution like the CDC in France, the BNG in the Netherlands or a revolving fund that could provide counter-cyclical funding might have proved to be very useful under these circumstances.

In both projects, the mix of uses, tenures, functions and phases, as well as off-plan sales and partnerships, was used effectively in both cases in order to manage market and construction risks. Substantial demonstration projects (WEQ, 'Chips', social housing) were utilised in order to reduce market uncertainty and create a positive dynamic about the areas targeted by the regeneration initiatives. However, no compensating strategy of that sort is able to tackle the lack of commercially available funds in projects that rely on them for the majority of their funding needs.

In New Islington, the alternative of giving a more prominent role to housing associations and of promoting tenures other than homeownership was pursued only to a limited extent, due to concerns about the future tenure composition of the site. Such concerns did not exist in Paddington, where, due to the depth of the London market, WCC was willing to allow changes in uses and tenures that better reflected the developers' perception of market conditions. Clearly, in terms of the physical attributes of the scheme, these rather flexible approaches create the preconditions for an evolving composition of the mix of uses, incomes, tenures etc. in both schemes. Given the situation in the property markets and the lack of state funding it may become very difficult for the strategic aims in New Islington to remain unaffected. Such concerns are less pronounced in Paddington, mainly due to the very nature of the planning approach followed there, which was less prescriptive to begin with.

Notes

1 This section was written in collaboration with Michael Manlangit.
2 This section was written in collaboration with Michael Manlangit.

Chapter 7
Conclusions

Public and private sector roles in urban regeneration

Property development can be viewed as the art and science of transforming space in the face of risk and uncertainty in order to match demand with supply in what is hoped to be the right place and, with some luck, at the right time. Seen this way, urban regeneration as it has been practised in Western Europe since the early 1990s at least, could also be seen as a process of spatial transformation with property development as a key factor in promoting economic growth but with a social welfare agenda underpinning it. The objectives of that agenda are usually achieved both by regulation and by negotiation.

In the preceding chapters we looked into three relatively different urban policy and regeneration regimes that apply in three Western European countries. Notwithstanding their other similarities and differences, the welfare regime in each country has been influenced by three rather different traditions – liberal in the UK, more corporatist in France and a rather social democratic one in the Netherlands (Arbaci, 2007; Esping-Andersen, 1990). By looking in detail at six regeneration schemes, we examined how private and public interests were combined and how outputs were delivered in each scheme, within each country's and locality's market and policy context. Of key interest was to explore how private and public actors devised and deployed strategies to deal with the risks and uncertainties to which they were exposed and how this in turn influenced the outcome of the regeneration projects in question, especially as regards the ability of those projects to fulfil policy objectives related to planning (like mixity etc.) and the provision of merit as well as public goods.

In dealing with MUURSs, one can distinguish three levels at which risk and uncertainty can be analysed: the systemic-contextual level, the scheme level and the project level. Similarly, the returns that any partner can expect should (in theory at least) reflect the level of risk that they are assuming. The six different case studies demonstrate that it is possible, generically speaking, for actors with a social mission to assume market risks (as do the housing associations in the Netherlands) and that it is also possible for private sector actors to take a long-term view (as Development Securities in Paddington, for example), even if this means that they risk suffering a short-term loss. This is not to say, however, that any actor is ideally placed for any role: the wider institutional and cultural context and the strategic orientation, capacities and competencies that actors have developed prior to engaging with any specific scheme or project will affect their willingness and suitability to deal with specific aspects of risk and uncertainty relating to urban regeneration schemes. Thus, of paramount importance is the capacity to manage 'perceived' and 'virtual' risks, which is affected by pre-existing mental schemata.

Our research framework was based on the premise that public, private and third sector actors become involved in regeneration schemes each with their own goals to pursue and their own strategies and competencies to help them achieve those goals. There may be elements of competition between them, but there is cooperation as well. It would be nearly impossible for a production process to operate without some level of cooperation between actors. Apart from anything else, the uncertainties and the costs for any actor approaching MUURSs through a non-cooperative strategy are too great to take on in the specific historical period that we are living in.

Crucially, it is the level of control over the property value chain that each actor has that affects their ability to generate and capture value as part of this process. This control is not exclusively to do with the ownership of property rights or with regulatory requirements, although in many ways it is expressed through those regimes. From a substantive point of view, the level of control that each actor exerts on the value chain is inextricably linked to the capacity of that actor to tackle the expected risks and uncertainties that this control brings with it, taking into consideration the anticipated returns.

The problem is that uncertainty, by its very nature, is impossible to estimate, most notably when it comes to Donald Rumsfeld's 'unknown unknowns'. Returns are equally hard to fully monetise when it comes to the production of the built environment, which is a mix of public, merit and private goods in a context of positive and negative externalities, the present and future size of which it is also impossible to entirely quantify. Thus situations where actors assume risks and uncertainties that do not result in subsequent higher returns or, even worse, situations where one actor or set of actors tackle most risks and uncertainties but another actor or set of actors get most of the returns are not uncommon and have been the cause of much of the critique launched at PFI schemes (NAO, 2011; Siddiquee, 2011).

The process of value generation, its monetisation and its capture in urban regeneration schemes is often viewed as a dichotomy, whereby private sector actors generate and monetise this value whereas the public sector tries to extract as much of that value as possible in order to achieve social policy objectives. Our research reaffirms that the processes taking place are much more complex and symbiotic than this rather polarised representation.

In the case of the built environment, the production of private goods is intertwined with the production of merit and public goods (such as parks and amenities, social infrastructure, non-market housing etc.). In fact, public goods provision by the state is actively used in all case studies as a means to further increase both the development potential and the value generated in a development, reflecting the point made by McGreal *et al.* (2000, p. 129), who claim that the "perception of the quality of the neighbouring environment is shown to be a major factor deterring investment". Indeed, up to a point, the provision of merit and public goods causes positive externalities that are captured to an extent in the pricing of private goods but also generate unmonetisable positive effects (from better health and higher productivity to the increase in the local tax base). Equally, excessive provision of merit and public or private goods can give rise to negative externalities and detrimentally affect the desirability and the financial viability of a scheme (see the critique that has been launched at New Islington).

It is, however, almost impossible to come up with a precise formula as to what proportions between the two lead to some sort of maximum benefit or ideal living environment. Thus, it is also extremely hard for the partners in public–private collaborations to estimate in advance their desired risk exposure and the expected returns that come with that exposure. That is not only because of the difficulty in fully monetising positive and negative externalities but also because the desirability and functionality of any form of built environment is culturally constructed to a large extent, and thus bound to change within the lifetime of a MUURS. The relationship between actors is therefore an exercise in contingency planning within a dynamically evolving process (see Doak and Karadimitriou, 2007). The first paragraph of this chapter referred to property development as an art and science: hopefully it is now clearer why we hold that view.

So far as the roles of actors are concerned, the state (due to its size and remit) appears to have an unparalleled capacity to affect the development potential of any given site, mainly through infrastructure provision, land assembly and actor coordination and by alleviating, through policy means, uncertainty about the site's future. It is characteristic that the approach of the British government so far as Crossrail, the Paddington Health Campus and the Metrolink were concerned was a major source of uncertainty in Paddington and in New Islington.

In all MUURSs that we looked into there was a clear need to involve actors at the systemic, scheme and project levels who would play this stabilising role. The ability to play that role depends on the strategies, values and remit of any actor and on the actor's capacity to absorb short-term and/or long-term monetary losses that may or may not eventually materialise. As it became evident following the onset of the financial crisis, the state is rather better suited to such a role, effectively reminding us of the Weberian justifications of the state as a means of reducing uncertainty through rational organisation. Not only does the state have the capacity to mobilise vast financial and other resources (which occasionally allow it to bail out several banks at once), but it also has the ability eventually to monetise its debt (not necessarily recommended or desirable as a policy, but widely implemented as of late).

That capacity to reduce uncertainty, however, is not purely down to financial resources but is also political, an aspect that became evident during the lifetime of the UDCs but that is also evident if one considers the social and economic implications of debt monetisation (inflation, wealth redistribution etc.). To put it another way, several private developers in all three countries were comfortable with taking a long-term view and with tackling risks and uncertainties so long as they could put a price on their potential exposure. Development Securities' approach to the Crossrail platform is a good example of how size, perspective and that type of financial backing can allow a private actor to tackle an uncertainty with a defined net cost (£30 million). It would be extremely difficult for a sound-minded developer to tackle uncertainties with undefined costs unless, to put it crudely, it had the capacity to impose taxes and print its own money. Urban regeneration, however, is full of situations in which uncertainties with undefined costs and benefits have to be tackled. Therefore, from an investor's point of view, "risk reduction measures are considered to be of fundamental importance. Principal mechanisms comprise grant aid, provision of tax breaks, pre-lets, forward funding, rental guarantees, simplified land assembly and basic infra-structure provision" (McGreal *et al.*, 2000, p. 129).

By the same token, private sector and third sector actors can be particularly apt in converting development potential into monetised value by producing dwellings, offices etc. that satisfy short- to medium-term market demand. One can imagine that a public sector entity could also play that role, but then they would also have to adopt the values, goals and strategies of their private sector competitors. 'Hybrid' organisations like the Dutch housing associations are called on to play that role, although even they eventually had to pool their expertise with private sector developers. The French *sociétés d'economie mixte* SEMs or the Dutch municipal land-development bodies (like the OBR) are interesting in that respect because they operate as private sector entities but have a social mission, and on occasion they are owned by the state. What these examples demonstrate is that there are limits imposed by the scope of an organ-isation and that there are certain advantages to specialisation.

By bringing a wider array of actors together, partnerships should in theory be able to pool their resources and specialisations and thus be able to tackle more complex tasks and a wider range of risks and uncertainties. With that in mind, the pressure that the European Union and national governments put on 'hybrid' organisations in the name of market competition seems to be missing one important point. It appears that these organisations can actually play a very useful role by assuming risks that neither purely private nor purely public bodies would be able or willing to take on.

Risks and uncertainties revisited

A key ingredient of the approaches pursued in all three countries was to modify the risk/reward profile of proposed regeneration schemes by increasing the development potential of the sites concerned and therefore to attract private developers and investors.

At project level, risk-management practices and responses to the financial crisis are quite similar between the three countries: the mix of uses, tenures, actors, functions and products as well as off-plan sales and flexible planning regulations are all used effectively. Although the situation can vary from country to country, the state mainly engages with extra investment in merit and public good provision and affects the mix of uses via planning policy, while the private sector manages financial risks and market uncertainties through phasing, forward sales etc. There is obviously a reciprocal relationship between planning stipulations and developer strategies within the context of MUURSs. Partnering is also widely used as a tool by which risks can be shared, and also as a mechanism through which returns can increase (via synergies, lower transaction costs etc.).

At the scheme level, practices diverge more because they rely on the specific institutional arrangements and on the institutional thickness and social capital built up in the partnership undertaking the regeneration. Trust appeared to be a crucial factor, as it facilitates flexibility and adaptability and lowers transaction costs. At that level, the role of long-term stability becomes more important and therefore the role of the state becomes more pronounced, either through planning mechanisms and contracts between government bodies or through the involvement of the state in the provision of infrastructure and public facilities, amenities and the public realm. Indeed, many difficulties in New Islington and in Paddington were caused by the lack of organisational capacity and long-term commitment on behalf of central government. That having been said, in Paddington the long-term commitment of the private partners was ensured through a careful selection strategy by the local authority, which itself took the long-term view. In the Dutch cases, long-term developer commitment was to a large extent ensured by giving a prominent role to housing associations. In all cases, market actors with a short-term view were enrolled only when what was required was a short-term monetisation of value that would serve the purposes of the scheme by testing the market, sharing short-term financial risk, generating a positive cash flow, creating marketing or political benefits etc.

At the systemic-contextual level, there is a distinct difference between the UK and the other two countries regarding mechanisms to mitigate risks and uncertainties and to balance out profits and losses. In the Netherlands, for example, funding can be secured via the BNG, and housing associations can borrow cheaply by using their assets effectively as collateral. Moreover, because of their capacity to act as land developers, municipalities (when they choose that role) can have a fund where proceeds go to balance out losses in some projects with gains in others, both across space and also across time. This model has attracted criticism following the onset of the crisis as several municipalities faced losses that proved difficult or impossible to manage. Central government funding is made available under a regime that emphasises adherence of the funded entity to central government policy. As a response to the downturn in the property markets, for example, central government started to provide subsidies for dwellings built for homeownership. However, the policy landscape, though subject to change, is rarely subject to disruptive alterations, and more often than not policies evolve in an incremental, path-dependent way. This reflects the capacity of the Dutch governance system to reach compromises reflecting a wider array of interests. Even the grossing exercise, which admittedly was a major change in the provision of non-market housing, did not aim at the disappearance of housing associations.

In France, there is a tradition of cooperation between central, regional and local governments as well as between neighbouring local or regional authorities. Central government funding is tied to policy goals and is delivered on the back of a contract system that effectively ties partners to a set of strategic objectives (similar covenants exist in the Netherlands, too). The advantage of this approach is the certainty that it induces and the leveraging potential that it unleashes. The disadvantage is the potential lack of flexibility and responsiveness to rapid changes in the contextual circumstances. The institutional framework in France is quite prescriptive in the sense that potential funding and implementation mechanisms are clearly set out and codified. Here, in a way similar to the Netherlands, policy regimes change in an incremental rather than a disruptive way and, as a result, the actors engaging in urban regeneration can use a palette of policies and mechanisms, some of which are quite new but others of which are decades old. Hybrid entities, like the SEMs or the EPFs, also give the state the capacity to engage in the land-development process if and when necessary. Equally unique is the concept behind the CDC, which gives public sector actors and projects access to financing at better than market terms.

In the UK, reliance on property market dynamics is greater than in the other two countries and state support for regeneration is largely focused on ensuring that market opportunities are realised. Since the UDCs were phased out there are no mechanisms through which the state can play an active role in land development, no equivalent of the CDC or the BNG that can fund regeneration projects during a credit crunch and no strong will to develop such institutions. Thus, public sector actors' choices when it comes to financing projects are rather more limited. It is very likely that the existence of such finance mechanisms would have allowed a greater degree of local autonomy and could have proved to be crucial in the case of New Islington.

The analytical framework that we have used in this book and that has underpinned our reading of the six cases suggests that the outcomes of MUURSs depend on how risks, uncertainties and returns are apportioned amongst key actors through the way in which the projects are organised and competing interests are coordinated. Both scheme organisation and actor coordination were, in turn, a result of possibilities presented by the particular contextual set-up of each scheme. The expected outcomes of that apportionment allow projects with significant market-oriented elements to be counted upon to deliver merit and public goods and therefore to be thought of as instruments of social policy.

Our six case studies have allowed us to explore in some detail not only how actors came together under the particular urban regeneration context of each country but also how the projects were organised within the prevailing development practices, planning legislation, funding systems etc. in order to deliver both commercial and non-commercial elements while managing associated risks.

In Chapter 3 we looked at Byrne's classification of risk-generating tasks in a development project (Byrne, 1996). It would be useful here to revisit his six categories and to try to explain how mechanisms of actor coordination, forms of project organisation and contextual constraints shaped the way that risks and uncertainties were managed in our case studies.

The first category relates to the perception and estimation of demand for the different components of a project, in our cases rendered more complex due to their mixed-use nature. In all the cases, the perception of potential demand for the developments was shaped to varying degrees by policy objectives from the central and local state. In all of our cases the perception that development was needed in those locations, the general character it should have and what policy objectives it should help to meet were not directly determined by commercial viability – and thus by a carefully calculated assessment of risks and returns, no matter how important these became in later stages of those projects.

This is not surprising, given the policy-delivery dimension inherent in urban regeneration and the very nature of the effort to turn around declining (and therefore more uncertain and commercially unattractive) areas. However, the policy-led approach meant that risks, uncertainties and their implications could not be considered in full in the initial stages of those projects, and risk-management strategies were employed in a rather retrospective way. Partnership mechanisms were essential as an arena for negotiating risk allocation and mitigation and for securing the viability of the projects. In practice, in the UK the partnerships had looser remits than in France or the Netherlands.

In both UK cases, although more so in Paddington than in New Islington, the partnerships worked to a looser strategic framework, with key elements such as use and tenure mix, phasing etc. being negotiated and revised as market conditions changed. These projects rely largely on market returns for their viability, they are more sensitive to market fluctuations and therefore all strategic elements are more prone to change if viability is to be secured. Dutch development partnerships had their own degree of flexibility, as evidenced by changes in tenure composition or start-up dates, so that developer risks could be mitigated. However, these partnerships worked to a much more defined strategic programme, determined by the local authority and not normally open for renegotiation. Municipal landownership and direct public funding of infrastructure seem to have contributed to reducing developer risk and therefore ensuring that public sector strategic frameworks and masterplans could be maintained relatively unaltered in the face of market fluctuations. Similarly in the French cases, intermediary landownership, whether used from the start or not, allowed the national and the local state to maintain a more robust development framework, and at the same time delimited more clearly the roles of the different partners and their ability to shape the overall project. In both countries, however, there was a degree of renegotiation in view of the severe market downturn, which may affect the long-term trajectory of the projects if it is maintained.

The second of Byrne's six categories of risk refers to those associated with the identification and securing of sites and obtaining planning and other statutory consents. By the very nature of these projects, sites were identified and secured a priori, as part of state-sponsored regeneration strategy. The problem here was not the risks and uncertainties related to identifying and securing the right sites to match predicted demand, but the reverse, i.e. what sort of demand could be attracted by the development of those preselected sites, and thus it conflates with the issue discussed in the previous paragraphs.

Uncertainties that would normally be associated with statutory consents (planning permission etc.) have been attenuated in all cases through partnership mechanisms and the manifest commitment of the relevant public bodies to seeing those projects completed. It was not just that local authorities were involved in the design of those developments, either as clients or as authors. Partnerships seem to have been effective in providing an arena for harmonising different views, thus reducing the uncertainties surrounding the approval of plans and designs. This was even more important in a discretionary system, as is the case with the UK. As demonstrated elsewhere (Adair *et al.*, 2003; Nappi-Choulet, 2006), regeneration partnerships contribute to reducing the uncertainties associated with planning and other regulatory requirements, and our cases were no exception.

The third category of risks and uncertainties encompasses those associated with designing the project, i.e. finding the best way to accommodate the predicted demand on the site, plus public space design and specification. The repeated changes to tenure and use mix, building specification and project phasing in all of our cases are symptomatic of efforts to adjust expectations of risk and returns as the projects evolved. The different degrees of flexibility embedded in each of the six projects are revealing of how variations in risk and returns were absorbed by the different players. Almost all of our cases were subdivided into development lots, which could have their specifications modified in order to adjust to changes in demand, availability of finance, etc. Once again, the deeper the connection between project outcomes and property-market dynamics, the more flexibility was required and the more likely it was that in the end the final outcomes would diverge from initial policy objectives. New Islington is perhaps emblematic in this regard, in the sense that market dynamics (or lack thereof) combined with uncertain funding commitments from the state and a lack of funding alternatives to create a situation where it is difficult to achieve the strategic aims of the scheme.

However, and more importantly, risks and uncertainties associated with the design of those projects (in its broadest sense) also encompasses the way that responsibility for planning, funding and implementing infrastructure of various sorts was distributed among public and private players. In all the projects except Paddington, basic investment in site infrastructure was undertaken by public actors operating locally, as an explicit means of reducing the perceived risk of locations that were outside the normal geographies of the property market of their respective cities. In some cases this involved significant up-front investment that should be able to be recouped at a later stage (where the public sector owned the land) as plots or completed buildings are sold off. As the cases demonstrate, this has been traditional practice in both the Netherlands and France, albeit through different mechanisms. The transfer of risk to municipalities makes it potentially more manageable and less decisive for the outcomes of the project: municipalities might lose money or earn money in the short term, but are less likely than a private developer to go bankrupt if they cannot sell promptly a parcel of serviced land (for a discussion of this approach see Needham, 2007). In other cases, notably the UK examples, public investment in infrastructure was often not up front but was conditioned on the sale of land and/or buildings, or transferred entirely to private developers through planning obligations. Although this approach may avoid excessive public commitment to projects that may never come to fruition, it also increases uncertainty and decreases development viability in the name of land-market efficiency. As our cases show, in a market recession the withdrawal of private developers may end up compromising the achievement of intended policy objectives altogether (including the aim of establishing a functioning local property market).

The fourth category of risks includes those related to the processes of getting short- and long-term development finance. All our cases relied on a mix of public and private sources of finance. Land infrastructure and public facilities were mostly funded through public sector funds (with the exception of Paddington), and in the early days of a project. Some key buildings may have received urban regeneration grants in the expectation that they would attract private funding. Components like non-market housing would have been partly cross-subsidised by the proceeds of private development and partly financed by public funds too. Private buildings were financed through private institutions and investors (banks, pension funds, wealthy individuals etc.). The main difference between our cases is the extent to which private finance was required and how it was organised. The size of private development contained in each project is linked to what is deemed necessary to deliver the intended policy objectives.

The way in which this link affected risks and uncertainties depended on how dysfunctional, in property market terms, each of these areas was and how credible was the strategy to transform them. The differences in the organisation of finance for each case have to do firstly with the structure of development financing in each country for each property sub-market. In the UK, for instance, bank finance is often the main source of short-term finance for development, especially in housing, with the addition of some government grants for non-market housing or equity from the developers themselves. Institutional investment is a significant source of long-term funding for development, especially in the commercial sector. On occasion, wealthy private individuals can also become involved.

In the Netherlands the state is much more active in ensuring that finance is available at an acceptable cost at the right time. Finance for commercial buildings comes from similar sources as in the UK, but finance for housing is often channelled through large housing associations that sometimes also act as longer-time investors. Government subsidies were made available for private house-building as an emergency measure. This seems to have introduced more adaptability in the Dutch cases, allowing short- and long-term changes in the housing tenure mix as a way of adjusting those projects to variations in demand and thus managing the associated risks.

In France the state has been more stable in its commitment and more proactive at both the central and the local levels in securing the availability of finance for regeneration areas. Even so, Carré de Soie faced difficulties because there was little that the public sector could do to revive developer interest. Dedicated municipal revolving funds in the Netherlands play a similar stabilising role. In the UK, a swift change in the flow of regeneration grants and HCA/ NWDA funding meant that availability of finance for our cases has relied much more on the dynamics of the property market (booming at the time when the two schemes were conceived) and on developers' skills in obtaining private finance. The risks that this brings were evident in the funding difficulties present in both cases as the recession bit, especially in areas of low demand.

The fifth category of risks has to do with the management of the design and construction process. All of our six cases involved complex partnership arrangements, with their own division of responsibilities between the municipality, central and/or regional government bodies, public services providers, private developers and public housing agencies as well as residents. Equally, complex contractual instruments were deployed to regulate the roles and responsibilities of the various parties and reduce the risk of non-compliance with agreements. In this, the six cases were no different from any large, multi-partner development scheme. In several of the cases, the schemes were broken down into smaller parcels as a way of avoiding the much larger risks associated with large developments, where, for example, the exit of one partner might lead to collapse. This was clearly the case in IJoevers, where an initial unsuccessful attempt to develop the whole site as one project was replaced by its division into seven relatively separate developments with their own management structures. In New Islington, Urban Splash could subcontract other developers to take over individual plots and thus spread the risks. In the French cases, special institutional instruments such as the ZAC and the PAE, with strong legal powers, were deployed to secure a coordinated management of the projects. However, parcelling the projects into smaller lots and bringing in several partners brought its own uncertainty, namely a difficulty in coordinating the development of all the intended sites that was, in most cases, addressed through a specialised coordination office (except in Paddington, where WCC and PWP shared the role, depending on the task and the actors involved).

Coordination of infrastructure provision is an essential part in the management of such complex projects and in reducing uncertainties for private developers, investors and potential occupiers. This worked better where partnerships had strong powers to decide on infrastructure investment and to compel utilities, public transport agencies etc. to work to a particular timetable. The French and Dutch partnership structures seem to have been better at this, with the necessary infrastructure mostly delivered ahead of development, although this may represent a larger risk for infrastructure providers, especially if the reduction in the pace of development brought by the recession is not reversed. The two UK cases were affected in differing degrees by uncertainties about transport infrastructure and public realm investment, which often were outside the remit of the development partnership. Management of land development seems to have been a key feature in reducing uncertainties in the implementation of the projects.

The more robust land-development powers and capacities of the state (in its various guises) in France and the Netherlands were a key element in securing the coordination between development and infrastructure provision, between the aims of the different players and between project objectives and outcomes, thus removing considerable uncertainty. The absence of such powers in the UK might have reduced the short-term exposure of local authorities and other public bodies to the financial risks associated with land development, but may have increased uncertainty for the projects as a whole. Interestingly enough, when faced with the collapse in demand, the state became involved in supporting both schemes, either directly or indirectly, but more in the form of emergency measures and not as part of a framework with strategic priorities reinforcing a long-term commitment.

Finally, the last category of risks is represented by those related to the letting and long-term management of the property and spaces created by the development. None of our cases has been fully completed and therefore not all issues related to letting and long-term management have been resolved. Whether or not all the commercial space and private housing in our projects are acquired by investors or occupiers and end up fully occupied will be a function of the condition of the property market. However, all the projects included mechanisms to try to reduce risks and uncertainties associated with the commercialisation and use of the completed development. Forward sales and pre-letting were widely used in the Netherlands, France and the UK, and our cases show that developers would often start a building only if a set proportion of units had been presold/pre-let. This approach is directly linked to the type of finance that is used and the conditions that come with it. Purely speculative buildings were rather infrequent, and when they did happen it was because of a particular opportunity or circumstance in the market, contractual obligations to develop or their use as a demonstration project. Changes in building specification (e.g. from large to small flats or from flats to houses), use (e.g. from offices to housing) and tenure mix (e.g. from flats for sale to flats to rent, from private housing to housing association housing) during development were also found in most of our cases, as attempts to match the nature of demand at the point of completion.

As regards the long-term management of the projects, the main issue is how the long-term value of public and private investment in these areas could be secured. For commercial buildings and private houses, all our cases rely on traditional forms of property management – which for commercial buildings may mean service charges paid to a facilities manager for the upkeep of the building. Public housing estates have their own forms of management, carried out by housing associations, tenants' organisations or municipal housing departments, and our cases adopt combinations of those. It is in the management of public facilities, and especially public space, that some of our cases diverge most from the norm. In the Dutch and French cases it is envisaged that public facilities and public space, even if produced by private developers, will have their ownership transferred to public agencies who will then manage them as they do with all other facilities and public spaces, all funded by municipal or agency budgets. In the UK cases the solution is different: in New Islington most public space created in the development will be transferred to a trust, funded through a levy on all adjacent properties and run by residents, property owners, the local authority and other stakeholders. Similarly, in Paddington many public spaces have remained privately owned. This is part of an on-going controversy in the UK involving the ability of local authorities to maintain the quality of public space over the long-term (see ODPM, 2004) and the appropriateness of committing dispropor-tionate parts of shrinking municipal budgets to the management of a few areas. In these cases, uncertainties about long-term management have been dealt with through mechanisms that directly link expenditure to income sources, mirroring the arrangements used for commercial and housing estates.

Merit and public goods provision and the importance of politics

Having discussed how the main categories of risk were managed in the six cases, we can now discuss how various risk-management strategies shaped the way in which those projects provided private, merit and public goods. A key aspect of the development value chain is land servicing in preparation for development. In France and in the Netherlands this is often taken on by public sector actors, although the task can be performed equally well by private actors, in technical terms at least. The argument in favour is that the state actors play that role in order to enhance their capacity to capture value and channel it into the provision of merit and public goods. The counter-argument is that there are more efficient mechanisms for capturing value (taxation, levies etc., see Buitelaar *et al.*, 2010). This may indeed be another policy option so far as capturing value is concerned, assuming that one can find a politically acceptable and technically suitable level of taxation (a big if); it also appears to be risk free from the public sector point of view, although this perception may indeed be mistaken, as financial risk is often transformed into political risk. However, the involvement of public actors in land development plays a crucial role in reducing uncertainty both by dampening volatility and by reinforcing the commitment of the public sector to taking the development forward. This active role is often well received by private actors, who see the state's involvement as part of a fairer distribution of risk and return, instead of an effort to tax hard-earned profits.

As is evidenced by our case studies, an instinctive response of private developers when faced with a downturn in the market is to reduce their level of production, leading to stop–go situations that reinforce volatility. The involvement of the public sector in land development acts as a backstop to dampen that volatility, as it creates a strong incentive for the public sector to sustain its engagement throughout the slump, in some cases by recycling the proceeds from previous profitable rounds of development. This changes the risk perceptions of other actors, thus making it easier to initiate and sustain investment in urban regeneration.

In France, in our case studies the state became involved in rather prescriptive and prescribed ways. There is a robust legal framework specifying the mechanisms and tools that can be used under different circumstances and the role of the public sector actors is also prescribed by law. Thus, depending on the goals of the regeneration initiative, the state may assume an active developer role or a more passive role. Each regime has its own toolkit that defines how value can be extracted from the development process in order to fund infrastructure and other merit and public goods. A separate legal framework determines the central government subsidies that are to be expected in each case. The state in its various guises, however, is perfectly entitled (and feels obliged) to become involved in the land market not only as an intermediate landowner who prepares and services land for a profit (ZAC) but also as a key active landowner (through pre-emption rights or market purchases) even in cases where it has assumed a passive role in land preparation and public good provision (PAE).

The Netherlands has a longer tradition of local devolution of power and a more policy-oriented regime. Thus local authorities operate remotely (albeit still controlled via funding and policy guidelines) from the central government and have developed substantial capacity to profit from land servicing and trading. Although since 2008 municipal authorities can use statutory tools that allow them to extract value without engaging in land development, they still use permanent or intermediate landownership in order to extract value and guide development along the outcomes desired by development plans. They can also develop their own mechanisms to manage those funds counter-cyclically and in accordance with their own infrastructure and merit and public goods provision priorities.

In the UK, however, there is little ambition on the part of the state in any of its guises to be involved in land development, reflecting a broader ambivalence as to whether and how the state should be involved in welfarist activities altogether. There are two issues worth considering in this respect: the first has to do with the proportion of value that can be extracted from land development. The state assumes no development risk and, in so doing, it foregoes the potential to reap substantive returns that could be used to fund infrastructure and the provision of goods such as non-market housing. Twice in the past, Labour governments have passed legislation to tax this 'unearned increment', and twice thereafter Conservative governments have repealed the legislation, a fact that has its own significance, as it highlights the highly political nature of the negotiation surrounding the capture of land development value.

Paddington Waterside is part of a rather uniquely deep, diverse and internationalised market, so the developers and their investors were robust enough to take the hit of the downturn and adjust their strategies accordingly: they slowed down the pace of development and altered the use mix to tap into international demand or unique opportunities such as the 2012 London Olympics. Even so, securing finance and finding clients are still major challenges. In New Islington, in spite of the investment in public good provision, there is a real need for stop-gap funding and, given that the central government has not been willing to provide it, the scheme's promoters are considering turning to sources of funding that not only may compromise the strategic aims of the project but also may undermine its desirability and financial viability. Thus, while the involvement of central government supported the development through infrastructure provision and the funding of alternative tenure schemes, it also increased uncertainty through the competitive and insecure nature of the funding regime, which even affected funding programmes designed to support developers in completing projects during the crisis.

All of our cases are examples of MUURSs that relied on the monetisation of value through the market mechanism for the funding of non-market components and, consequently, for achieving planning and urban regeneration policy objectives. In this light, the various risk-management strategies discussed are part of an effort to find a balance in how risks and rewards are apportioned between the public and private sector partners, thus keeping the projects viable. Given that, by definition, these regeneration projects were taking place in areas that had remained at the margins of mainstream property markets, this balancing meant essentially an effort to reduce the risk to private developers and investors through public sector intervention, whilst simultaneously keeping the exposure of the public sector and its resource commitments to acceptable levels. This was reflected in the ways in which objectives were chosen, the projects were designed and managed, the partnerships were formed, the partners were bound together and the arrangements operated.

In all projects, albeit to different degrees, the delivery of non-market housing was a key part, whether as a replacement for inadequate old stock or as part of the formation of mixed communities or even city-wide 'rebalancing'. The delivery of non-market ('affordable', 'social') housing to meet housing-policy objectives in these projects was, at least partly, linked to the profits that could be obtained from the sale or rental of property in the open market. This was also the case for many other public facilities: public space in New Islington was funded directly or indirectly by leasing land to developers, all predicated on the profitability of private property sales. Interestingly enough, when the downturn occurred, the social rental sector was called upon to play a bigger role in keeping the schemes afloat.

Land sales predicated on the profitability of commercial or residential property did indeed assist with the funding of infrastructure of all kinds in our projects, especially in the Dutch and French examples. In the UK cases, planning obligations come out as key instruments for capturing part of the profits of private development and reinvesting them in non-market project components: planning obligations secured part of the non-market housing and public space in New Islington, and allowed the creation of a fund for investment in neighbouring deprived areas in Paddington.

Whatever other issues the funding of public facilities, infrastructure and non-market housing through the extraction of value from the property value chain might raise, our cases show that one of the consequences of this approach is the reinforcement of a link between the provision of merit and public goods, the delivery of public policy and the dynamics of property and development markets. Although, if properly managed, it might be beneficial in a buoyant market, it has proved to be problematic in periods of crisis. In all of our cases, policy objectives have had to be readjusted and reduced in order to face the recession. Worse still, in some cases the financial and market risks carefully transferred to private partners returned to the public sector agencies, compounded by political risks, when developments froze and the private profits that would pay back public investment suddenly disappeared. This suggests a more serious point for reflection, which is the extent to which the policy outcomes associated with urban regeneration are dictated by the dynamics of the market. This includes not just the narrow policy outcomes related to the regeneration of specific areas, but also issues of welfare provision, human well-being and the legitimisation of the state in the eyes of its citizens.

As the cases show, the three countries have different approaches or models for trying to capture value in MUURSs and to channel it into the delivery of policy objectives. Our two French cases suggest that the allocation of risks and rewards between public and private sector partners and the connection between development profits and the provision of non-market housing and other public facilities and infrastructure happen within robust national and local policy and policy implementation frameworks, with clear and stable definition of roles and responsibilities. Our Dutch cases point to strong strategic policy frameworks closely linked to municipal land-development powers and the dominance of housing associations as both market and non-market housing providers. Conversely, in the UK the cases suggest weaker strategic direction (especially at the level of the central government), with a stronger reliance on private development and property-market dynamics to deliver policy objectives and a more hands-off role for the public sector, focused on actor coordination and on responding to property market conditions.

Based on the evidence gathered in the case studies, these three models have demonstrated degrees of success, but also limitations in how strategic policy objectives can be effectively delivered, and especially in how much they can be relied upon to ensure the desired provision of non-market housing and other merit and pubic goods. However, the evidence also suggests that these models have by no means been exhausted: the recent recession and credit crisis have pointed to shortcomings, but the pressures that have led to a redefinition of the roles of the public and private sectors in the delivery of public policy are still very much present.

The likelihood of a growing role for markets and civil society in setting and delivering urban policy objectives makes it imperative that lessons are learned about the limits and potential of the forms of collaboration that have been used so far, in urban regeneration as in other fields of urban policy. In our view, this book opens a crucial question as to why specific approaches to the well-being of the citizens of each country develop and are adhered to within the context of economic globalisation, and the challenges these bring for national and local economic growth.

As mentioned in the first chapter, the forces affecting each society may be roughly similar, but the answers that each society gives are deeply political. Similarly, our analysis has illustrated how the role of the state in regeneration is greatly influenced by a political imperative, namely the role that each society expects the state to play in so far as citizen well-being is concerned. The work of political theorists stresses the importance of democratic institutions in shaping the welfare regime of capitalist democracies (Birchfield and Crepaz, 1998; Swank, 2001). They argue that the degree of inclusiveness of the institutionalised forms of representation (electoral or other) is directly related to the egalitarianism of policy goals in the long run. Forms of representation that allow for more pluralist power-sharing arrangements to take place have been linked to more egalitarian systems of welfare provision. Apart from any contribution to the subject of planning, regeneration and property development, we hope that this book will contribute towards that discussion too.

References

Adair, A., Berry, J. and McGreal, S. (2003) "Urban regeneration and property investment performance", *Journal of Property Research* 20(4), pp. 371–386.

Adair, A., Berry, J., McGreal, S., Deddis, B. and Hirst, S. (2000) "The financing of urban regeneration", *Land Use Policy* 17, pp. 147–156.

Adams, D., Watkins, C. and White, M. (eds) (2005) *Planning, Public Policy and Property Markets*. Oxford: Blackwell.

Adams, J. (1995) *Risk*. London: UCL Press.

Adams, J. (1999) "Risk-benefit analysis: Who wants it? Who needs it?", paper presented at Cost Benefit Analysis Conference, Yale University, October.

Adams, J. (2007) "Risk management is not rocket science: it's much more complicated", *Public Risk Forum* (May), pp. 9–11.

Albrechts, L. (2009) "Enhancing creativity and action orientation in planning", in Hillier, J. and Healey, P. (eds) *Companion to Planning Theory*. Farnham: Ashgate, pp. 215–232.

Alexander, E.R. (2001) "Why planning and markets is an oxymoron: asking the right question", *Planning and Markets* 4(1), pp. 1–6.

Anderson, H. and van Kempen, R. (eds) (2001) *Governing European Cities: Social Fragmentation, Social Exclusion and Urban Governance*. Aldershot: Ashgate.

Arbaci, S. (2007) "Ethnic segregation, housing systems and welfare regimes in Europe", *International Journal of Housing Policy* 7(4), pp. 401–433.

Bailey, N., Barker, A. and MacDonald, K. (1995) *Partnership Agencies in British Urban Policy*. London: UCL Press.

Balchin, P. (ed.) (1996) *Housing Policy in Europe*. London: Routledge.

Balchin, P., Sýkora, L. and Bull, G. (1999) *Regional Policy and Planning in Europe*. London: Routledge.

Barker, K. (2004) *Review of Housing Supply: Delivering Stability: Securing our Future Housing Needs: Final Report*. Norwich: HMSO.

Barlow, J. and Duncan, S. (1994) *Success and Failure in Housing Provision: European Systems Compared*. Oxford: Pergamon.

Beauregard, R. (2003) *Voices of Decline: The Postwar Fate of US Cities*. Cambridge, Mass.: Routledge.

Beck, U. (1992) *Risk Society*. London: Sage.

Becker, F. and Patterson, V. (2005) "Private partnerships: balancing financial returns, risks, and roles of the partners", *Public Performance & Management Review* 29(2), pp. 125–144.

Birchfield, V. and Crepaz, M.M.L. (1998) "The impact of constitutional structures and collective and competitive veto points on income inequality in industrialized democracies", *European Journal of Political Research* 34, pp. 175–200.

Blanc, M. and Bertrand, L. (1996) "The promotion of social housing: France", in Balchin, P. (ed.) (1996) *Housing Policy in Europe*. London: Routledge, pp. 125–147.

Bonneville, M. (2005) "The ambiguity of urban renewal in France: between continuity and rupture", *Journal of Housing and the Built Environment* 20(3), pp. 229–242.

Brandsen, T. and Pestoff, V. (2006) "Co-production, the third sector and the delivery of public services", *Public Management Review* 8(4), pp. 493–500.

Buitelaar, E., Bregman, A., van de Broek, L., Evers, D., Nieuwenhuizen, W. and Sorel, N. (2010) *Ex-durante evaluatie Wet Ruimtelijke Ordening, eerste resultaten*. The Hague: NAI Uitgevers/PBL.

Byrne, P. (1996) *Risk, Uncertainty and Decision-making in Property Development*. London: Taylor & Francis.

CABE and DETR (2001) *The Value of Urban Design*. Tonbridge: Thomas Telford.

Cadell, C., Falk, N. and King, F. (2008) *Regeneration in European Cities: Making Connections*. York: Joseph Rowntree Foundation.

CAH and Rottenberg, F. (2007) *WIMBY! Hoogvliet. Future, Past and Present of a New Town*. Rotterdam: NAi Publishers.

Cameron, S. (2006) "From low demand to rising aspirations: housing market renewal within regional and neighbourhood regeneration policy", *Housing Studies* 21(1), pp. 3–16.

Canniffe, E. (2010) "A surfeit of surface and an excess of space: New Islington and Spinningfields, Manchester", paper presented at the AESOP conference, Helsinki, Finland, July.

Castells, M. (1989) *The Informational City: Information Technology, Economic Restructuring and the Urban–Regional Process*. Oxford: Blackwell.

CEC (1990) *Green Paper on the Urban Environment*. Brussels: CEC.

Chaline, C. (1999) *La regeneration urbaine*. Paris: PUF.

Chaline, C. (2003) *Les politiques de la ville*. Paris: PUF.

Cheshire, P. (2007) *Segregated Neighbourhoods and Mixed Communities*. York: Joseph Rowntree Foundation.

Childs, P. D., Riddiough, T.J. and Triantis, A.J. (1996) "Mixed uses and the redevelopment option", *Real Estate Economics* 24(3) pp. 317–339.

Clarke, M. and Stewart, J. (1997) *Handling the Wicked Issues: A Challenge for Government*. Birmingham: INLOGOV.

Colenutt, B. (1999) "Deal or no deal for people based regeneration?", in Imrie, R. and Thomas, H. (eds) *British Urban Policy: An Evaluation of the Urban Development Corporations*. London: Sage, pp. 233–245.

Comby, J. (2001) "Savoir choisir une stratégie de renouvellement urbain", *Etudes foncières* 89, pp. 26–31.

Conseil Communautaire du Grand Lyon (2004) Délibération du 29 mars 2004.

Conseil Communautaire du Grand Lyon (2006) Délibération no. 2006-3204.

Couch, C. (2003) "Economic and physical influences on urban regeneration in Europe", in Couch, C., Frazer, C. and Percy, S. (eds) *Urban Regeneration in Europe*. Oxford: Blackwell Science, pp. 166–179.

Couch, C., Frazer, C. and Percy, S. (2003) *Urban Regeneration in Europe*. Oxford: Blackwell Science.

Couch, C., Sykes, O. and Börstinghaus, W. (2011) "Thirty years of regeneration in France, Germany and Britain: the importance of context and path dependency", *Progress in Planning* 75(1) pp. 1–52.

Cour des Comptes (2002) *La politique de la Ville, Rapport Public Particulier*. Paris: Direction des Journeaux Officiels.

Crook, A.D.H. and Whitehead, C.M.E. (2002) "Social housing and planning gain: is this an appropriate way of providing affordable housing?", *Environment & Planning A* 34, pp. 1259–1279.

Crook, A.D.H., Monk, S., Rowley, S. and Whitehead, C.M.E. (2006) "Planning gain and the supply of new affordable housing in England: understanding the numbers", *Town Planning Review* 77(3), pp. 353–373.

Crook, A.D.H., Currie, J., Jackson, A., Monk, S., Rowley, S., Smith, K. and Whitehead, C.M.E. (2002) *Planning Gain and Affordable Housing: Making It Count*. York: Joseph Rowntree Foundation.

de Kam, G. (1996) *Op grond van beleid: locaties voor de sociale woningbouw, grondbeleid en ruimtelijke spreiding van welstand in en rond Den Haag*. Almere: Nationale Woningraad.

de Magalhães, C. (1999a) "Institutional capacity-building, urban planning and urban regeneration projects", *Futura* 18(3), pp. 117–137.

de Magalhães, C. (1999b) "Social agents, the provision of buildings and property booms: the case of São Paulo", *International Journal of Urban and Regional Research* 23(3), pp. 445–463.

de Magalhães, C. (2004) "Centres of excellence for urban regeneration: promoting institutional capacity and innovation or reaffirming old ideas", *Planning Theory and Practice* 5(1), pp. 33–47.

Deakin, N. (2001) "Putting narrow-mindedness out of countenance: the UK voluntary sector in the new millennium", in Anheier, H. and Kendall, J. (eds) *Third Sector Policy at the Crossroads*. London: Routledge, pp. 36–50.

DETR (1997) *The Way Forward for Regeneration*. London: HMSO.

Dikec, M. (2006) "Two decades of French urban policy: from social development of neighbourhoods to the republican penal state", *Antipode* 38(1), pp. 59–81.

Doak, J. and Karadimitriou, N. (2007) "(Re)development, complexity and networks: a framework for research", *Urban Studies* 44(2), pp. 209–229.

DoE (1995) *Our Future Homes: Opportunity, Choice, Responsibility*. London: HMSO.

Dormois, R., Pinson, G. and Reignier, H. (2005) "Path-dependency in public–private partnership in French urban renewal", *Journal of Housing and the Built Environment* 20(3), pp. 243–256.

ECTP (2003) *The New Charter of Athens*. Lisbon: ECTP.

Eiser, J.R. (2004) *Public Perception of Risk. Report prepared for "Foresight" Office of Science and Technology.* Sheffield: University of Sheffield.

Ekkers, P. (2002) *Van volkshuisvesting naar woonbeleid.* Den Haag: SDU Uitgevers.

Esping-Andersen, G. (1990) *The Three Worlds of Welfare Capitalism.* Princeton, NJ: Princeton University Press.

Esping-Andersen, G. (2002) *Why We Need a New Welfare State.* Oxford: Oxford University Press.

FDP Savills (2003) *Investment in Mixed Use.* London: FDP Savills.

Forrest, R. (1987) "Spatial mobility, tenure mobility, and emerging social divisions in the UK housing market", in *Environment and Planning A* 19, pp. 1611–1630.

Fraser, C. (2003a) "Change in the European industrial city", in Couch, C., Fraser, C. and Percy, S. (eds) *Urban Regeneration in Europe.* Oxford: Blackwell, pp. 17–33.

Fraser, C. (2003b), "The institutional and financial conditions of urban regeneration in Europe", in Couch, C., Fraser, C. and Percy, S. (eds) *Urban Regeneration in Europe.* Oxford: Blackwell, pp. 180–199.

Giddens, A. (1984) *The Constitution of Society.* Berkeley: UCP.

Goldsmith, M. (1993) "Local government", in Paddison, R. *et al.* (eds) *International Perspectives in Urban Studies.* Glasgow: University of Glasgow.

Goodchild, B. and Cole, I. (2001) "Social balance and mixed neighbourhoods in Britain since 1979: a review of discourse and practice in social housing", *Environment and Planning D: Society and Space* 19, pp. 103–121.

Goss, S. (2001) *Making Local Governance Work: Networks, Relationships and the Management of Change.* Basingstoke: Palgrave.

Gregory, J. (2011) *Can Housing Work for Workers?*, The Fabian Society Touchstone Pamphlet No. 11. London: TUC.

Guy, S., Henneberry, J. and Rowley, S. (2002) "Development cultures and urban regeneration", *Urban Studies* 39(7), pp. 1181–1196.

Hall, P. (1990) *Cities of Tomorrow.* Oxford: Blackwell.

Hall, P. and Tewdwr-Jones, M. (2011) *Urban and Regional Planning.* London: Routledge.

Hall, S. and Hickman, P. (2002) "Neighbourhood renewal and urban policy: a comparison of new approaches in England and France", *Regional Studies* 36(6), pp. 691–707.

Hamnett, C. (1998) "Social polarisation, economic restructuring and welfare state regimes", in Musterd, R. and Ostendorf, W. (eds) *Urban Segregation and the Welfare State: Inequality and Exclusion in Western Cities.* London: Routledge.

Harloe, M. (1995) *The People's Home: Social Rented Housing in Europe and America.* Oxford: Blackwell.

Healey, P. (1991) "Urban regeneration and the development industry", *Regional Studies* 25(2), pp. 97–110.

Henderson, S. (2010) "Developer collaboration in urban land development: partnership working in Paddington, London", *Environment and Planning C: Government and Policy* 28(1), pp. 165–185.

Henderson, S., Bowlby, S. and Raco, M. (2007) "Re-fashioning local government and inner-city regeneration: the Salford experience", *Urban Studies* 44(8), pp. 1441–1463.

Henneberry, J., Guy, S. and Rowley, S. (2002) "Development cultures and urban regeneration", *Urban Studies* 39(7), pp. 1181–1196.

Henneberry, J., Rowley, S., Crook, A., Smith, R. and Watkins, C. (2008) *Valuing Planning Obligations in England: Update Study for 2005–06*. London: DCLG.

Hills, J. (2007) *Ends and Means: The Future Roles of Social Housing in England*, ESRC CASE report 34. London: LSE.

Hoekstra, J. (2003) "Housing and the welfare state in the Netherlands: an application of Esping-Andersen's typology", *Housing, Theory and Society* 20(2), pp. 58–71.

Høj, J. (2011) "Improving the flexibility of the Dutch housing market to enhance labour mobility", *OECD Economics Department Working Papers*, No. 833. Paris: OECD Publishing.

Hoppenbrouwer, E. and Louw, E. (2005) "Mixed-use development: theory and practice in Amsterdam's Eastern Docklands", *European Planning Studies* 13(7), pp. 967–983.

Hudson, R. (2005) "Re-thinking change in old industrial regions: reflecting on the experiences of North East England", *Environment and Planning A* 37(4), pp. 581–596.

Hurst, W. (2010) "HCA forced to reveal details of poor housing", *Building Design* (3 December). Available from http://www.bdonline.co.uk/news/hca-forced-to-reveal-details-of-poor-housing/5009847.article.

Iglesias, T. (2009) "Our pluralist housing ethics and public private partnerships for affordable housing", in Davidson, N. and Malloy, R. (eds) *Affordable Housing and Public Private Partnerships*. Farnham: Ashgate.

Imrie, R. and Thomas, H. (eds) (1999) *British Urban Policy: An Evaluation of the Urban Development Corporations*. London: Sage.

IPD (2008) *IPD Regeneration Index*. London: IPD.

Investment Property Forum (2006) *Institutional Investment in Regeneration: Necessary Conditions for Effective Funding*. London: IPF.

Jacobs, J. (2000) *The Death and Life of Great American Cities*. London: Pimlico.

Jaeger, C. *et al.* (2001) *Risk, Uncertainty and Rational Action*. London: Earthscan.

Jeffrey, P. and Pounder, J. (2000) "Major themes and topics: physical and environmental aspects", in Roberts, P. and Sykes, H. (eds) *Urban Regeneration: A Handbook*. London: Sage, pp. 86–108.

Karadimitriou, N. (2005) "Changing the way UK cities are built: the shifting urban policy and the adaptation of London's housebuilders", *Journal of Housing and the Built Environment* 20(3), pp. 271–286.

Kemeny, J. (1995) *From Public to the Social Market. Rental Policy Strategies in Comparative Perspective*. London: Routledge.

Kemeny, J. (2001) "Comparative housing and welfare: theorising the relationship", *Journal of Housing and the Built Environment* 16(1) pp. 53–70.

Kemeny, J., Kersloot, J. and Thalmann, P. (2005) "Non-profit housing influencing, leading and dominating the unitary rental market: three case studies", *Housing Studies* 20(6), pp. 855–872.

Kleinhans, R. (2009) "Does social capital affect residents' propensity to move from restructured neighbourhoods?", *Housing Studies* 24(5), pp. 629–651.

Kooiman, J. (2003) *Governing as Governance*. London: Sage.

Korthals Altes, W.K. (2002) "Local government and the decentralisation of urban regeneration policies in the Netherlands", *Urban Studies* 39(8), pp. 1439–1452.

Lai, R.N. *et al.* (2004) "Sale before completion of development: pricing and strategy", *Real Estate Economics* 32(2), pp. 329–357.

Le Galès, P. (2003) *Le retour des villes Européennes: Sociétés urbaines, mondialisation, gouvernement et gouvernance*. Paris: Presses de Sciences Po.

Le Monde (2002) "Un grand projet de ville de 60 millions d'euros pour le 9ᵉ arrondissement", (24 May).

Leach, R. and Percy-Smith, J. (2001) *Local Governance in Britain*. Basingstoke: Palgrave.

Lindblom, C.E. (2001) *The Market System: What It Is, How It Works and What to Make of It*, New Haven, CT: Yale University Press.

Louw, E. and Bruinsma, F. (2006) "From mixed to multiple land use", *Journal of Housing and the Built Environment* 21(1), pp. 1–13.

McCarthy, J. (2007) *Partnership, Collaborative Planning and Urban Regeneration*. Aldershot: Ashgate.

McGreal, S., Adair, A., Berry, J., Deddis, B. and Hirst, S. (2000) "Accessing private sector finance in urban regeneration: investor and non-investor perspectives", *Journal of Property Research* 17(2), pp. 109–131.

MacLaran, A. (ed.) (2003) *Making Space: Property Development and Urban Planning*. London: Arnold.

Majoor, S. (2006) "Conditions for multiple land use in large scale urban problems", *Journal of Housing and the Built Environment* 21(1), pp. 15–32.

Marcuse, P. and van Kempen, R. (eds) (2002) *Of State and Cities. The Partitioning of Urban Space*. Oxford: Oxford University Press.

Medda, F. and Nijkamp, P. (1997) "Waterfront revitalization projects: a comparative study of London Docklands and Yokohama Minato Mirai 21", *Research Memorandum 1997-16*. Amsterdam: Vrije Universiteit Amsterdam.

Mejean, P. (2003) "La politique de la ville à l'épreuve de la loi Borloo", *Etudes foncières* 106, pp. 30–34.

Meyer, C. and Davis, S. (2003) *It's Alive. The Coming Convergence of Information, Biology and Business*. New York: Crown Business.

Ministerie van Algemene Zaken (2007) *Brief minister president ter aanbieding van het beleidsprogramma "samen werken, samen leven", voor de periode 2007–2011*, bijlage kamerstuk 31070 no. 1 (15 June). Den Haag: Ministerie van Algemene Zaken.

Ministerie van VROM (2001) *Housing Statistics in the European Union*. The Hague: Ministerie van VROM.

Miraftab, F. (2004) "Public–private partnerships. The Trojan horse of neoliberal development?" *Journal of Planning Education and Research* 24(1), pp. 89–101.

NAO (2006) *The Paddington Health Campus Scheme*. London: The Stationery Office.

NAO (2011) *Lessons from PFI and Other Projects*. London: The Stationery Office.

Nappi-Choulet, I. (2006) "The role and behaviour of commercial property investors and developers in French urban regeneration: the experience of the Paris region", *Urban Studies* 43(9), pp. 1511–1535.

Needham, B. (2006) *Planning, Law and Economics*. London: Routledge.

Needham, B. (2007) *Dutch Land-use Planning: Planning and Managing Land-use in the Netherlands, the Principles and the Practice*. The Hague: SdU Uitgevers.

Needham, B. and Verhage, R. (1998) "The effects of land policy: quantity as well as quality is important", *Urban Studies* 35, pp. 25–44.

Nevin, B. and Leather, P. (2006) "Understanding the drivers of housing market change in Britain's post-industrial cities", in Malpass, P. and Cairncross, L. (eds) *Building on the Past. Visions of Housing Futures*, Bristol: The Policy Press, pp. 97–126.

Nijkamp, P., van der Burch, M. and Vindigni, G. (2002) "A comparative institutional evaluation of public–private partnerships in Dutch urban land-use and revitalisation projects", *Urban Studies* 39(10), pp. 1865–1880.

Oakley, A. and Williams, A.S. (eds) (1994) *The Politics of the Welfare State*. London: UCL Press.

ODPM (Office of the Deputy Prime Minister) (2000) *Our Towns and Cities: The Future: Delivering an Urban Renaissance*. London: The Stationery Office.

ODPM (2003) *Sustainable Communities: Building for the Future*. London: ODPM.

ODPM (2004) *Living Places: Caring for Quality*. London: RIBA Enterprises.

ODPM (2006) *State of English Cities: A Research Study*. London: ODPM.

Ouwehand, A. and van Daalen, G. (2002) *Dutch Housing Associations: A Model for Social Housing*. Delft: Delft University Press.

Pierre, J. and Peters, B.G. (2000) *Governance, Politics, and the State*. Basingstoke: Macmillan.

Pierson, P. (1996) *Dismantling the Welfare State? Reagan, Thatcher and the Politics of Retrenchment*. Cambridge: Cambridge University Press.

Piron, O. (2002) *Le renouvellement urbain: une analyse systémique*. Paris: PUCA.

Priemus, H. (2006) "Regeneration of Dutch post-war urban districts: the role of housing associations", *Journal of Housing and the Built Environment* 21(4), pp. 365–375.

Priemus, H. (1998) "Redifferentiation of the urban housing stock in the Netherlands: a strategy to prevent spatial segregation?", *Housing Studies* 13(3), pp. 301–310.

Priemus, H., Verhage, R. and Kruythoff, H.M. (2002) "De stedelijke investeringsopgave 2003–2014", *Stedelijke en regionale verkenningen* no. 30, Delft: Delft University Press.

Raco, M. (2008) "Key worker housing, welfare reform and the new spatial policy in England", *Regional Studies* 42(5), pp. 737–751.

Raco, M. and Henderson, S. (2009) "Flagship regeneration in a global city: the re-making of Paddington Basin", *Urban Policy and Research* 27(3), pp. 301–314.

Rhodes, R. (1997) *Understanding Governance: Policy Networks, Governance, Reflexivity, and Accountability*. Buckingham: Open University Press.

Richards, S., Barnes, M., Sullivan, H., Gaster, L., Leach, B. and Coulson, A. (1999) *Crosscutting Issues in Public Policy and Public Service*. London: Department of the Environment, Transport and the Regions.

Roberts, P. (2000) "The evolution, definition and purpose of urban regeneration", in Roberts, P. and Sykes, H. (eds) *Urban Regeneration: A Handbook*. London: Sage, pp. 9–36.

Rodney, B. and Clark, P. (2000) "Financing urban regeneration", *Research Paper 2000.04*. London: City University.

Roussel, F.X. (1997) "La ville renouvelée", *Urbanisme* 296 (Sept./Oct.), p. 75.

Sassen, S. (1991) *The Global City: New York, London, Tokyo*. Princeton, NJ: Princeton University Press.

Schoon, N. (2001) *The Chosen City*. London: Spon.

Scott, P. (2001) "Industrial estates and British industrial development, 1897–1939", *Business History* 43(2), pp. 73–98.

SEU (1998) *Bringing Britain Together: A National Strategy for Neighbourhood Renewal*. London: HMSO.

Siddiquee, N.A. (2011) "Rhetoric and Reality of public–private partnerships: learning points from the Australian experience", *Asian Journal of Political Science* 19(2), pp. 129–148.

Stewart, J. and Walsh, K. (1992) "Change in the management of public services", *Public Administration* 70(4), pp. 499–518.

Stoker, G. (2004) *Transforming Local Governance: From Thatcherism to New Labour*. Basingstoke: Palgrave.

Stouten, P. (2010) *Changing Contexts in Urban Regeneration: 30 Years of Modernisation in Rotterdam*. Amsterdam: Techne Press.

Sullivan, H. and Skelcher, C. (2002) *Working across Boundaries: Collaboration in Public Services*. Basingstoke: Palgrave.

Swank, D. (2001) "Political institutions and welfare state restructuring", in Pierson, P. (ed.) *The New Politics of the Welfare State*. Oxford: Oxford University Press.

Swyngedow, E., Moulaert, F. and Rodriguez, A. (2002) "Neoliberal urbanisation in Europe: large-scale urban development projects and the new urban policy", *Antipode* 34(3), pp. 542–577.

Syms, P. (2002) *Land, Development and Design*. Oxford: Blackwell.

Taleb, N. (2007) *The Black Swan: The Impact of the Highly Improbable*. New York: Random House.

Trache, H., Green, H. and Menez, F. (2007) "Public–private partnership in urban regeneration", in Booth, P., Breuillard, M., Fraser, C. and Paris, D. (eds) *Spatial Planning Systems of Britain and France: A Comparative Analysis*. London: Routledge.

Turok, I. (1992) "Property-led urban regeneration: panacea or placebo?", *Environment and Planning A* 24(3), pp. 361–379.

Uitermark, J., Duyvendak, J.W. and Kleinhans, R. (2007) "Gentrification as a governmental strategy: social control and social cohesion in Hoogvliet, Rotterdam", *Environment and Planning A* 39, pp. 125–141.

Urban Land Institute (2003) *Mixed Use Development Handbook* (2nd edn). Washington DC: Urban Land Institute.

Urban Task Force (1999) *Towards an Urban Renaissance*. London: E & FN Spon.

van Beckhoven, E. and van Kempen, R. (2003) "Social effects of urban restructuring: a case study in Amsterdam and Utrecht, the Netherlands", *Housing Studies* 18(6), pp. 853–875.

van der Krabben, E. and Jacobs, H. (2011) "Public land development as a strategic tool for redevelopment: lessons for American cities from the Netherlands", paper presented at the AESOP Conference, Perth: Australia.

van der Schaar, J. (2005) *Over rollen en partijen in de stedelijke vernieuwing*. Rotterdam: KEI.

Verhage, R. (2005a) "Towards a territorialised approach to urban renewal: a comparison of policies in France and the Netherlands", *International Planning Studies* 10(2), pp. 129–143.

Verhage, R. (2005b) "Renewing urban renewal in France, the UK and the Netherlands: introduction", *Journal of Housing and the Built Environment* 20(3), pp. 215–227.

Verhage, R. and Sluis, R. (2003) "Samenwerking bij stedelijke vernieuwing", *Stedelijke en Regionale Verkenningen* vol. 31. Delft: Delft University Press.

Watson, M. (2009) "Planning for a future of asset-based welfare? New Labour, financialised economic agency and the housing market", *Planning Practice & Research* 2(1), pp. 41–56.

Wellings, F. (2006) *British Housebuilders*. Oxford: Blackwell.

Whitty *et al.* (1994) "Making sense of the new politics of education", in Oakley, A. and Williams, A.S. (eds) *The Politics of the Welfare State*. London: UCL Press.

Wildavsky, A. (1988) *Searching for Safety*. Oxford: Transition.

Index